Verse Going Viral

Verse Going Viral

CHINA'S NEW MEDIA SCENES

Heather Inwood

A China Program Book
UNIVERSITY OF WASHINGTON PRESS *Seattle and London*

THIS BOOK IS MADE POSSIBLE BY A COLLABORATIVE GRANT FROM THE ANDREW W. MELLON FOUNDATION.

This book was supported in part by the China Studies Program, a division of the Henry M. Jackson School of International Studies at the University of Washington.

18 17 16 15 14 5 4 3 2 1

University of Washington Press
PO Box 50096, Seattle, WA 98145, USA
www.washington.edu/uwpress

Library of Congress Cataloging-in-Publication Data

Inwood, Heather, author.
Verse Going Viral : China's New Media Scenes / Heather Inwood.
pages cm
Includes bibliographical references and index.
ISBN 978-0-295-99369-0 (hardback)
ISBN 978-0-295-99370-6 (paperback)
1. Chinese poetry—21st century—Criticism and interpretation. 2. Literature and society—China. 3. Digital media—China. 4. Popular culture—China. I. Title.
PL2333.I59 2014
895.11'609—dc23 2014001454

The paper used in this publication is acid-free and meets the minimum requirements of American National Standard for Information Sciences—Permanence of Paper for Printed Library Materials, ANSI Z39.48–1984.∞

CONTENTS

ACKNOWLEDGMENTS

Like any book, this one has been on a journey and many people have helped it along the way. I would like to thank all the poetry scene participants in China who kindly provided me with mountains of research materials and made this project feasible. They include A Xiang, An Qi, Bei Ta, Duoyu, Fu Mahuo, Huang Lihai, Jiang Hao, Lao Chao, Li Shaojun, Pidan, Shen Haobo, Shi Zhongren, Tan Kexiu, Tang Xiaodu, Wang Mingyun, Xie Youshun, Xu Jiang, Xu Xiangchou, Yang Ke, Yi Sha, Yu Jian, Yudu, Zhou Zan, and the poets who completed my online poetry questionnaire. My gratitude also goes to my poet friends and teachers who welcomed me during my time at Peking University, in particular Hu Xudong, Jiang Tao, Leng Shuang, Wang Pu, Zang Di, Zhang Li, and members of the May Fourth Literature Society, all of whom were instrumental in getting me involved in poetry activities in China. Special thanks to Li Wei, Xu Xiangchou, Yang Li, and Wang Yin for generously granting me permission to include my translations of their poems in the epigraphs to the chapters of this book, and to Li Zhenghu (Su Shansheng) for allowing me to cite his viral earthquake poem in full in Chapter 4.

Funding for this project was provided first by the Arts and Humanities Research Council (AHRC) of the United Kingdom and later by a generous start-up grant from The Ohio State University (OSU) for tenure-track faculty, which enabled me to return to China to conduct additional fieldwork. In the U.K., I am most grateful to my teacher at the School of Oriental and African Studies (SOAS), Michel Hockx, who continues to be a source of wisdom and guidance, as well to Henry Zhao for his energetic classes on critical theory and other members of the SOAS community including Cosima Bruno, Margaret Hillenbrand, and Andrew Lo. Chris Berry and Maghiel van

Crevel provided invaluable feedback on my research that helped see me through the process of writing this book. In the United States, my thanks go to everyone in OSU's Department of East Asian Languages and Literatures for their friendship and support, and in particular to my colleagues in Chinese literature, each of whom shared their advice on this project at one stage or another: Mark Bender, Kirk Denton, Meow Hui Goh, and Patricia Sieber.

Some parts of this book were originally published as articles. An earlier version of part of Chapter 1 appeared as "Identity Politics in Online Chinese Poetry Groups," in the Postmodern China edition of *Berliner China-Hefte/Chinese History and Society* 34 (2008): 77–94, and a section of Chapter 4 appeared in a slightly different form in "Multimedia Quake Poetry: Convergence Culture After the Sichuan Earthquake," *China Quarterly* 208 (2011): 932–50. All of the translations in this book, unless otherwise noted, are my own.

Finally, I would like to express my thanks to the three readers at the University of Washington Press for their incisive and in some cases extremely detailed feedback and to Lorri Hagman for her patience, optimism, and seemingly miraculous achievement of guiding such an interdisciplinary book through to publication. Last but not least, thank you to all my friends and family around the world for your humor and love, and most of all to my partner, Di, whom I am incredibly lucky to have by my side no matter where life takes us.

Verse Going Viral

Is Zhang Ziyi beautiful or not?
Some think she's beautiful
Some think she's not
Liu Ping who works in the same office as me
Definitely thinks not
But Zhang Yimou thinks she's beautiful
Ang Lee thinks she's beautiful
Jackie Chan thinks she's beautiful
Wong Kar-wai thinks she's beautiful
Henry Fok's grandson thinks she's beautiful
Steven Spielberg thinks she's beautiful
Now even Feng Xiaogang thinks she's beautiful
So *is* Zhang Ziyi beautiful or not?
My opinion is
Zhang Ziyi is more beautiful than Zhang Yimou
More beautiful than Ang Lee
More beautiful than Jackie Chan
More beautiful than Wong Kar-wai
More beautiful than Henry Fok's grandson
More beautiful than Steven Spielberg
And more beautiful even than Feng Xiaogang
But
Not as beautiful as Liu Ping who works in the same office as me

—LI WEI, "*Is Zhang Ziyi Beautiful or Not?*" (Zhang Ziyi piaoliang bu piaoliang?)

My opinion has long been that there is no need for modern poetry or poets to exist, as they are of zero value. These days paper is pretty expensive, so why not just write some decent prose and fill the whole page?

—HAN HAN, "*How come modern poetry and poets still exist?*" (Xiandai shi he shiren zenme hai cunzai?)

Introduction

Modern Chinese poetry can often seem like a bundle of contradictions. On the one hand, many Chinese people take pride in belonging to a "nation of poetry" (*shi de guodu* or *shiguo*) whose written poetic history can be traced well over two thousand years to the *Shijing* (Book of Songs), supposedly compiled by Confucius himself. This is a country that boasts such poet greats as Li Bai, Du Fu, Li Qingzhao, and, in the twentieth century, the almost equally revered Xu Zhimo, Shu Ting, and Haizi. Many children are taught to recite Tang poems as soon as they can talk and continue to study canonical works of classical poetry all the way through high school. Even Chairman Mao with his predilection for continuous revolution and the smashing of anything old spent his spare time composing classical-style poems like a member of the traditional literati. Any educated person in China can recite the canonical adage "poetry expresses what is intently on the mind" (*shi yan zhi*).[1] Indeed, it was toward poetry that many people first turned as a means of self-expression after the death of Premier Zhou Enlai in January 1976 and in the aftermath of the devastating Sichuan Earthquake of May 2008. To this day, the title "poet" carries an aura of intellectual and aesthetic cultivation that rests on the achievements of millennia of writers and the central position that poetry long occupied within China's civil service examination system.

But the status of *modern* poetry—the kind mostly written in free verse using vernacular Chinese—within the People's Republic of China (PRC) is far from assured. Vociferous critiques from journalists, academics, and celebrities (including the popular author and race car driver Han Han) were widely circulated in the media in the 2000s and embraced by a population that seemed only too happy to ridicule a nation's poets for their collective shortcomings. Li Wei's poem on the much-debated beauty of actress Zhang Ziyi, for example, made a splash when it found itself listed at number two on the country's first ever Mediocre Poetry Chart in 2007 (I return to the journey of this poem in the conclusion). Media organizations and literary critics alike portray modern poetry as a literature in crisis, marginalized by its inability to adapt to the climatic shift from the utopianism of high-culture fever (*wenhuare*) in the 1980s to the money-oriented tides of commercial popular culture in the 1990s and beyond. Even China's central news agency, Xinhua, published reports in the mid-2000s with such quizzical headlines as "Who still writes poetry and does China still have poets?" and "Why is contemporary poetry so lonely?"[2]

Verse Going Viral sets out to make sense of some of the paradoxes that characterize modern Chinese poetry in an age of the Internet and the market economy by adopting a cultural studies approach that examines contemporary poetry activity from the perspective of scenes and the media that support them. Far from being perilously close to extinction as news reports often have it, modern poetry is alive and well in twenty-first-century China. Evidence of its vitality can be found in the number of active poetry groups across the country and in the wealth of poetry writing and related activities taking place daily on the Internet, in print publications, and at face-to-face events, activities that together give structure to poetry scenes.[3] What is "new" about the new media scenes this book explores is not so much the media themselves, which have been in existence from at least two decades (in the case of the Internet) to over a thousand (in the case of print) or hundred thousand (in the case of oral communication) years, but rather the dynamics between them and the discourses and behaviors they embody.[4] One defining feature of poetry scenes in the new millennium is the prevalence of contention between poets and poetry groups surrounding just about every poetry-related issue imaginable. Again, this is in many ways neither novel nor unexpected: as scholars have attested, the statesman-cum-poet-theorist Cao Pi's observation in the third century that "literary men disparage one another—it's always been that way" holds true for modern Chinese literature as well.[5] Nonetheless, the forms of contention that surround poetry in the early twenty-first century go far beyond personal differences and need to be contextualized in light of broader developments in media, culture, and society since the 1990s.

In order to understand the multiple meanings that modern poetry carries in China for both poets and non-poetry-reading publics, it is necessary to supplement the study of individual poems as static artistic objects produced by recognized authors with the ideas of poetry as culture and poetry scenes as dynamic networks of people, practices, and discourses connected across multiple media spaces and conditioned by the current historical moment. In China, all media continue to be subject to surveillance and control by the Chinese party-state, a reality that has been a central focus of existing scholarship in this area.[6] The simple presence of media control does not, however, predetermine the uses to which media are put, although it can and does have an effect. Poetry can be considered a vivid example of how developments in media and society play out in the hands of individuals and communities whose primary interest is not in challenging or enacting state power or defending citizen rights but in furthering their chosen area of culture and sharing the value of what they do with like-minded creators and audiences. The activities and discourses that shape poetry scenes can tell us much about the changing dynamics among the Chinese state, economy, media, and society, as well as the ways in which these forces interact and clash in China today.

POETRY AND CULTURAL STUDIES

Cultural studies is a notoriously slippery area of study that has in its relatively short lifespan been accused of many shortcomings, not least among which are its supposed lack of methodology, fixation on mass or popular culture, and tendency to reduce all cultural creation to struggles over identity and power or race, class, and gender.[7] A more generous take is that cultural studies tells us things we don't already know by explaining cultural phenomena in a way that embraces their complex, contingent, and often contentious nature, while avoiding grand claims to universal truth.[8] This requires an interdisciplinary methodology, as contexts—like culture itself—can rarely be described in purely cultural terms. A cultural studies approach to literature also involves deferring aesthetic judgment, as this, too, can be the subject of analysis, bound as it is within political, social, and economic realms. When approaching poetry, the first question a cultural studies researcher would usually ask is not "How good is this poem?" or "What does this poem mean?" but "What is this poem good *for* and for whom?"[9]

My reason for treating poetry as culture is that the meanings and uses of poetry in China extend far beyond the assemblages of words that some would call (and others, inevitably, would not) a "poem." Poetry, as Joseph Harrington aptly puts it, is "not reducible to poems" and can instead be considered a "social form" that is dispersed across multiple textual and institutional sites. Its definitions, moreover, shift in response to changing aesthetic and ideological beliefs and always exist in the plural; there is no universal agreement as to what exactly a poem "is," despite thousands of years of efforts to pin poetry down.[10] This does not, however, stop many people from having their own idea of what a poem *should* be, even if they have never written one themselves and do not read poetry for pleasure. This holds especially true in China. As a genre that for many hundreds of years represented not only the zenith of literary accomplishment but also a means of entrance into China's imperial bureaucracy (as well as a source of self-comfort after failing to get in) and which, during the tumultuous twentieth century, was used for purposes that included aiding the War of Resistance against Japan (1937–45), stirring up proletarian passions during the disastrous Great Leap Forward (1958–61),[11] and returning psychological normality to the nation after the upheavals of the Cultural Revolution (1966–76), it stands to reason that poetry in twenty-first-century China is also subject to multiple political, economic, and emotional demands.

The cultural studies understanding of the conjuncture is useful for uncovering some of the structures that underpin poetry early on in the twenty-first century. Conjunctures are specific historic moments formed by the coming together of different kinds of context and circumstance that include discourses, everyday life practices, and regimes of power. As complex networks of social forms and forces, conjunctures are shaped by the conflicts that invariably exist among them as well as by attempts to resolve these conflicts through struggle and negotiation. Conjunctures serve as descriptions of the fragmented nature of social formations, which means that they do not exist a priori but have to be, as Lawrence Grossberg puts it, "constructed, narrated, fabricated."[12] The complexity of any individual historical moment makes description or storytelling an essential part of conjunctural analysis.

Conjunctures are not always defined by the nation-state, and neither can the regimes of power that help structure cultural activity be reduced to the simple opposition between domination and resistance or, as it is usually understood in commentary on the PRC, the struggles between state and society or between mainstream political ideology and the needs and desires of "ordinary citizens." Ban Wang suggests that typical polarizations between state, society, and community could be reframed from a performative perspective as a series of interactions among participants in modern society, thus creating potential for a more democratic mode of public life that depends on concepts such as justice, values, and norms.[13] In a similar vein, cultural studies proposes to replace the dichotomy between domination and resistance with the more fluid interplay of agency and resistance,[14] a way of problematizing culture that offers a distributed understanding of power and emphasizes the potential of individuals to use existing resources to satisfy their desires.

Closely connected to the interplay between agency and resistance is subjectivity, or selfhood produced by social means.[15] By exploring the subjectivities of cultural producers and consumers, who in today's age of participatory culture are often one and the same, culture can be understood as the culmination of individual consciousness and experience. This is linked to the idea that identity is not essential or absolute but is rather the product of semiotic constructions of difference, which for poets might include differences in socioeconomic status, gender, and geography, as well as cultural ideology and aesthetics.[16] In the social form of modern Chinese poetry, one of the key ways that subjectivities are expressed and fashioned is through gatekeeping, a concept most commonly employed in information and communication studies. Gatekeeping is central to the role of the media in modern public life and can be defined as "the process of culling and crafting countless bits of information into the limited number of messages that reach people every day."[17] Gatekeepers (*baguanren*) of poetry include not just people working for media outlets (websites, book publishers, newspapers, and so on) and the government-run agencies responsible for surveying and controlling information flows but also poetry critics and poets themselves, who have an interest in preserving the boundaries of poetry scenes and in asserting their poetry citizenship based on their own definition of modern poetry.

Poetry citizenship is a poetry-specific version of cultural citizenship, a term that has been used in English-language scholarship since the 1980s as way of understanding the relationships among individuals, culture, and society, especially in an increasingly cosmopolitan and technologically interconnected world.[18] Cultural citizenship denotes the right to belong to a larger community and to have one's belonging recognized by others; it also carries with it a responsibility to defend the dignity of the cultural community of which one is part.[19] Being a poet-citizen is about far more than simply writing poetry, keeping it in a drawer at home or filed away on a computer, and from time to time posting a poem or two on a blog or Internet forum. It also involves declaring membership in a broader poetry community through participation across multiple media spaces, adherence to specific interpretive strategies for reading and writing poems, and being recognized as a poet-citizen by other poets, critics, and academics—in other words, passing through the numerous gatekeeping mechanisms that surround the publication and evaluation of poetry in China. Gatekeeping practices hinge on individual subjectivities as well as on the shared literary beliefs of poetry groups and are a central means by which poets and the communities to which they belong make their agency felt. They are shaped not just by the historical conjuncture of the early twenty-first century but also by the dynamics associated with the different media spaces in which poetry is made public: the Internet, print publication, and face-to-face events, as well as by the Chinese discourses that underpin what are known in English as poetry "scenes."

THE CONJUNCTURE OF THE EARLY TWENTY-FIRST CENTURY

Researchers of contemporary Chinese culture and media have employed various terms in their attempt to name the historical period that begins in the early 1990s with Deng Xiaoping's Southern Tour of 1992, widely seen as his affirmation of capitalist development as the proper direction for the nation, and continues into the 2000s and 2010s. Xudong Zhang acknowledges the difficulty involved in so doing, describing the 1990s as heterogeneous to the point of defying categorization. "Postsocialism," Zhang's preferred descriptor for this decade over "postcolonialism," denotes a tension-filled mixture of value systems and modes of production, a central characteristic of which is the perceived need to defend and explain the legitimacy of socialist revolution in a global context that is defined largely by capitalist modernity. Zhang suggests that the imperative task facing researchers is to explore the differences that exist between postsocialist nations such as China and other parts of the world while trying to make sense of the continued existence of the socialist state and its indispensable role in constructing China's new socioeconomic system. A new dialectical way of thinking is needed to underscore the lively debates taking place across China in the 1990s on the future of the country.[20]

Growing numbers of scholars have adopted the idea of postsocialism to conceptualize changes in Chinese culture, society, and politics since the 1990s and make sense of the contradictions inherent in an increasingly pluralistic and fragmented Chinese society.[21] Sheldon Lu characterizes Chinese postsocialism as a battlefield between neoliberals and New Leftists, with the former celebrating the coming of bourgeois civil society and its protection of private ownership rights and the latter calling for greater equality between the social classes and a fairer system of wealth distribution across the country. Lu draws a line between the post*socialism* in the more cautious reform era of the 1980s and the *post*socialism that defines the period from the 1990s to the present, an age of "grandiose transnational capitalism."[22] Haomin Gong in his discussion of "uneven modernity" in postsocialist China examines the complicated relationship between the cultural and the socioeconomic, which he similarly sees as being characterized by both tensions and cooperation, conspiracies and negotiations, incorporation and conflict.[23]

Neoliberalism (Xin Ziyouzhuyi) and New Leftism (Xin Zuopai) are two major critical paradigms that convey China's ideologically conflicted landscape in the 1990s and beyond. David Harvey was the first to identify "neoliberalism with Chinese characteristics" as the outcome of the Chinese market economy's integration of neoliberal elements with centralized authoritarian control.[24] In her study of communications in China, Yuezhi Zhao frames her discussion around the concept of neoliberal revolution, borrowing Richard Robison's understanding of neoliberalism as an ideological system that calls for large-scale social and political change centered on the goal of extending market values and relations into broader social and political realms.[25] Neoliberal practices have been described as "predatory," involving "accumulation by dispossession" set in motion by the Chinese party-state in its embracing of market rationality and unleashing of entrepreneurial interests.[26]

In the context of the formation of China's middle class, neoliberalism has been seen as a window through which to examine changes in class and citizenship, with the government promoting its vision of neoliberal citizenship or "the entrepreneurial way of living or the self-reliable and self-responsible way of life" as a way of managing the multiple risks at stake in Chinese society, not the least of which is the legitimacy of single-party rule. The middle class (*zhongchan jieceng*) has emerged as a key governmental construct aimed at building a new nation-state centered on rationalized society.[27] Culture is an essential tool in this process. Employed by the government to enforce its neoliberal policies and promote harmonious society (*hexie shehui*), culture brings the principles of economic rationalism into the domain of everyday life and portrays individualization as the normative way of living in which risks are, in fact, distributed "unevenly and unequally."[28] The current political discourse of harmony, as Hai Ren suggests, is the product of a Confucian worldview that bases state sovereignty on the consensus of the people.

Given neoliberalism's tendency to enhance social and economic inequities and the residual influence of socialist ideology in China, the concomitant rise of New Leftist thinking is unsurprising. Like neoliberals, New Leftists are aware of the growing collusions between political power and economic capital that result from capitalist marketization but see them as more problematic than productive. Though they do not currently constitute a clearly defined group or political movement, New Leftist thinkers are united in their desire for justice and social equality, which they see as being threatened by the neoliberal model of development on display in China. Intellectual engagement, rather than political activism, is their preferred means of intervening in the mounting instances of oppression and exploitation that accompany the country's neoliberal economic practices.[29] Interventions take the form of cultural initiatives that involve a diverse range of people from political activists and social scientists to migrant workers and artists—or in the case of poetry, artists who happen to be migrant workers and who are championed as literary representatives of China's grassroots (*caogen*).[30]

In short, there is a growing consensus that China in the early twenty-first century is in the midst of a period of transition characterized by conflict and negotiation between ideologies and forms of power, although not everyone agrees on the direction or destination toward which China is transitioning. Negotiation and conflict are recurring themes in this book. In the case of poetry, they help precipitate shifts in who holds discursive power within poetry scenes, which are related in turn to developments in the media through which people gain access to cultural communities and make their voices heard. The concept of the conjuncture can help illuminate both the underlying historical conditions in which poetry is produced as well as the temporary collusions among a diverse array of people, texts, institutions, resources, and forms of capital that constitute poetry activity and shape poetry scenes.

Though these arrangements may seem to suggest a widespread passion for poetry and could be used as proof that it is still capable of acting as a unifying sociocultural force, beneath their surface lie simmering tensions between divergent ideologies and subjectivities. They are the product of both top-down political and economic uses of culture and bottom-up gatekeeping practices and cultural behaviors, although as we will see in the course of this book, this dichotomy usually falls apart upon closer examination. Tensions erupt in the form of debates surrounding, for example, the ambitions of online poetry groups, the contents of poetry anthologies, the practice of poetry recitation, the behaviors of poetry activists, and the reception of modern poetry online. Even the terms used to describe poetry scenes have been subject to contention. It is these clashes, as much as the vitality of poetry writing in the new millennium, that make the social form of modern Chinese poetry such a fascinating area of study.

POETRY SCENE DISCOURSES

Scenes are a part of everyday English vocabulary for discussing the production and consumption of culture, but on a theoretical level they are usually left undefined. Books on Chinese literature and culture are peppered with references to China's "intellectual scene," "cultural scene," "unofficial literary scene," and so on but almost never explain what is meant by these terms. A reluctance to define the term "scene" might stem from the rhetorical flexibility that its vagueness allows, as users of the word need only observe "a hazy coherence between sets of practices or affinities." This haziness is exacerbated by the number of tasks scenes are expected to perform: on top of their theatrical connotations (a scene within a play or film), they can also refer to the single site of a cultural activity, performance, or event (as in the scene of a music concert or book signing), as well as the sum of all activities that surround a cultural genre in a particular country or around the world (as in the global art scene).[31]

In Chinese, a variety of terms are used to refer to the collective areas of culture that are known in English as scenes. They include *jie* (realm or world), *tan* (altar or arena), and *quanzi* (circles). Like "scene," these terms point to an assortment of people who share an interest in a particular area of culture and who come together to create and evaluate the contents of their chosen cultural form. Within the overarching "world" of poetry are found a number of smaller communities or collectives referred to as groups (*qunti* or *tuanti*), societies (*she*), schools (*liupai*), movements (*yundong*), tides or waves (*chao*), isms (*zhuyi*), and generations (*dai*), bound by factors such as an intentionally or unintentionally shared poetics; a site or location of poetry activity such as a website, journal, or city of residence; and age or decade of birth. All active poets are considered part of China's poetry world (*shige jie*) and most find themselves assigned to a specific generation of writers whether they like it or not; some might also be representatives of one or more poetry groups or isms depending on their literary inclinations, while others prefer to maintain an individual approach to writing and disassociate themselves from any form of poetry collectivism.

While "world" and "circles" are relatively value-neutral terms for depicting a shared area of cultural interest, two concepts stand out within post-1990 Chinese poetry criticism as embodying noticeable discursive strategies in the conceptualization of poetry scenes. I refer to them as discourses to indicate that they both reflect existing power relations and exert an effect on social relations by producing power; they are dynamic rather than stable and can be understood in various ways by different people.[32] The first is *shitan*, which I translate as "poetry arena" to avoid confusion with the English "poetry scene." This term has been in use since premodern times and regularly appears in the titles of anthologies and histories of modern and classical Chinese poetry.[33] The original meaning of *tan* as a raised earthen platform used for ritual offerings has echoes in its modern usage as a platform for elite cultural or sporting activity (as in the literary arena or *wentan*, the sporting arena or *titan*, and the cinematic arena or *yingtan*).

A second discourse that has emerged much more recently surrounds the word *xianchang*, which I translate as "live scene" and which other scholars have rendered as "on the scene," "on the spot," "actual scene," and "on site."[34] *Xianchang* is a compound of *xian* (to reveal, actual, or of the present) and *chang* (a scene, field, or level open space) and was brought into the modern Chinese vernacular in the early twentieth century from Japanese, which pronounces it *genba*.[35] In both languages it can refer to the location of an incident or action; the spot where an activity is required to take place; the place where an organization or enterprise carries out activities; or a site of research that takes place outside the laboratory.[36] Used as a countable noun, "live scene" can denote individual sites of poetry-related activity such as online interactions, print publications, and face-to-face events. It also has a related adjectival meaning indicating either that a person is currently on the scene of an event that is occurring in real time or that an event or activity has arisen or been completed on location. This adjectival usage is best translated in English as "live," as in live performance (*xianchang biaoyan*) or live broadcasting (*xianchang zhibo*). When employed in cultural criticism, the term "liveness" (*xianchangxing*) is comparable to the contemporary spirit (*dangxiaxing*) or "here and now" (*ci shi ci di*) of cultural creation and activity.

The concept of the poetry arena needs to be understood in light of the close connection between poetry and the nation in twentieth-century China, itself a continuation of the political importance attached to poetry in imperial times. The modernization of poetry that began in the late nineteenth century with calls for a "poetry world revolution" (*shijie geming*) and that became entrenched during the New Culture Movement of the 1910s and 1920s through the efforts of poetry reformists such as Hu Shi and Guo Moruo was intended to open the gates of poetry by adopting the vernacular language and thus making poetry accessible to a broader segment of the reading public. Vernacular Chinese (*baihuawen*) had already been in use to a lesser extent in literary narratives of the Ming and Qing dynasties but was reimagined in the early twentieth century as a way of helping literature participate in the nation-building agenda that followed the collapse of the Qing dynasty (1644–1911).

The sense of historical mission (*shiminggan*) carried by many Republican-era poets did not mean that their efforts at modernizing poetry were fully accepted by readers at the time. As Michelle Yeh argues, modern poetry has always represented the avant-garde of cultural and literary trends in China, meaning that its effects have not always been appreciated by the general population; it is both "challenging and challenged," its newness rendering it "strange and suspicious" to general readers and intellectuals alike.[37] Michel Hockx has shown that the so-called New Poetry (Xin Shi) that was pioneered during the Republican era (1911–49) was mostly produced and theorized within tight-knit literary societies whose members shared their writings via small-scale print publications and meetings and whose activities went largely unknown to the majority of the Chinese population.[38] The insular nature of many of these communities, combined with the high levels of literacy traditionally required to write poetry in China, is partly what gives the poetry arena its exclusive connotations.

The other important historical context of the poetry arena is political. Since the mid-twentieth century, the mainland Chinese poetry arena has become equated with the cultural bureaucracy of the Chinese Communist Party (CCP), which after its Civil War victory over the Nationalist Party in 1949 subsumed all cultural activity under its auspices with the creation of the Chinese National Federation of Writers and Artists (Zhongguo Wenxue Yishujie Lianhehui, or Wenlian for short), an umbrella structure that contains within it culture-specific organizations such as the Writers' Association (Zuojia Xiehui) and the Film Artists' Association (Dianyingjia Xiehui), each represented at provincial and municipal levels. Recognized authors were (and many still are) formally employed within the Writers' Association, receiving publishing opportunities and a state salary in exchange for their adherence to government ideology.[39] Many poets and researchers have attempted to distinguish China's state-sponsored or official (*guanfang*) poetry arena from the nongovernmental/popular/of the people (*minjian*), unofficial (*fei guanfang*), or avant-garde (*xianfeng*) kind, especially since the end of the Cultural Revolution, a time when the divide was especially stark.[40] Nonetheless, attitudes toward the poetry arena remain colored by a suspicion of complicity between national politics and China's cultural elites, regardless of whether the poets contained within it identify with state-approved or unofficial definitions of poetry. Such attitudes are reflected in sarcastic puns on "poetry arena" as a *shitan*, "arena of shit," or *sitan*, "arena of the dead."

These historical contexts are essential for understanding the rise of the term "live scene" as an alternative to "poetry arena" in contemporary China. As a discourse, live scenes have gained currency in several fields of contemporary Chinese culture since the early to mid-1990s, roughly concurrent with the acceleration of China's economic reforms. From news reports to documentary cinema, theater, music, and literature, live scenes are taken to mean, in simplest terms, "where it's at." They embody an ideology of spontaneity and the here and now, of fleeting moments rather than big schemes and grand narratives, and of the increasingly permeable boundaries between participant and observer, performer and audience, author and reader. Live-scene discourse is especially prominent in cultural forms whose value has been brought into doubt by the growth of China's market economy. It offers a way for cultural producers to assert their authenticity and lay claim to the symbolic capital accruable simply by being there, present and involved, rather than measured according to external indicators of success such as sales volume, financial revenue, or popularity charts.

A number of cultural scholars in China have noted the importance of live-scene discourse to post-1990 cultural production and consumption. Dai Jinhua argues that live scenes featured as a salient part of China's postmodern landscape of the 1990s and identifies a "feeling of live scenes" (*xianchanggan*) as a central characteristic of 1990s Chinese culture. As she sees it, the sense of discontinuity and contemporaneity evident in live-scene narratives record a world in which any sense of a cultural center has dissipated if not disappeared entirely.[41] Dai explains the growing prominence of cultural forms such as rock music, experimental theater, performance art, and documentary cinema as a continuation of patterns of artistic development begun in hidden corners in the late 1980s, unable to enter public vision until sociopolitical changes allowed. A discursive shift toward live scenes thus does not imply the creation of new phenomena but rather an emphasis on reality, "naked textures," and "bearing witness."[42]

Such arguments about the cultural importance of live scenes are echoed in critical and scholarly writings on performance art, theater, and documentary film. Performance art theorist Qiu Zhijie argues that a live-scene approach requires physical presence during the production of culture and suggests that even the slightest movements of hand or foot have the potential to influence the live scene.[43] Another critic, Zhang Xinyu, makes a similar point in a discussion of the liveness of performance art, a quality that he suggests requires a perceptual rather than a rational examination of the artistic work and emphasizes "the here and now of the original work and its authenticity."[44] Thomas Berghuis also comments on the importance of live scenes (which he translates as "actual scenes") to Chinese performance art, suggesting that they indicate a preference for live action over documentation and can be understood as a model for remediating the space and time of artistic performance.[45] In contemporary drama, Huang Zhenlin points to the amplification of a "feeling of live scenes" as a key factor in opening up more immediate channels of communication between performers and their audiences and argues that theater offers a kind of aura, a coming together of breaths, sights, and sounds with which flat-screen arts cannot compare.[46]

Although film, unlike performance art and theater, does not require the physical co-presence of producers and audiences in order for the work of art to transpire, live-scene discourse has also been a prominent feature of documentary film criticism since the 1990s. It can be viewed as a strategy to highlight the processes involved in the authentic representation of a scene or happening. The documentary filmmaker Wu Wenguang is among the most vocal theorists of live scenes in China and has edited three editions of the journal *Document* (Xianchang), published in 2000, 2001, and 2005, which document scenes of cultural activity including art, literature, theater, cinema, and music. Wu emphasizes the importance to the journals of the "present tense" (*xianzaishi*) and "on the scene presence" (*zaichang*),[47] conveyed through the inclusion of personal information about cultural producers as well as work notes, photographs, and other documentary materials. Wu claims to value live scenes for their capacity to convey something essential and gritty (*juyou keligan*), unlike fictional forms of cinema whose objects are fabricated, "non-live scene," and thus less essential.[48]

This preoccupation with live scenes may be seen as emblematic of the urban generation of Chinese cinematographers and amateur cinema in particular.[49] According to Zhen Zhang, *xianchang* captures the contemporary spirit of this generation of filmmakers and refers to a space that challenges the divide between professional and amateur cinematic practice and blurs the boundaries between documentary and fiction. An insistence on boundary blurring is in part this generation's reaction to its marginalization in the hands of major film studios and its exclusion from conventional, more costly channels of cinematic production. The scene is thus shifted to low-cost or cost-free filming locations such as streets, markets, and residential compounds: "in short, the vast 'location' outside the walls of the system." Jia Zhangke's film *The Pickpocket* (Xiao wu) is a typical example of this production style, set and filmed entirely in Jia's hometown of Fenyang, Shanxi province. Thus located, *xianchang* becomes a kind of aesthetic or poetics in itself, founded in shared social space and experience. It is "contingent, immanent, improvisational and open-ended"—in Jia's own words, an "adventure on the scene of shooting, which will yield unexpected situations but also possibilities."[50]

Zhang links live-scene discourse to a mediated representation of reality—an "edgy realism"—enabled in part by giving ordinary people the right to participate in cinematic productions of and about themselves. As a result of this expansion in participation, cinematic space becomes filled with the textures of daily life and multiple voices emanating from different experiences and realities. Live scenes, therefore, constitute "a particular social and epistemic space" in which the specificity of individual and social experience can be recorded and acknowledged, and voices and performances can be expressed via aesthetic means.[51] A live-scene approach to realism is a reaction to the historical dominance of orthodox or more culturally entrenched realisms, in particular socialist realism and the historical allegories evident in the work of fifth-generation filmmakers such as Chen Kaige and Zhang Yimou. The resulting form of documentary realism is commonly referred to in Chinese film criticism as *jishi zhuyi*, which Chris Berry translates as "on-the-spot realism"—*jishi* meaning, literally, "recording the real" rather than *xianshi*, or "revealing the real."[52] At the same time, any representation of reality is inevitably an intervention into that reality, or as Dai Jinhua sees it, a way of overturning the culture of the moment. Dai observes how the emphasis on live scenes as an antidote to official talk (*guanfang shuofa*) has gradually turned into a peculiarly Chinese type of cultural performance in itself.[53]

These cultural understandings of live scenes are echoed in the live-scene discourse that surrounds modern poetry. This was confirmed by a qualitative survey I conducted of Chinese poets that consisted of a questionnaire disseminated via Internet forums, email, and blogs. It included ten open-ended questions designed to elicit their thoughts on various aspects of contemporary poetry activity.[54] The first question, pertaining to their understanding of the terms "poetry arena" and "live scene," generated some revealing responses. Several poets expressed unfamiliarity with the poetry arena; one compared it to a neighbor whose mother's last name he did not know; another claimed that he had no idea where the poetry arena was located but was certain that it was "far behind" (*luohouyu*) live scenes. Many poets communicated distrust, if not active dislike, of the poetry arena. One wrote, "poetry arena, in my eyes, is a dirty word. 'Arena' has performative connotations that imply the existence of strategies, of clowns and spectators; its scope is narrow, but because they have an amplifier, the voices are loud and drown many ears." Another participant suggested that the arena is a "cliquish entity" that grants its members entrance through a partisan gate (*menkan*); this acceptance must be openly acknowledged in order for it to have taken place. The poetry arena, according to this respondent, has become "stale and stubborn," despised and distrusted. One described the poetry arena as an "arena of the dead," and another drew a sharp comparison between the arena and a live scene, comparing the former to an "unchanging platform" and the latter to a "current location."

Most poets shared a vision of live scenes as current, individual, and exciting, as the places and moments where and when poetry happens, often outside the control of the poetry arena. One defined live scenes as "the places where living poets set foot, where they bear witness, and through which they gain entrance to and interact on the 'true veins' of the activities of poetic creation." Some saw a connection between live scenes and poetry writing, arguing that "live scenes are creation, experimentation; as long as you are creating and experimenting, you can say you are on a live scene." Others offered a medium-specific understanding of live scenes, explaining them as Chinese Internet poetry phenomena that supplement the poetry arena that is constituted, instead, by print poetry journals. This is because the Internet is where poetry "happens"; as one poet put it, "it is changing, happening, and growing, whereas the poetry arena is pre-existent and static. Take, for example, someone who has not written a poem for many years: unless his or her poetry is still influencing current poetic writing, he or she is a person of the poetry arena, and not of live scenes of poetry."

Thus, in general, the poetry arena is associated with high levels of gatekeeping, and the people assumed to belong to it tend to be established writers who have published poetry and/or poetry criticism in print journals and anthologies and are regularly invited to attend poetry events such as recitals, conferences, and awards ceremonies, regardless of whether or not they are still writing poetry. Live scenes, on the other hand, are constituted of whoever is present in poetry activity that evolves in real time in physical or mediatized space. Live-scene discourse sometimes appears as an expression of resistance against the perceived discursive power (*huayuquan*)—or gatekeeping authority—of the poetry arena to decide which poets and poems are worthy of publication. There is a parallel here with the focus on live scenes among documentary filmmakers such as Wu Wenguang and Jia Zhangke who feel excluded from conventional channels of cinematic production. At the same time as it reflects a quest for immediacy and authenticity shared with performance artists and filmmakers, the emphasis on presence, liveness, participation, and the here and now could be seen as an attempt to recapture what has been called the "sacred aura" of poetry as high culture during an era in which it is widely thought to have been lost due to the inexorable rise of mediated commercial culture.[55]

MEDIA DYNAMICS

Another explanation for the tensions between the discourse of the poetry arena and that of live scenes is connected to media dynamics. As Hartley, Burgess, and Bruns suggest, media dynamics can be both endogenous, pertaining to change that occurs within a particular medium, and exogenous, pertaining to shifting relationships across different media.[56] The first three chapters of this book address the three primary media spaces that constitute poetry scenes in the early twenty-first century: the Internet, print publications, and face-to-face events. Considering these spaces separately allows us to examine how individual and communal approaches to poetry activity relate to the particular media space in use and to explore how dynamics within and between these spaces contribute to poetry scene productivity (and contention) and thus enhance their accompanying sense of eventfulness or "liveliness." The discourse of the poetry arena reflects media dynamics associated with what John Miles Foley calls the "textual arena" or tAgora and its concomitant ideology of the text. These include qualities such as "fixity, single authorship, exact replicability, resistance to morphing, free-standing status, proprietary nature, and a lack of pathways."[57] To this list one could add authority, editorial control, and containment, which relate to the function of texts to mask contingency, or to remove uncertainty and replace "the conditional with the factual."[58] As a discourse, the poetry arena carries a sense of authority as a purveyor of texts intended to stand the test of time.

Live-scene discourse, on the other hand, has more in common with what Foley calls the "arena of oral tradition" or oAgora.[59] Participation in this arena takes place:

> via face-to-face transaction, not by swapping texts. Everything happens "in the moment"—right now, not at some convenient future time to be chosen by a detached, independent reader and forestalled until the time seems right. The oAgora event is all-consuming for audience and performer alike because it is unmediated by texts, with nothing held at arm's length.

Rather than facilitating ownership over fixed texts, the oAgora is public and open-access. Instead of an assembled collection of objects, as we find in a printed book, the oAgora is a linked system of potentials consisting of "sets of intangible pathways activated by navigators making their own decisions and choosing among ever-contingent realities."[60] And rather than replacing the conditional with the factual as the tAgora tries to do, the oAgora depends upon contingency, making it "a system of openly acknowledged, dynamic 'What ifs?'" If this is beginning to sound as much like a description of surfing the Internet as communicating and transmitting culture orally, that is because, according to Foley, the two experiences are fundamentally alike. Both depend on continuous processes rather than static products and on vectors of magnitude and direction rather than stationary points; in other words, "not on 'What?' but on 'How do I get there?'" The upshot is that both the oral tradition (OT) and Internet technologies (IT) echo the way that humans think "by navigating along pathways within an interactive network."[61]

The case studies investigated in this book suggest that the three media spaces of the Internet, print publication, and face-to-face events are best thought of as hybrid agoras: rather than operating purely according to the rules of play of the three arenas of communication identified by Foley, each space contains traces of the others and functions according to a complex mixture of dynamics and discourses. While the dominant ideology in all three spaces remains the ideology of the text (the way of thinking that underpins the discourse of the poetry arena), a more open and contingent approach to poetry is taking hold in the discourse of live scenes. Live-scene discourse suggests that who is "on the scene" and worthy of poetry citizenship depends not so much on poets' past publication history or how many literary prizes won but on how active poets are in the present and how involved they are in the processes of poetry writing, sharing, reacting, and debating.

The contingency and ephemerality emphasized in live-scene discourse have not, however, prevented some poets from using it as a way of enacting an alternative style of gatekeeping within poetry communities. In an interesting twist of logic, the poet Yi Sha has complained about the inability of editors at publishing houses to understand the true workings of poetry scenes, largely due to their being "people who are not present [on the scene]" (*bu zaichang zhe*); that is to say, they are "not on the already existent and ever growing live scenes of Chinese new poetry." Because these editors "do not understand the means of existence and constitutive state of outstanding poets," any poetry anthologies they compile and publish through "proper" (*zhenggui*) channels are, conversely, "suspicious and improper." A satisfactory understanding of the ins and outs of Chinese poetry can only be gained, he argues, through participation online: "In the new century, the Internet has clearly already become the primary live scene for contemporary poets' daily existence and for the open circulation of contemporary poetry."[62] This is undoubtedly an expression of gatekeeping authority, the implication being that Yi Sha and his fellow Internet-savvy poets have the best grip on which poems and poets are worth publishing.

My research on Internet-based poetry communities, presented in Chapter 1, supports Yi Sha's conclusion that the Internet is now the main space in which poetry is produced and circulated in China. The Internet has also, however, made poetry susceptible to new modes of reception and circulation that are not quite like those of either print publication or Foley's arena of oral tradition. As I explore in Chapter 4, poems have on several occasions "gone viral" by being rapidly passed from person to person hundreds of thousands of times via social media such as blogs, forums, and microblogs (*weibo*). If the poetry arena is understood as representing an economy of authority based primarily on access to print publication and live scenes symbolize an economy of authenticity based on the immediacy of face-to-face and online interactions, then what is at work when texts or ideas go viral online is an economy of attention, dependent on what often seems to be the random ability of images and words to hit upon something so fundamental to human psychology that they get repeatedly viewed and shared up to millions (or, in the case of the South Korean pop star Psy's music video "Gangnam Style," billions) of times.

Carolyn Miller and Dawn Shepherd propose that the phenomenon of viral circulation can be explained by the "volume and volatility of information, fragmentation of attention, speed of dissemination, [and] multiplicity of connection" that characterize the Internet. These result in what they call "the facile replication of form," which can be the product of habit, technology, or deliberate action.[63] I argue that the instances in which Chinese poetry has gone viral suggest a mass form of gatekeeping in which China's otherwise non-poetry-reading online public behaves like a collective consciousness or what some are calling the "hive mind," using the acts of clicking and forwarding as a means of expressing an attitude toward modern Chinese poetry.[64] Although this is not to say that all Internet users hold the same opinions of the texts being shared, the ultimate effect of viral circulation is to subject poetry to different values from those of either the poetry arena or live-scene discourse. In other words, going viral is usually not as "facile" as Miller and Shepherd suggest: it can be construed as a form of popular and often highly creative resistance against elitist intellectual or political uses of culture and in this sense takes on ideological implications of its own.[65]

The discursive practice that usually comes to the fore when verse goes viral on the Chinese Internet is that of the *egao* or spoof, succinctly defined by Haomin Gong and Xin Yang as "technology-enabled online parody."[66] Rather than a tool for the production and dissemination of high culture, the web for the majority of Chinese Internet users is a space for community-based participation, contention, and entertainment. It is the latter of these that has had the biggest effect on poetry in the twenty-first century: while modern Chinese poetry has been many things during the first one hundred years of its development (iconoclastic, experimental, educational, propagandistic, liberating, cathartic, soothing, and intentionally provocative, to name a few), entertaining is not usually high on the list. In the new millennium, poetry's ability to go viral is closely linked to its potential for producing humor and enjoyment. In order to understand how this potential is realized and the ways in which the public's spoofing practices clash with the discourses of the poetry arena and live scenes, we must first familiarize ourselves with some key facets of the communication and cultural sectors in contemporary China.

COMMUNICATIONS AND THE CULTURAL ECONOMY

The interactions between poetry scene discourses and media dynamics are a product of the historical conjuncture of early twenty-first-century China, a time in which the viability of print is being challenged by the ease of publication on the Internet and when the uses of all media are still dominated by the dynamics of print and oral communication. At the same time, communication technologies in China operate under the watchful eye of the party-state, which continues to use the media as channels for the "correct guidance of public opinion" (*zhengque daoxiang*).[67] The media, according to Yuezhi Zhao, are a tool for the acquisition of economic and sociocultural privileges and political power and thus facilitate the Chinese party-state's ability to rule.[68]

Underlying the government's practices of media control is an awareness of the inequity that abounds in Chinese society across class, ethnic, rural-urban, and regional divides. Consequently, as Zhao argues, the issues of access and control surrounding tools of social communication are more critical than ever and "'the power to discourse' (*huayuquan*) has never been so central to the unfolding process of social struggle."[69] Since 1989, the government has attempted to ensure that disciplinary power is more evenly dispersed across all levels of the propaganda hierarchy, resulting in a system of censorship and discipline that requires each media entity to "bear the responsibility of defending its own territory" (*shoutu youze*).[70] Thus media control has subtly shifted from a strategy of total control to one of effective domination. Censorship, accordingly, is now shaped more by negotiation than negation and is differentiated across media outlets depending on the size and nature of the audience. This has produced a seemingly paradoxical situation in which media control appears to have been tightened at the same time as the public's space for expression has grown.[71]

In addition to the growth of the Internet into what is arguably China's most important and contentious discourse space (*huayu kongjian*), discussed in more detail in Chapters 1 and 4, another key aspect of communications in China is the increasing importance of the media and cultural sector within the Chinese economy. Two trends can be observed in this regard, both of which have had a salient effect on the interactions between poetry and media organizations in the new millennium. The first is the shift in media-based understandings of culture away from the socialist high-culture connotations of literature and art (*wenyi*) toward entertainment (*yule*) and leisure (*xiuxian*), a process that began in the 1990s and has been described by Geremie Barmé as "kowtowing to the vulgar" (*meisu*).[72] Evidence for this is ubiquitous in contemporary media and culture and includes the rise of provincial satellite television channels such as Hunan Satellite TV, which specializes in producing uplifting entertainment rather than the more serious-minded news shows and dramas typical of China's state-run television company, China Central Television (CCTV).[73]

The second trend is the changing function of culture itself, which according to Yuezhi Zhao has been relieved of both its Marxist legacy of belonging to the "superstructure" and its elitist overtones, thereby transforming itself into a means by which money is made and citizens engage in symbolic forms of consumption.[74] Through a series of reports and directives, the Chinese party-state has made it clear that it now considers culture to be a larger category that subsumes the news media within it and is capable of "mutually interpenetrating" with politics and economics, or as Jing Wang puts it, "political, cultural, and economic capital in post-1992 China now emerge as interchangeable terms of value."[75] A recurring theme in government reports is "cultural system reforms" (*wenhua tizhi gaige*). These reforms, which aim to support the development of China's culture industry (*wenhua chanye*) and promote the use of soft power in competitive global contexts, have effectively replaced the agenda of media reform as a central component of political reform.[76] The interchangeability between cultural and economic capital is encapsulated in the concept of the cultural economy (*wenhua jingyi*) and the catchphrase "using culture to promote business" (*yiwen cuxiao*).[77] It is resulting at all administrative levels in the synergistic use of culture to boost local commerce, consolidate brand images, and distinguish cities and regions from their neighbors in order to attract financial investors and consumers.

In his examination of themed spaces in neoliberal China, Hai Ren employs the concept of the "life spectacle" to emphasize the importance of media and culture to contemporary capitalism and to shaping the ways that people think, act, and function in everyday life. Spectacles, Guy Debord's term for a mode of social life in which "all that was directly lived has become mere representation," are a form of governmental apparatus used to "communicate 'life' as a *strategic* response to a given historical urgency."[78] The resulting aestheticization of everyday life is marked by "a rich visual poetry," a sequence of concrete activities that serve the government's need to promote a harmonious middle-class society yet contain, nonetheless, unresolved tensions and ambiguities. Examples include ethnic minority theme parks, folklore museums, and "life television" programs that reminisce on ordinary people's lived experiences. An emphasis on life spectacles is but one example of the Chinese state's changing style of communication, which has moved away from the top-down, centrally planned propaganda model toward a "public relations model of communication that cultivates a message's effects and is interested in the audience's responses."[79]

Central to this public relations model of communication in China and the media's portrayal of life spectacles are the actions of individuals, in particular entrepreneurs, who avail themselves of the freedoms offered by the do-it-yourself (DIY) way of life by, for example, becoming CEO of their own company, making films that star themselves, or marketing their talents through social media.[80] While do-it-yourself lifestyles may seem hopeful and empowering, Ren suggests that they also carry considerable risks, leaving individuals vulnerable to their own mistakes and to the uneven opportunities for success in Chinese neoliberal society.[81] The DIY approach might also seem to contradict what Zhao describes as the dominant "consumerist mode of cultural citizenship enfranchisement";[82] the former suggests a productive self-reliance, while the latter values individuals primarily for their ability to consume, spend money, and thus contribute to economic growth. Both, however, mark a significant change from the old socialist understanding of citizenship, which was organized collectively through the work unit (*danwei*) and commune and centered on the working class. As a result of the individualization process, citizenship is now reimagined as an individual undertaking, with each person delinked from the collective and responsible for his or her own well-being.[83]

What, then, does all this mean for modern Chinese poetry? Although poetry might easily be assumed to exist in isolation from broader socioeconomic forces, many of the conflicts and tensions that enliven poetry scenes can be connected to China's transition toward a capitalist mode of life and the accompanying changes in media and culture. Tensions can be observed between the power of the collective and the desires of the individual, between the government's strategic use of the media to foster economic growth and the uses to which media are put by poetry scenes, and between entertainment-oriented understandings of culture and the expectations of both poets and non-poetry-reading publics that poetry, as a core part of China's national cultural identity and a key representative of high culture, has a duty to rise above the cacophony of materialist desires that dominates media and culture in China today. "Rising above" requires that somebody has to do gatekeeping to ensure that the descriptive categories of "poem" and "poet" still carry value. Gatekeepers of poetry include established poets and critics who control access to print publication (people usually associated with the poetry arena), as well as those who consider themselves active on live scenes of poetry. They also include members of the public, who use spoofing and humor as a means of commenting on the direction in which modern poetry seems to be heading.

The entrepreneurial way of life is on display in the actions of wealthy poets who use their own resources to sponsor (*zanzhu*) poetry activity and boost their individual reputations as poet-citizens and poetry activists (*shige huodongjia*). Combined with the sponsorship of poetry events by real estate companies and other big businesses (discussed in Chapter 3), one might conclude that poetry has been subsumed within the cultural economy to the extent that it has become just another mediated life spectacle or one of many ways in which businesses can use culture to enhance profits.[84] To make this argument, however, would be to ignore the agency of poets themselves and the communities to which they belong. The conjuncture at which poets find themselves in the early twenty-first century is marked not just by innovative political and economic uses of culture but also by the unrelenting desire of poets to control their creative destiny and narrate their own history of poetic development, as well as by the cultural memory that continues to surround the genre of poetry in China.

POETRY HISTORY AND CULTURAL MEMORY

For all the emphasis on the here and now of poetry activity that is suggested by live-scene discourse, poetry history remains a very real force within Chinese poetry scenes. This is evident in the huge volume of books and essays that deal with the historical development of modern Chinese poetry, many of which are written by poets and critics as well as by literary scholars such as Hong Zicheng, Cheng Guangwei, Zhang Xin, Zhou Zan, and Luo Zhenya, among others.[85] Books on the history of modern (*xiandai*, usually understood to mean Republican era and beyond) and contemporary (*dangdai*, which according to CCP versions of history begins in 1949 but is increasingly being understood to mean post-Mao) poetry are typically divided into different groups, generations, and movements, emphasizing the continuities and discontinuities between them as well as the contributions of individual poets who exert a particularly strong influence on the content of poetry.

That writing history is seen as such a vital undertaking among contemporary poets and critics is in itself significant; as Maghiel van Crevel points out, unlike poets of the Republican era whose modernizing efforts were considered central to the nation-building project, the contemporary avant-garde has had no such "singular purchase on the making of literary history."[86] From one perspective, even the act of writing modern poetry in China today is a form of resistance against the sweeping tides of history, in which capitalist economics and the transformation of culture into entertainment and a site for profit-making are thought to have rendered poetry and other forms of high culture obsolete. In this sense poetry might even be considered, to appropriate a phrase from Yomi Braester, a witness *against* rather than *for* history.[87] Taking control of poetry history by narrating its development and mapping its terrain acquires further significance as a way for poets to "achieve a new aesthetic aura for themselves as producers of history."[88] Writing history and remembering the past are a means of emphasizing poetry citizenship and connecting the genre of poetry to specific people and groups; it also reinforces the existence of poetry as a social form and not just a series of individual texts, thus highlighting the agency of poets to determine their own path of literary development.

The need to produce history and not simply be governed by it takes on additional urgency in light of China's often-stated identity as a "nation of poetry" and the public's resulting sense of ownership over the cultural memory of poetry. Jan Assmann explains the importance of cultural memory to national identity, defining the former as a collective understanding of knowledge that is disseminated across the generations through social interactions and that shapes human experience and behavior. Assmann makes a distinction between cultural memory, which takes time to accumulate and is removed from the everyday, and communicative memory, which is based on everyday communications and characterized by a lack of organization and specialization, as well as by thematic instability and reciprocity of roles.[89] Which communicative memories of poetry any given person holds depends on a variety of factors including age and education; what I refer to in this book as the "non-poetry-reading public" is by no means a uniform whole that possesses identical attitudes and values. To the extent that one can speak of a cultural memory of poetry in China, in the early twenty-first century it is still dominated by classical rather than modern poetry. This has the potential to change, however, as communicative memories develop into cultural memory over time via the processes of objectification and transmission through the media and among networks of people.

The generations that came of age during the Maoist years from the establishment of the PRC in 1949 to Mao's death in 1976 are most likely to remember the revolutionary zeal and theatrical style of poetry recitations during that time and appreciate the classical verse of Chairman Mao himself.[90] They may recall attending public recitation events and having to memorize Mao's poetry when they were young; some might have been aware of the Tiananmen Square incident of 1976, when a mass public display of grief for Zhou Enlai manifested in an outpouring of classical- and modern-style poems that were recited aloud, scribbled on scraps of paper and twisted into wreaths of flowers, stuck onto lampposts and security fencing, and hung among the branches of the trees that surround the square.[91] Those who were born during the 1950s, 1960s, and early 1970s who experienced China's high-culture fever as students and artistic youths (*wenyi qingnian*) may feel the most nostalgia toward the more individualistic, lyrical poetry of that decade. Many will have gone through a phase of writing modern poems themselves, perhaps as part of one or more of the hundreds of campus poetry societies that were formed across the country during the 1980s.

Today's younger generations, born into Reform-era (post-1978) China, have been exposed to a mixture of classical and modern poetry through their education, although the volume of classical Chinese and foreign works they read far outweighs the modest number of modern Chinese poems included in school textbooks.[92] Most have been taught standardized readings of canonical texts (*jingdianzuo*) such as Xu Zhimo's "Second Farewell to Cambridge" (Zaibie kangqiao) and Dai Wangshu's "Rainy Alley" (Yuxiang) and trained to appreciate their beauty and emotional effects. Patriotism features heavily, as demonstrated by poems such as Ai Qing's "I Love This Land" (Wo ai zhe tudi), Haizi's "Motherland, Or a Dream as a Horse" (Zuguo, huo yi meng wei ma), the Taiwanese exile poet Yu Guangzhong's "Nostalgia" (Xiangchou), and Shu Ting's "Ah Motherland, My Dear Motherland!" (Zuguo a, wo qin'ai de zuguo).[93] Consequently, these younger generations tend to associate poetry with patriotic or romantic lyrical verse and with the classical genre as distinguished by a singularly difficult set of textual attributes such as rhyme, rhythm, tone, meter, form, allusion, metaphor, and so on. To their minds, any poem that fails to demonstrate at least some of these characteristics can be declared, in unequivocal terms, to be "not a poem," a charge that has plagued modern Chinese poetry since its earliest experiments in the Republican era.

The distinction I am alluding to between a history of modern poetry articulated by participants in poetry scenes and the cultural and communicative memories held by the non-poetry-reading public is not absolute. As Ban Wang shows in his work on memory and history in modern China, it is often difficult to distinguish between the two: history, for example, is kept alive through the creative acts of memory, which in turn can help wage a struggle against new mythologies that disguise themselves as history.[94] Modern history begins by critiquing tradition and memory, but as historical narratives become set in stone and start to dominate the public consciousness, memory can offer a necessary contrasting vision of the past. Such dynamic motion between memory and history results in a critical historical consciousness, which Wang defines as "the ever-intensified self-conscious discourse that criticizes the 'natural,' embodied, inherited practice based on memory."[95] Still, there is clearly a massive discrepancy in China between, on the one hand, poets' experience of modern poetry as dynamic, forward-moving, and full of life and, on the other, the general public's perception that modern poetry mostly exists in ossified form in school textbooks, perhaps occasionally appearing on television and the radio in the form of stylized recitations by famous actors.[96]

In order to grasp the full extent of this disconnect, it is necessary to have an understanding of some of the major events and discourses that are described in poetry history books as marking the development of modern Chinese poetry since the late twentieth century. Just as current cultural discourses impact the production and reception of culture, so too can the discursive formation of history shape the way that poets approach their own writing and involvement in poetry activities. The Republican and Maoist eras of modern Chinese poetry have been detailed in a number of other books;[97] I will focus on the period since the end of the Cultural Revolution and the poetry activities that constitute what is often called the poetic "avant-garde." What follows is not intended to be a comprehensive overview of the post-Mao development of Chinese poetry but a discussion of the general patterns of most historical narrations, as well as of a few key events, concepts, and debates that influence current Chinese poetry scenes.

POETRY SINCE THE DEATH OF MAO

Despite the subordination of culture to politics under Chairman Mao's rule between the establishment of the People's Republic of China in 1949 and his death in 1976 and the risks involved in defying his vision of culture as a political tool to serve the CCP, Chinese poets' modernizing ambitions and desire for individual expression did not dry up during this time. Instead they continued in the PRC, and more openly in Hong Kong and Taiwan, in the efforts of poets who were willing to risk political retribution by writing a more emotionally honest style of poetry. During the Cultural Revolution, poems were passed around in secret by hand and by word of mouth among readers who craved an alternative to the orthodox literature that dominated the public stage.[98] Of these "underground" poets, Shi Zhi ("index finger," the pen name of Guo Lusheng) and Huang Xiang are the best known, the former for iconic poems like "Believe in the Future" (Xiangxin weilai), a defiant statement of youthful optimism written before he succumbed to mental illness in the 1970s, and the latter for his participation in the Wild Duck Salon (Yeya Shalong), a Guiyang-based secret literary society that was active in the late 1960s and 1970s. Huang Xiang's 1968 poem "Beast" (Yeshou) appeared to epitomize the mind-set of these poets with the line, "Even if I have only one bone left / I will stick it in the throat of this abominable age."[99]

Most historical narratives of contemporary poetry begin in earnest with the appearance in Beijing in the late 1970s of a group of writers who created the literary journal *Today* (Jintian), now widely celebrated as China's first unofficial poetry journal. *Today* was produced on a shoestring budget between December 1978 and September 1980 before being declared an illegal publication and ordered to cease all literary activities. It was in its pages that many of China's best-known contemporary poets first published their works: Bei Dao, Mang Ke, Shu Ting, Yang Lian, and Gu Cheng, among others. Their poetry became collectively known as misty or obscure (*menglong*) after it was described in this way by a hostile critic in a 1980 issue of the Writers' Association journal *Poetry* (Shikan). Such criticisms were nothing new to these poets, whose writings were regularly declared weird (*guguai*), incomprehensible (*nandong*), and opaque (*huise*) by readers more accustomed to the socialist transparency of Mao-era poetry.

At the same time as this new wave of poetry drew criticism from establishment-oriented critics and older-generation poets, it was its misty or highly imagistic nature that gave it such broad appeal in Reform-era China. The poet and critic Xu Jingya, writing in 1981, announced his delight with the new poetry: "The poetry arena has given rise to a new kind of beauty!"[100] The individual frustrations and desires expressed within many Misty poems resonated with a public that was thirsty for any form of culture that might speak to their own emotional and ideological ambivalences. The *Today* group in particular won legions of fans and imitators across the country. As early as 1979, open-air poetry recitals held in a Beijing park drew crowds in the thousands, attracted by what Tian Xiaoqing described as the "celebrity effect" of poets like Bei Dao, Shu Ting, and Duoduo.[101] The subsequent canonization of Misty Poetry in the 1980s was so rapid that it soon found itself the target of attack by a younger generation of writers, mostly born in the 1960s, who declared their intention to "pass Bei Dao" and thus mark the beginning of a new post-Misty (*hou menglong*) era.

The 1980s are often remembered as a golden age for modern Chinese poetry, a time in which poets had been granted freedom from the political repression of the Mao years and were taking part (even if they did not realize it) in China's national modernization project.[102] Cultural pluralism was on the rise, reflected in the vast array of poetry schools and isms that sprang up across the country. In 1986, Xu Jingya embarked on the ambitious task of gathering them together in what he called the "Grand Exhibition of Modernist Poetry Groups on China's Poetry Arena in 1986" (Zhongguo shitan 1986 xiandaishi qunti dazhan). A total of sixty-five groups of varying sizes were included, most of which claimed membership of the Third Generation (Di san dai) of poets, self-anointed successors to the early PRC generation of writers and the Misty poets.[103] They included the colloquial poetry of Them (Tamen) in Nanjing, the irrepressible chauvinism of the college-aged Macho Men (Manghan) in Sichuan, the not-rational, not-sublime cultural philosophy of the Not-Not (Feifei) group, also from Sichuan, and the playful irreverence of Shanghai's School of Coquetry (Sajiao pai). The Grand Exhibition thus marked a decisive public declaration of the vitality of the Chinese poetry arena, which had moved into a time of newfound "pluriformity and abundance" and further freed itself from the ideological restrictions of the Cultural Revolution and early 1980s.[104]

But by the end of the decade a sense of alienation had begun to spread among Chinese poets. As Michelle Yeh suggests, this can be attributed in part to political movements that impacted writers and intellectuals in the 1980s, such as the Anti-Spiritual Pollution campaign of 1983, the Anti-Bourgeois Liberalization campaign of 1987, and the nationwide crackdown on pro-democracy protests in June 1989. National politics, however, do not tell the full story. Poets were equally disenfranchised by the effects of China's economic reforms, which were resulting in an increasingly visible divide between the extravagant lifestyles of China's new rich—as well as the writers who were still employed with generous salaries by the China Writers' Association—and the far more modest circumstances of those on the lower rungs of the country's economic ladder, which included many poets.

One result of poetry's perceived marginalization was the emergence of a religiously inflected discourse and poetics that Yeh describes as a "cult of poetry" (*shige chongbai*). Religious symbolism could be detected in numerous unofficial poetry journals and writings in the late 1980s and early to mid-1990s, in some cases taking on explicitly Christian overtones, in others suggesting that poetry offers spiritual nourishment during times of material paucity. The impression that China's poets were suffering was compounded by the suicides of the poets Haizi in 1989, Ge Mai in 1990, and Gu Cheng in 1993. In death, these poets have been hailed as poet-heroes and saints, their writings scoured for signs of creative genius and psychological torment. Even the tragic manner in which Gu Cheng killed his wife before taking his own life has not stopped him from being canonized within what Yeh characterizes as a genealogy of poet-martyrs, traceable all the way back to the "father of Chinese poetry," Qu Yuan, who drowned himself in 278 BC.[105]

And so the 1990s began in a somber mood, brought on in part by the events of June 1989 and the deaths of well-known poets, and in part by the dawning realization that the central role that poetry had played in the intellectual life of Reform-era China had come to an end. Several poets who had risen to prominence in the 1980s spent the next decade living outside of China in a state of exile, concerned about their safety and the limitations on their freedom back home. In China, the decline in public enthusiasm for poetry had led many critics to talk of a crisis of confidence and to question modern poetry's legitimacy as a literary genre. Professional critics were frustrated by what they saw as poets' failure to deal in any meaningful way with the transformations occurring within Chinese society and culture in the post–New Era (*hou xin shiqi*), a critique that echoed broader intellectual discussions in the early to mid-1990s around the loss of humanistic spirit. As many poets believed these critics did not possess the creative experience necessary to explain the intricacies of poetry to a general public, they took it upon themselves to offer their own analyses of the development of contemporary poetry, thus displaying an increasingly pervasive literary historical consciousness.[106]

A prevailing assumption among the media and the non-poetry-reading public that nothing much happened to poetry during the 1990s can be explained in part by the fact that most activity took place within campus environments such as those of Peking University and Beijing Normal University and in "unofficial," independently financed poetry journals (*minjian shige kanwu* or simply *minkan*) that had limited circulation because they lacked an International Standard Serial Number (ISSN or *kanhao*) required for legal publication and thus rarely attracted the attention of the government or mainstream media. Poets, too, appeared disillusioned with the multitude of isms that marked literary life in the previous decade. This attitudinal shift was encapsulated in the discourse of individualized writing (*gerenhua xiezuo*). By using this concept, poets and critics disavowed the collectivism that had characterized modern poetry in the second half of the 1980s as well as its subordination to the kinds of "shared themes of the era" promoted by the Chinese state. Individualized writing seemed a welcome alternative during a decade many considered to be "not a time for poetry" (*fei shi shidai*) and heralded what Luo Zhenya claims was the first era in modern Chinese history in which poetry had not been subservient to ideology.[107]

With the declining influence of political ideology, however, came the rise of poetry politics, or the interpersonal maneuverings that decide who is who within the poetry arena and affect distributions of discursive power. By the late 1990s, many writers in cities and provinces outside Beijing had become fed up with what they saw as an imbalance in publishing opportunities in favor of poets in the capital, especially those who were employed within higher education establishments. The publication in February 1998 of a poetry anthology edited by Renmin University professor Cheng Guangwei titled *A Portrait of Years Gone By: Literature of the Nineties, Poetry Volume* (Suiyue de yizhao: Jiushi niandai wenxue shuxi shige juan) proved to be the tipping point. Rather than selecting poets from across China who represented diverse backgrounds and writing styles, Cheng's anthology consisted predominantly of Beijing-based poets whom Cheng referred to in the preface as his "friends": male writers such as Wang Jiaxin, Zhang Shuguang, Xi Chuan, Zang Di, Sun Wenbo, Ouyang Jianghe, and Chen Dongdong, many of whom were known for their academic credentials and partiality toward foreign poetry.

A young student of Beijing Normal University named Shen Haobo was among the first to react. In October 1998, a student-run newspaper published his inflammatory essay "Who's Fooling 'the Nineties'?" which accused Cheng of promoting a highly biased understanding of "poetry of the nineties." Shen, with biting sarcasm, referred to Cheng as a "so-called 'famous' poetry critic whom I have always disliked" and lampooned the poets featured in the anthology for their lack of talent and servility toward Western culture.[108] Many more poets responded in a huge volume of critical essays published over the following years, mostly either supporting Cheng's representation of poetry of the 1990s or joining in the attacks on the overly academic nature of much poetry writing and anthologizing in China. The polemic quickly established itself around the divide between "Intellectual Writing" (Zhishifenzi xiezuo), a term that Xi Chuan first used in 1987 to describe the poet-intellectual's spirit of independence, and the "Popular Standpoint" (Minjian lichang), which Han Dong defined in similar terms as an "independent spirit and free creation" and which Yu Jian described as "freedom, independence, originality, and democratic spirit."[109]

Much could be written about the Intellectual-Popular polemic from a poetic perspective as well as from a poetry-political one. Dian Li describes it as an attempt at reconfiguration and a "battle of [modern Chinese poetry's] own making—the battle of how to name itself in the changing cultural and social landscape of China."[110] Van Crevel also considers the polemic from a more literary standpoint, connecting it to the two "broadly defined aesthetics" in contemporary poetry that he calls the Elevated and the Earthly. Elevated poetry, associated with the Intellectual Writing side of the polemic, demonstrates qualities such as the heroic, literary, cultural, lyrical, mythical, sacred, utopian, absolute, elitist, academic, Westernized, central, northern, and the mind. Earthly poetry, by contrast, tends toward the quotidian, colloquial, anticultural, antilyrical, antimythical, mundane, realist, relative, ordinary, authentic, indigenous, local, Southern, and corporeal and is associated with the Popular Standpoint.[111] Although in reality all poetry exists somewhere on the spectrum between these "outer limits," this dichotomous approach to both poetry aesthetics and politics has nonetheless exerted an undeniable influence on narrations of literary history since the 1990s and is still evident in poetry discourse in the 2010s.

The poetry-political side of the Intellectual-Popular polemic became more apparent at a conference held in April 1999 in the Panfeng Hotel on the outskirts of Beijing, jointly organized by the contemporary literature department of the Chinese Academy of Social Sciences, the Beijing branch of the Writers' Association, and the editorial boards of *Poetry Exploration* (Shi tansuo) and *Beijing Literature* (Beijing wenxue). The meeting was titled "Turn of the Century: A Forum on Creative Trends and Theoretical Construction in Chinese Poetry" (Shiji zhi jiao: Zhongguo shige chuangzuo zitai yu lilun jianshe yantaohui) but has since become known simply as the Panfeng Meeting (Panfeng shihui). Around forty well-known poets and critics were present, many meeting in person for the first time. They included a number of writers who had recently finished production of a Guangzhou-based counteranthology that supported the Popular Standpoint, the *1998 Chinese New Poetry Almanac* (1998 nian Zhongguo xin shi nianjian), including Yu Jian, Yi Sha, Yang Ke, and Xu Jiang. The Intellectual-Popular divide thus marked a confrontation between competing poetry publications as well as a clash of minds between writers who had shared the national stage in the 1980s but felt compelled to stand their ground in the more limited public space available to modern poetry in the following decade.

The Panfeng Polemic (Panfeng lunzheng or lunjian) has been widely acknowledged as a major turning point in the history of post-Mao poetry. Its effects can be detected in many areas, including the proliferation of face-to-face poetry meetings in the 2000s and 2010s, poets' attempts to involve the news media in poetry activity, and the rise in national influence since 1999 of all those associated with the Popular Standpoint. The Panfeng Meeting also fed into an awareness that in order to be considered part of poetry scenes one had to be present in live scenes of poetry, not just by seeking publication in national poetry journals and anthologies but by making oneself visible at the kinds of events that give rise to contentious incidents (*shijian*) and attract media attention in the process. This was connected to the personalization of interpoet debates and what Van Crevel argues is a heavier focus on poethood, or the real person and personality behind the poems.[112]

Another term for poetry communities also emerged around this time that can tell us much about the changing social form of modern

Chinese poetry: "poetry rivers and lakes" (*shi jianghu*). "Rivers and lakes" is a term popularized by modern martial arts fiction to indicate the world occupied by knights-errant (*xiake*). It represents a fictional social space in which men and women are always searching for something, in the process being shaped by the rivers and lakes as much as they mold them with their actions.[113] Scholars have noted the term's conceptual ambiguity: while the knights-errant who live within the rivers and lakes often yearn for seclusion and for an "idyllic life and mystical destination," their significance lies in their attempts to bring order to the rivers and lakes and to prevent them from descending into anarchy.[114] Rivers and lakes became a common descriptor of the Chinese Internet in the 2000s; Guobin Yang describes it as a world that is characterized by intrigue and betrayal as much as it is by positive values such as freedom and adventure. The popularity of the term to describe poetry and Internet culture reflects suggestions that contemporary Chinese society as a whole is becoming a world of rivers and lakes, characterized by corruption and ill-functioning bureaucracy and requiring citizens to organize their own strategies for freedom and justice.[115]

"Poetry rivers and lakes," then, captures several aspects of contemporary poetry activity that are not fully conveyed by the discourse of either the poetry arena or live scenes. For one, poets in the early 2000s were conceiving of poetry scenes in playfully competitive terms, banding together to stake out a piece of literary turf and rescue poetry from a perceived state of stagnation and crisis. Among the biggest heroes of the rivers and lakes was Shen Haobo. In 2000, Shen cemented his reputation as an influential young upstart within China's poetry scenes by forming his own poetry group with Yin Lichuan, a graduate of Peking University, and several other poets also born in the 1970s (Nanren, Li Hongqi, Wu Ang, and Sheng Xing, among others). Their Lower Body (Xiabanshen) group became notorious for producing a kind of sexually explicit "body writing" (*shenti xiezuo*), a term previously associated with the novels of Wei Hui and Mian Mian, China's "Beauty writers" (*meinü zuojia*). The Lower Body established its headquarters in March 2000 in an online poetry forum called, appropriately, *Poetry Rivers and Lakes*, where its members continued to publish poetry and engage in debate both within the group and with other online poetry communities for much of the 2000s.[116]

In 1999, Bai Xiaosheng had fun mapping the new rivers and lakes of poetry in a piece of writing he called "Poetry arena heroes ranked by order of seating" (Shitan yingxiong zuoci paihangbang). This lengthy document consisted of humorous descriptions written in semiclassical Chinese of 108 poetry arena members of the previous twenty years, taking as its blueprint the 108 Heroes of Mount Liangshan from the classic martial arts novel *Water Margin* (Shuihuzhuan). Shen Haobo, still at an early stage in his poetry career, found himself at number 53 on the list, well below the Intellectual and Popular poets who had dominated the Panfeng Polemic. Occupying the throne of "heavenly king" was Shi Zhi, indicating his hallowed status as the forebearer of post-Mao Chinese poetry. Shi Zhi's significance goes far beyond the poems he wrote, which Zhang Qinghua describes as "immortal songs of life filled with an authentic spirit of witness to China's history."[117] He also symbolizes the belief that post-Mao poetry has its roots in the seemingly unassailable divide between official (state-sponsored and state-approved) and unofficial (non-state-sponsored and often state-disapproved) poetry activity that emerged in the Cultural Revolution era.

Today the lines between official and unofficial poetry scenes are far less clear-cut. As early as the 1980s, poets who identified with the independent, anti-establishment orientation of post-Mao avant-garde poetry were being published in state-run journals such as *Poetry*, *Poetry Monthly* (Shige yuekan) and *Stars* (Xingxing), essentially moving from one "world" of poetry to another, as Michael Day puts it, "without feeling they have 'compromised' anything."[118] Nonetheless, a binary division of poetry activity has persisted for several reasons. They include the enduring political sensitivity of the CCP toward poetry, explainable in part by post-Mao poets' deployment of a range of nonorthodox rhetorical strategies such as metaphor, irony, and innuendo and in part by poetry's long-lasting preeminence among literary genres in China and its traditional duty of "expressing what is intently on the mind." This, as Zhou Zan suggests, helps explain why poetry has encountered a markedly different contemporary fate from fiction, which, judging by sales figures alone, has adapted extremely well to market conditions.[119]

Since the late 1990s, a dizzying array of poetry groups, movements, generations, and incidents have punctuated overviews of contemporary poetry, indicating a whole-hearted return to the collectivism of the 1980s and giving the impression that history has been picking up speed rather than coming to an end, producing more styles of poetry and poetry-related incidents than those who attempt to document poetry scenes could possibly keep up with. Shen Haobo and Yin Lichuan's controversial Lower Body group was just one part of the post-1970 generation of poets who were widely lauded in the early 2000s as representing the younger, trendier face of Chinese poetry, unafraid of breaking social taboos and pushing the boundaries of poetic acceptability in their writing. Other influential figures include a number of less provocative poets sometimes described as belonging to the "academic group" (*xueyuan pai*) because of their connections to Peking University, such as Hu Xudong, Jiang Tao, Leng Shuang, Jiang Hao, La Jiadu, Wang Ao, and Han Bo. There are also a number of prominent post-1970 (*qiling hou*) poets based in China's southern provinces, several of whom are especially active in producing unofficial poetry journals and running poetry websites, such as Duoyu, Huang Lihai, Fu Mahuo, Liu Chun, Ma Fei, and Yan Wo.

The post-1970 poets were soon joined by the even younger post-1980 and post-1990 generations and accompanied by a flurry of criticism that attempted to draw attention to a group of poets left out in most decade-specific naming: the so-called Middle Generation (Zhongjian dai), which included An Qi (the main instigator of the naming of this generation), Yi Sha, Zang Di, Zhao Lihua, Bei Ta, Sang Ke, Shucai, Pan Wei, and many others, mostly born in the second half of the 1960s.[120] Poetry by women, too, has attracted renewed critical attention since the late 1990s, due in part to the efforts of poet-critics like Zhou Zan, founder of the poetry journal and website *Wings* (Yi), to support the work of female poets by organizing poetry activities and producing criticism of their writings. The category of "women's poetry" (*nüxing shige*), a term that dates back to the 1980s, maintains its discursive importance not least because of the heavily male-dominated atmosphere of poetry scenes and the sexism that female poets often encounter at poetry events.[121]

On the Internet, the blasé attitude toward sex and violence displayed in some poems by the Lower Body group has been challenged by even more "cutting-edge" poetry groups that demonstrate a radical approach toward Earthly poetics and have been collectively labeled the Low Poetry Movement (Di shige yundong or Di shichao). Like many Third Generation and post-1970 poets, Low Poetry writers adopt a colloquial, matter-of-fact tone of voice in their poetry and embrace the ugly side of life in contemporary China: topics such as death, disease, destruction, decomposition, poverty, oppression, depression, and defecation all loom large. Low Poetry is closely connected to the media dynamics of the Internet and represents one of the more intriguing aspects of what is known as "Internet poetry" (*wangluo shige*) (see Chapter 1).

One tendency evident in all these developments is the importance placed on naming (*mingming*), a topic that has been the subject of a number of essays by Chinese poets.[122] More than anything else, it is the act of naming that gives shape to historical narratives of modern Chinese poetry and gives poets a sense of control over their personal and collective literary histories. Ban Wang suggests that history writing is a kind of politics in itself and more than just a politically inflected search for "positive historical directions." Its urgency derives from the current conjuncture, a time in which history is widely thought to have ended, with no alternative in sight.[123] Live-scene discourse is impacting literary historiography, too. In his preface to a collection of essays by the poet-critic Liu Chun on China's post-Misty "poetry arena map" (*shitan ditu*), Cheng Guangwei describes Liu's approach to poetry as "criticism that confronts live scenes" (*zhimian xianchang de piping*) and contrasts it with the academic style of history writing that tends to be denser and more linear.[124] This live-scene approach, also evident in histories of May Fourth–era literature by Chen Pingyuan and Jiang Tao, is of critical importance to contemporary Chinese poetry scenes.[125] In going beyond teleological narrations of poetic development and emphasizing the ruptures, contentions, and incidents that reflect the contingency of poetry scenes, it implies that history is something that happens, in the present tense, and not simply a force imposed on poets from above.

SCENE-BASED METHODOLOGY

In this book, I use the English word "scene" to refer to historically conditioned and loosely affiliated networks of people involved in producing, circulating, and evaluating the contents of a cultural form and who assume primary responsibility for negotiating generic boundaries through a combination of discursive and performative practices. Like Foley's understanding of arenas (distinct from the Chinese discourse of *tan*), scenes are defined not by geography or other physical characteristics but by the activities that take place within them.[126] They are expressed in temporary collusions (and collisions) of people, texts, institutions, and resources that surround a specified cultural form. As Will Straw suggests, scenes should not be thought of simply as the overflows of sociability that accompany the more serious task of creating and evaluating culture; they also forge the "grooves to which practices and affinities become fixed."[127] There is an important distinction to be made between poems as texts and the social form of poetry as embodied in cultural networks. Foley argues that whereas texts "only offer an arithmetic of frozen, one-dimensional culture," networks provide the means for change.[128] It is my hope that directing attention toward China's poetry scenes will be helpful for understanding the gatekeeping processes through which modern Chinese poems are made public and meaningful, as well as the discourses and practices that inform participation in cultural scenes more generally and facilitate change. My approach offers an alternative way of looking at Chinese literature that does not privilege certain authors or texts on the basis of a perceived superior talent, reputation, or their availability in translation but instead explores the melee of figures and writings that exist prior to and during the processes of literary creation and canonization.

My research for this book involved spending lengthy periods of time immersed in poetry activities in mainland China. Between 2005 and 2010, including during eight months of fieldwork in 2007, I participated in a number of poetry events that stretched across the country (Hainan, Shenzhen, Guangzhou, Changsha, Suzhou, Xi'an, Tianjin, Beijing, and Inner Mongolia) and encompassed a diverse range of settings, ranging from university auditoriums and real estate offices to peach orchards and seaside resorts. More often than not, I found myself invited into the inner workings of the event, asked to act as host or emcee, meet with local government officials, share my thoughts on poetry, take part in drinking rituals, recite poems in Chinese and in English, and even accompany poets on all-expenses-paid excursions to foot massage parlors. These experiences were as educational as they were memorable: it is almost impossible to be an observer of such events without also becoming a contributor and acquiring participatory competence in the process.[129] While carrying out fieldwork in China, I also interviewed a number of poets, critics, academics, editors, and publishers about their involvement in poetry activity. Other research included reading and archiving several hundred pieces of poetry criticism and other poetry-related writings from the Internet, collecting a large number of print poetry journals and books, visiting poetry websites and interacting with poets on Internet forums and blogs, and conducting an online survey of forty-five poets (see Appendix).

As I hope to have made clear, it is not my intention to determine the historical value of specific poems or to assess the relative importance of individual writers, even if my choice of case studies inevitably gives more weight to some than others. While there is certainly value in the close reading of poems and I firmly agree with Michelle Yeh that literature deserves to be treated as more than simply representation, aesthetic interpretation is not the task that I have set myself in this book.[130] To some readers, my approach could be seen as reflecting what Gary Xu suggests is a "siege" on literature in the current era, in which literary studies is subordinated to cultural studies and foreign (i.e., non-U.S.) literature is only studied for the insight it gives into the bigger pictures of politics and culture. This is happening at a time when neoliberal policies are thought to be inflicting the logic of the free market on all forms of global culture and thus robbing it of its "aura," which Xu characterizes as "the non-conforming, the non-practical, the nonchalant, the not-so-orderly, the distanced."

I also concur, however, with Xu's suggestion that by emphasizing networks (or in this book's terminology the scenes in which authors operate), we can draw attention to two important truths: first, that governments can condition networks but not erase the creative imaginations of individual authors, and second, that understanding networks/scenes requires a considerable amount of work in comparing and combining perspectives that include, but are not limited to, those of the authors themselves.[131] While cultural studies offers a wide-angled lens through which to examine the conjuncture in which modern Chinese poetry finds itself in the early twenty-first century, I hope that through detailed analysis, contextualization, and a focus on the individual people and poetic ambitions that shape poetry scenes, this book can play its own small part in conveying the continued aura of this particular area of culture.

CHAPTER OVERVIEW

This book is divided into four chapters, each of which deals with a separate media space of poetry activity: the Internet, print publication, face-to-face poetry events, and the news media. The chapters are ordered to reflect the typical journeys that poems embark on in post-2000 China. In today's new media age, poems more often than not begin their life on the Internet, posted on an online forum or blog by individual poets before being selected for inclusion in webzines and "best of" selections of online poetry. Writings that are deemed worthy of more permanent documentation are then published in print poetry journals and anthologies, a channel of publication that is more politically fraught than the Internet in part because of the additional gatekeeping processes that stand in the way of making it to print. Poets whose writings constitute a visible presence online and in print are more likely to be invited as representatives of Chinese modern poetry to participate in the kinds of face-to-face events that have come to dominate poetry scenes in the new millennium.

Finally, poetry on occasion finds itself subject to another media dynamic much less under the control of poets and their poetry scenes, as poems make the news as a result of being circulated (and spoofed) through social media in the hands of non-poetry-reading publics. This is the most unpredictable of all the media dynamics explored in this book and relates to the Chinese public's cultural memory of poetry. Although the Internet is, despite the existence of online censorship, widely seen as the most open and participatory of China's media spaces, it is also subject to the government's strategic use of communication technologies to satisfy its own nation-building agendas, evident in the promulgation of certain narratives that highlight the unity or "harmony" that supposedly exists between poetry and the people.

Chapter 1, then, deals with poetry on the Internet, examining what has changed and what has not in poetry's post-2000 move online and exploring the role of the Internet in the functioning of China's poetry scenes. I consider predictions in the late 1990s that the Internet was set to revolutionize poetry writing by giving rise to exciting new hypermedia forms of poetry, then put these predictions to the test through a close analysis of a scatologically inclined poetry group, the School of Rubbish, whose poetry activities bore echoes of culturally oriented forms of online activism explored by Guobin Yang. The interactions and textual output of the School of Rubbish were also shaped by Internet-specific media dynamics and practices including anonymity and the searchability of online texts and suggested the importance of presence and participation in the live scenes of poetry represented by poetry forums or Bulletin Board Systems (BBS). Both individual poets and the communities to which they belong used the Internet's capacity for direct, real-time interaction and for archiving huge volumes of poetry-related texts in their quests for recognition and historical standing within China's poetry scenes.

In Chapter 2 I explore the shifting function of print publication in a new media age. Despite the development of the Internet into the most dynamic space of poetry activity, printed texts have retained their ability to stir the ambitions of Chinese poets. What is it about journals and books that set this medium apart from others and why go to the effort of publishing on paper when it is so easy to share poetry online? To answer these questions I take a close look at the finances, publishing politics, design, and editing of a long-running series of poetry anthologies, the *Chinese New Poetry Almanac*, which played an important role in attempts to redistribute discursive power within Chinese poetry scenes in the late 1990s and 2000s. Using information from interviews with editors and poets and from printed materials collected over the past decade, I show how the *Almanac* became implicated in national poetry debates, in particular the Intellectual-Popular polemic. One of the main objectives of print poetry publications in the age of the Internet is to document sites of poetry activity that are found at face-to-face events and online, an ambition that reflects both the ideology of the text and its associated values of permanence and authority *and* the more participatory discourse of live scenes. This goal can be understood in commercial terms, as a way of enhancing the spectacular appeal of poetry anthologies as physical objects, and historically as evidence of an anxiety of representation born from poetry's perceived marginalization within Chinese society and thus the relatively limited space available to a contemporary canon of poetry in the wider cultural realm.

The third media space explored in this book is the face-to-face space, that is, any occasion in which poets come together "in the flesh" and in the service of poetry. In Chapter 3 I question the positions of poems within large-scale poetry events and consider the role of China's cultural system reforms in encouraging entrepreneurs and businesses to invest in what many assume to be a hopelessly unprofitable cultural genre. From the perspective of Chinese poetry communities, attending face-to-face poetry events is an important means of acquiring poetry citizenship and constitutes a form of public performance that requires certain ritualized codes of behavior, including (but not limited to) the politically and aesthetically fraught act of poetry recitation. Although face-to-face poetry events often seem more like an excuse for heavy drinking and socializing than a serious occasion for the appreciation of poetry, their contingent dynamics help give rise to important poetry "incidents," documented and sensationalized by the media, which can exert a transformational effect on the power structures of poetry scenes and help steer the future direction of poetry-related discourse.

The final chapter moves away from the internal machinations of poetry scenes to consider what poetry looks like from the outside in the eyes of the news media and the media-consuming public. To do this, I analyze several interactions between modern poetry and the non-poetry-reading public that took shape in spoof poetry "forms" that went viral in the 2000s and the Quake Poetry movement of 2008. Media spectacles such as these show how the parameters of poetry scenes lie not just in medium-specific discourses and dynamics but also in the very genre of poetry, which is subject to conflicting aesthetic and political demands. But both mass spoofings and popular outpourings of modern poems suggest that the category of "poetry" still carries great symbolic weight in early twenty-first-century China. By lambasting China's contemporary poets, netizens inadvertently acknowledged the cultural memory that continues to surround Chinese poetry and that makes its presence felt in the somewhat contradictory media-led discussions of poetry's fatal marginalization in a consumer age and the occasions when nothing other than poetry will suffice for allowing Chinese people to respond emotionally to moments of national significance.

The conclusion summarizes my main arguments about the functioning of modern Chinese poetry as a social form and the importance of "scenes" for understanding the seemingly paradoxical situation in which poetry is widely written off as being out of touch with the times at the same time as poetry-related activity is burgeoning across the country, supported by business and political institutions and benefiting from the logic of the cultural economy. Poetry scenes have found a way around the contradictions between ideologies and forms of power that mark the contemporary conjuncture by engaging in processes of performative negotiation and relying on live-scene discourse as protection against some of the harsher criticisms that have been leveled at modern poetry and the "poetry arena" in recent years. I also trace the journey taken thus far across media space and time by Li Wei's poem "Is Zhang Ziyi Beautiful or Not?" and consider to what extent the "opening up" of poetry that is occurring in the age of participatory media represents a turning point in Chinese (and perhaps world) cultural history. Finally, I question whether the phenomenon of "verse going viral" explored in Chapter 4 marks not the beginning of the end for poetry as a core part of China's national identity but a return to more enduring patterns of cultural transmission and communal meaning-making that suggest that poetry's "aura" is far from being lost after all.

CHAPTER 1

Poetry on the Web

The East is black, the sun is bad
China has given rise to a School of Rubbish
you're black I'm even blacker than you
you're bad I'm even badder than you
Born as a Rubbish person
I'll die as a Rubbish ghost
I am the School of Rubbish
the School of Rubbish is me

—XU XIANGCHOU, "*Worshiping the High Is Exhausting*" (Chonggao zhen lei)

Poetry has always been destined to be the extreme avant-garde and light cavalry of literature. From the very start, it sniffed out the limitless potential for growth that comes with the age of the Internet, and embraced the Internet with open arms. As expected, the Internet gave poetry wings and made poetic exchange more intimate, as if poetry has returned to the glorious age of the Tang Dynasty. In a flash, live scenes of poetry shifted from print media to the Internet, like the early bird catching the worm.

—HONG ZHU, "*Why do we say the Internet has changed Chinese poetry?*" (Weihe shuo wangluo gaibian le Zhongguo shige?)

Most commentators agree that the development of the Internet had the single biggest impact on Chinese poetry activity in the first decade of the twenty-first century. According to typical narratives, the web injected much-needed life into poetry, rescuing it from the wilderness years of the 1990s, a time when more commercialized forms of culture were squeezing it from public view. As the poetry critic Li Xia described in 2004, "The Internet has brought the world into a new era, and brought poetry into a new era too—or you could say, the Internet has saved poetry's life. It is almost as though the Internet exists for the sake of poetry, and only there have poets been able to find their place and their value."[1] In the even more exuberant words of Chen Zhongyi, the love affair between poets and the Internet made it seem as though poetry had swallowed a dose of Viagra, thereby "sweeping away its impotency of the past few years and rediscovering its vitality, passion, and impulse."[2]

A production-oriented approach is useful for investigating the ways that online poetry communities have responded to the growth of the Internet and the opportunities for interaction and publication that it affords, and for examining the interplay between the media dynamics of the Internet, the broader communications environment in which they are situated, and the ambitions and activities of online poetry communities. Such an approach focuses not on what cannot be written online because of government-enforced censorship but on what is created and why.[3] Despite often being characterized as a unique culture or world unto its own, the Internet is inextricably entwined with the other media spaces explored in this book and its dynamics depend heavily on those of both print and face-to-face communication. The online space is, therefore, a hybrid agora that bears strong traces of the ideology of the texts at the same time as it is characterized by qualities such as contingency and real-time interaction.[4] Since the latter half of the 2000s, the majority of poems and critical essays that have been published in print journals and books previously appeared online in some form or other. Poetry recitals, summits, and gatherings are publicized online before the event, then documented and processed on forums and blogs in the following days, weeks, and years. Perhaps most significant of all, the Internet's effectiveness as a medium for poetry publication and community formation has meant that many poets appear to have ceased caring altogether about having their works published in print.

An examination of the Internet-based textual interactions of a particularly controversial poetry group, the School of Rubbish (Laji pai), suggests that China's online poetry communities demonstrate the robustness of the social form of modern Chinese poetry and the collective potential of literary activity in an era dominated by capitalist economics, individualization, and the commercialization of culture. They also embody the tension between the discourses of the poetry arena and live scenes: while Internet-based poets derive their sense of poetry citizenship first and foremost through presence and real-time participation in live scenes such as online forums and blogs, they also demonstrate a keen awareness of poetry hierarchies and the influence of text-based literary histories by engaging in debates with rival poetry groups. The School of Rubbish and the Low Poetry Movement to which its members belong offer a compelling case study of how cultural communities make creative use of the Internet to further their own aesthetic and ideological agendas, ignoring—if not flagrantly defying—the government agencies responsible for policing Internet content and promoting "harmonious society" online. Viewed from the perspective of cultural contention developed by Guobin Yang, Low Poetry's fixation on defecation, sex, and the dirty side of human existence not only stands in contrast to orthodox narratives of economically productive middle-class lifestyles promoted by the party-state but also implies a form of online activism aimed primarily at the gatekeeping authority of China's print-based poetry arena and at the "harmonizing" efforts of the country's media censorship schemes.

COMMUNICATION AND CONTENTION ONLINE

The development of the Internet has been the biggest factor in the expansion of space for public expression in China. Writing in 2008, Yuezhi Zhao states quite simply that the Internet has essentially become the public in Chinese public communication but notes that it is constituted of an unusual mix of people that includes "old lefts," humanistic intellectuals, university professors, white-collar workers, grassroots commentators, and a category of young people often subsumed under the label "angry youths" (*fenqing*).[5] China's Internet users, a population that in July 2013 stood at 591 million or approximately 44.1 percent of China's overall population and is expected to exceed 800 million by 2015, demonstrate a combination of social and political engagement and the need to communicate with each other and be entertained.[6] The diversity of cultural and social expression that exists online is not surprising; given the ever-growing proportion of the population that has access to the web, it makes sense that almost every facet of contemporary life is reflected online in some way.

A central theme in scholarship on the Chinese Internet is the tensions between various forms of power, especially political power, and netizen interests and concerns, tensions that are often conceptualized in terms of struggles or activism. Guobin Yang examines the complex nature of online activism, which he defines as any kind of contentious activity that involves the use of new communication technologies such as the Internet. Online activism, he argues, emerged after the revolutionary spirit of the 1989 student movement had died down in the 1990s and has since situated itself within a wide spectrum of "converging and contending forces" that are not just political but also social, economic, technological, and cultural.[7] Issues of contention are diverse but generally fall into seven categories: popular nationalism, rights defense, corruption and power abuse, the environment, muckraking, online charity, and cultural contention. Contention often takes place within online communities, which Yang conceptualizes as "spatial havens" and sites of resistance in which Internet users can create new identities for themselves while experimenting with new forms of organization and imagining new worlds.[8]

Attempts to limit the circulation of information online can often feel like a game of cat and mouse, whereby the government agencies responsible for policing Internet content and the companies who comply via self-regulation are forced to react on a minute-by-minute basis to the latest developments in Internet discourse, censoring "sensitive words" (*min'ganci*) and phrases almost as quickly as they appear. There are at least twelve government agencies that play a part in China's Internet content control regime, ranging from the State Council Information Office and the Ministry of Industry and Information Technology to entities such as the State Food and Drug Administration and the Ministry of Education. The array of regulations that they are expected to implement is vast, issued and amended periodically by the CCP's Propaganda Department as well as by lower-level organizations. A list of Internet content regulations assembled by Yang dates back to the "Regulation on Protecting Computer Information System Security of the People's Republic of China" released in 1994; more recent additions include provisions on administering Internet games and culture announced in 2011.[9]

Despite the best efforts of the Chinese party-state, limiting online discourse is considerably less feasible than controlling communication that takes place in print or through the broadcast media of radio, film, and television. Indeed, this may well be part of the government's overarching media strategy, in which the Internet is intentionally granted a greater degree of freedom than other media in order to allow Chinese citizens space to let off steam in a relatively contained environment.[10] Not only are netizens acutely aware, moreover, of the existence of censorship and the government's attempts to shape online public opinion, they also discuss them openly and make fun of them through subversive puns and other parodic practices.[11] The most well-known of these converts the characters for harmony (*hexie*, a stand-in for censorship) into the characters for river crab (*hexie*) and pits the crab in a battle against another mythological creature of the web, the "grass mud horse" (*cao ni ma*), whose name offers a tonal variant on a mother-related profanity that has come to symbolize the resistance of netizens against the government's attempts to sanitize Internet culture and society.

Having examined a range of forms of contention on the Chinese Internet, Guobin Yang concludes that online activism represents a "palpable revival of the revolutionary spirit" in China and a response to the condition of Chinese modernity. His research highlights the cultural nature of such activism: contention on the Internet relies on existing cultural tools and symbols at the same time as it demonstrates a high level of innovation and creativity.[12] If the Internet has given rise to a communication revolution then it is equally a social revolution and a cultural revolution, not least because the people involved in online creativity extend far beyond the intellectual elites who dominated cultural production in the 1980s to include "common people" and, increasingly, socially and economically disenfranchised groups such as migrant workers and the rural poor; this trend will continue as Internet access and literacy expand in the countryside and among older and less educated populations.[13]

Judging by their poetry alone, the School of Rubbish is about as far removed from the traditional image of China's intellectual elites as one could possibly imagine. Rather than an explicit means of "worrying about the nation and the people" (*youguo youmin*), writing poetry is a way of expressing belonging first and foremost to the online community that is the School of Rubbish. It is important to note that the kinds of poems produced by Rubbish poets would be highly unlikely to find their way into print publications, especially those legally available for sale through China's book and magazine distribution channels. In order to understand the school's poetics and approach to poetic interaction, we need to consider both the unique media dynamics of online communication and the historical conjuncture in which the School of Rubbish is situated. By turning poetry norms upside down and challenging the power of print gatekeepers to determine what writings are worthy of designation as "poems," communities such as the School of Rubbish can be considered an example of the "cultural revolution" that Yang suggests has been facilitated by the Chinese Internet, but one that is also inseparable from the historical consciousness and strong sense of communal belonging held by modern Chinese poets.

SITES OF POETRY

A large variety of website formats play host to the publication and discussion of poetry and poetry criticism on the Chinese Internet. They include portal sites dedicated solely to poetry such as the long-running website *Poemlife* (Shi shenghuo, www.poemlife.com); poetry-themed sections of larger culturally or literary-themed sites (for example, the poetry sections of www.hongxiu.com); poetry forums (*luntan*) or BBS (Bulletin Board Systems) hosted by commercial web portals as well as by educational, political, and media organizations; blogs (*boke*) and weibo such as those hosted by Sina (Xinlang) and Sohu (Souhu); video-sharing sites (like Youku, www.youku.com); news sites; and poetry-themed webzines or e-zines (*wangkan*), which can sometimes be downloaded and read offline. Of these, the most significant in the development of online poetry scenes are poetry forums, poetry-dedicated websites, blogs, and weibo. Together, these sites comprise the main stomping grounds, or live scenes, of online Chinese poetry.

As one of the earliest online communication tools, forums offer an open space for public discussion of clearly labeled topics, categorized according to subject matter, interest group, or theme and usually organized in order of most recent response. They are distinguished by the communal nature of their content management and authorship, functioning as a space in which registered members and guests alike can begin new conversations or "threads," respond to existing topics, seek and offer help or advice, interact and form new relationships, and browse for general interest or information-seeking purposes. As Guobin Yang shows, forums are also one of the main spaces in which contention occurs on the Chinese Internet, making them a powerful medium for online activism and a central space in which online communities take shape.[14] Literary forums have played a key role in the history of Chinese Internet literature and were the first types of website to emerge in the mid-1990s as spaces for literary production. By the mid-2000s there were over three hundred websites dedicated to poetry on the mainland Chinese Internet, the vast majority of which were forums. Their ubiquity led Wang Pu to comment in 2005 that they represent a whole way of life for poetry on the Internet.[15]

By 2008, however, activity levels on poetry forums were on the wane. Reasons for this include a heightening of Internet censorship in the lead-up to and duration of the summer 2008 Beijing Olympic Games as well as a gradual shift in interest toward individually authored blogs, social networking sites, and other community-based services provided by commercial Internet portals such as Sina and Douban. The decline in forum-based poetry activity was accelerated in early June 2010 when the Chinese government's tightening of media control around the anniversary of June 4, 1989, led commercial server NetEase (Wangyi) to shut down nearly two hundred poetry forums without any warning. They included some of the most influential sites in the past decade of online poetry, such as *Poetry Rivers and Lakes*, home of the Lower Body group, and *Beijing Review* (Beijing pinglun), birthplace of the School of Rubbish.[16] The sudden disappearance of so many poetry forums not only resulted in the loss of all associated content but also further spurred Chinese poets' mass migration to website formats that allow a greater degree of networking and individual control, such as blogs, weibo, and other social media. A neat line was thus drawn at the end of 2010: a whole decade of forum-led online poetry production had come to a close.[17]

The importance of poetry forums to Chinese poetry scenes during the first decade of the twenty-first century can hardly be overstated. At the peak of their popularity, sites such as *Modern Poetry Forum* (Xiandai shige luntan) were attracting nearly 100,000 hits a month; one survey showed that 251 poetry-related posts were left on the popular forum *Tianya Poetry Society* (Tianya shihui) on a single day in 2005, a number that was by no means out of the ordinary at the time. It was poetry forums that led to what Chen Zhongyi calls a "great leap forward" in poetry writing in the age of the Internet, a vast increase in poetic output and in the accessibility of poetic experiments by writers across China and elsewhere in the world who write in Chinese.[18]

As the name "forum" suggests, the primary function of these sites has been to provide an open space in which poets, readers, and critics can publish their writings and engage in text-based interactions. Although forum moderators (*banzhu*) command the greatest power because of their editorial privileges and name recognition, the majority of poetry forums are open-access and visible to all, giving them a symbolic value akin to that traditionally held by offline public spaces and media such as town squares, wall posters, or notice boards.[19]

Chinese terms used to refer to forum-based interaction include platform (*pingtai*), stage (*wutai*), and square (*guangchang*).[20] While "stage" implies a higher degree of performativity and a separation between poets and their audiences, these terms all suggest an open space in which activities, interactions, and performances are visible to anyone with a connection to the Internet.

Since the mid to late 2000s, the free-for-all, communal environment of poetry forums has been supplemented by more complex and structured forms of individual expression and social networking, particularly blogs and weibo. Although blogging has been in existence on the Chinese Internet since 2002, it was not until 2005 that it began to really take off, due in part to a number of blog-writing competitions sponsored that year by the Internet service providers Sina, Sohu, and Bokee (Boke wang).[21] By June 2006 there were nearly 17.5 million bloggers in China, accounting for 14 percent of China's Internet population.[22] By the end of 2012 that number had swelled to 373 million. With around 64 percent of all Internet users owning a blog or personal space, blogging had become the fourth most popular activity on the Chinese Internet.[23]

Microblogging, in particular China's most popular weibo platform hosted by Sina (www.weibo.com), has also proved extremely attractive to poets since Sina launched the service in 2009. The ability to share chunks of information in weibos of 140 or fewer characters, as well as post photos and links to longer blog essays, turns each poet into a potential hub of information and strengthens the ability of poets to communicate in real time within the scenes or networks to which they belong.[24] Weibo have enabled Chinese poets to stay in contact with each other to an unprecedented extent, regardless of geographic distance, group affiliation, or poetic preference. Instead of having to enter separate URLs in order to visit individual poetry forums or blogs, poets can read updates from all of their contacts on the same page, thus learning at a glance what is currently being talked about within poetry circles. By the early 2010s, blogging and microblogging had usurped poetry forums to become the primary means by which contemporary Chinese poets keep their fingers on the pulse of poetry scenes.[25] As participants in the "First Chinese Poetry Weibo Forum Online Poetry Conference" declared in September 2010, Chinese Internet poetry had entered a "post–poetry forum era."[26]

POETRY LITERACY IN ONLINE POETRY GROUPS

This poetry conference, held online by the poetry group Third Pole (Di san ji), was part of a bout of end-of-decade contemplation within poetry circles regarding how the Internet had changed Chinese poetry. Among the issues discussed was the proper definition of Internet poetry, a category of writing whose parameters have long been subject to debate. Since the early days of Chinese poetry on the Internet, a common assumption has been that its creation in an interactive digital environment will have a predictable impact on form and content, usually meaning the incorporation of hypertext writing or multimedia elements such as sound and image files or flash video. Poetry critic Yang Xiaomin made such a prediction in 1999 when he suggested that "on the Internet, the poetic text as we currently know it will mix together with calligraphy, fiction, advertising, drama, essays, drawings, short sketches, popular music, film, television, acrobatics, and so on, and thus an intertextual, typically postmodern text—the hyperpoetry text—will have been born."[27] Sang Ke, cofounder of *Poemlife* and an important figure in the early stages of online poetry development, expressed similar sentiments in 2001: "I personally believe that hyperlink and multimedia poetry will be the main direction for the development of 'Internet-form poetry' [*wangluoti shige*] in the immediate future. . . . I believe that in this respect (multimedia poetry writing, hypertext poetry writing, etc.), the Internet will bring about big, revolutionary changes to poetry."[28]

As we shall see in Chapter 4, such predictions of multimedia poetry have come true to an extent but thus far have mostly been confined to poems produced outside the kinds of communities that are the focus of this book. Instead, examining the interactions of groups like the School of Rubbish reveals that the Internet, and poetry forums in particular, favor linear text poetry and a particular style of poetic interaction or what I term "online poetry literacy." Learning how to interact in an appropriate way with other poets and how to produce an appropriate style of poetry through participation in the social processes of poetry writing and evaluation is a prerequisite for acquiring poetry literacy and achieving citizenship within online poetry scenes. Of interest here are three central features of the School of Rubbish's approach to online poetry literacy, each of which demonstrates the tensions between textual and oral modes of communication and reflects the coexisting dynamics of the poetry arena and live-scene discourse.

The first is a particular attitude toward online identity that takes advantage of the anonymous nature of forum-based communication to enhance a sense of intimacy and liveliness within the poetry community. Poems produced by the School of Rubbish also reflect these strong connections between individual poets and the community by demonstrating a high level of self-reflexivity and referring to community members by name within the text of the poems. They could be considered metapoetry in the sense that they are poems *about* poems and draw attention to the socially constructed nature of poetry. Related to self-reflexivity is the colloquial, casual style that dominates most online poetry writing and criticism and that enables poets to respond as quickly as possible to contingencies of online communication. Colloquial writing could be considered an example of what Thomas Pettitt calls a "lettered quasi-orality" or "speaking through the fingers."[29]

The second feature of poetry literacy that defines communities like the School of Rubbish is the close connection between the metatextual writings of the group and the poems they produce, or in other words, the importance of interpretive strategies to the formation and operation of the poetry community. This suggests that the School of Rubbish was invested in exercising its own gatekeeping authority to maintain the boundaries of the group, a strategy that calls to mind the textual ideology of the poetry arena and its strategies of editorial control and containment. Third, the group was also interested in asserting a place for themselves within China's poetry scenes, if only as the most extreme representatives of the Earthly end of Van Crevel's poetic spectrum. From the way that its members announced their arrival in 2003 by engaging in online contention with Lower Body poets on forums that included the Lower Body headquarters, *Poetry Rivers and Lakes*, we can see that the School of Rubbish sought the attention of more than simply like-minded Rubbish poets; they also had one eye on their textual connections with competing poetry communities and another on their potential representation in future literary histories. In exhaustively naming and documenting their poetic beliefs, manifestos, debates, criticisms, individual poetic theories, forum-based discussions, and so on, the school embodied a live-scene approach to literary history writing in which documentation of the here and now serves as a means of asserting one's subjectivity and creative agency against the broader tides of contemporary Chinese history that have little room for modern poetry in general, let alone subversive poetry communities like the School of Rubbish.

IDENTITY POLITICS

All media have a potential role to play in identity management in that they possess a series of qualities that enable, limit, and give structure to communication and action. As well as facilitating communication between parties who do not simultaneously occupy the same physical space, media allow individuals to shape understandings of specific social situations through both verbal and nonverbal communicative means and to decide the outer limits of their interations with others.[30] As Stig Hjarvard and others have demonstrated, media in general and the Internet in particular allow for the selective presentation or performance of one's identity. According to one scholar, the Internet offers digital authors an unprecedented level of freedom with which they can invent themselves, limited only by the constraints of the medium itself.[31]

Attitudes toward online identity can, however, vary across the world. In Europe and North America, the default approach in human-computer interactions is to associate online identities with specific offline individuals. Who you are online, in other words, broadly corresponds to and is anchored in your offline self. According to this model, the future development of the Internet hinges upon the creation of a network of associations between online services and offline identities, enabled by the online storage of information about each user. In China, on the other hand, there is a more strenuous avoidance of connections between online and offline identities.[32] Despite recent government attempts to close the anonymity gap by requiring real-name registration for many online services, for much of the 2000s Chinese netizens were comparatively free to select how they present themselves and what identities to perform online.

Karsten Giese has pointed out that modern forms of mass media have offered Chinese citizens models for identification that were previously provided by the individual's workplace. China's ongoing telecommunications revolution has enabled the formation of a space for private communication that confirms and consolidates shared identities.[33] It is not just the confirmation and consolidation of shared identities but also the formation and expression of individual identity within a community or scene that is a key part of cultural interactions on the Internet. According to the scene theorist John Irwin, the scene or "activity system" is in a fundamental sense theatrical in that it requires individuals to make a self-conscious decision to manage their behavior and participate in a way that conforms to the meanings and language they share with others.[34] Impression management is an integral part of being an active participant on online poetry scenes and many poets have taken the scene-as-theater metaphor to its logical conclusion by performing multiple online identities, either consecutively or simultaneously.

The possibilities for play and deception inherent in online identity have seduced sociologists and media studies scholars since the early days of Internet studies in the mid- to late 1990s.[35] Writing in 1995, Sherry Turkle expressed a typically utopian view of the disruptive potential of online communication by examining the rapidly disappearing divides between the single and the multiple self, between animate and inanimate beings, and between the "real" and the "virtual."[36] The behaviors of Chinese poets on the Internet seem to confirm the flexibility, if not total erosion, of these boundaries by encompassing a variety of approaches toward online and offline identity and the relationship between the two. At one end of the scale are those whose online identity is fully anchored in their offline existence, down to the use of their legal name and verifiable statements of profession, age, gender, and residence. This is the case for poets who began publishing poetry on the Internet after establishing a name for themselves in the print and face-to-face spaces of poetry in the 1980s and 1990s, referred to in Internet slang as "ground surface poets" (*dimian shiren*).

At the other end of the scale are those who participate solely under the guise of one or more fictional web-names (*wangming*) or IDs and whose geographic whereabouts, email address, and legal identity remain hidden to most Internet users. Most of these, known simply as "Internet poets" (*wangluo shiren*) or in early Internet slang "aborigine poets" (*tuzhu shiren*), had not previously made a substantial impact on poetry scenes. In some instances, the choice to operate under a pseudonym can be explained by a desire to reduce traceability, especially in cases when a politically sensitive style of writing could compromise the offline security or professional reputation of the writer. For poets who stick to one web-name and use it to establish a reputation for themselves through participation on poetry forums and other online poetry activities, the reward can be fame or notoriety capable of rivaling that of established print-culture poets. Once an online social circle has been established, the web-name starts acting as a receptacle for cultural associations, power relations, and symbolic capital. Potential associations include negative preconceptions and discrimination, consequences that might seem at odds with the principles of equality and free speech so often claimed for online communication.[37]

A combination of one or more pseudonymous online identities with a provocative approach to writing can be employed to increase the perceived popularity (*renqi*) or symbolic capital of a writer, and in some cases, ambiguity surrounding a poet's "true" identity can add to a carefully managed air of mystique. One poet who has exploited these possibilities is the creator and central figurehead of the School of Rubbish, a poet who went by the web-name Old Man (Lao Touzi). For two years after establishing the school in March 2003, Old Man remained an enigmatic figure, closely guarding the secret of his offline identity and invoking much speculation as to who he really was. He often found himself the target of online impersonation by other poets, to such an extent that in late 2003 one participant on *Beijing Review* suggested they hold open elections for the "post" of Old Man, implying this was a replaceable position within the school rather than the identity of an individual author. The mystery surrounding the person behind the ID caused poetry critic Lao Xiang (pen name of Zhang Jiayan) to refer to Old Man's identity as an "unbreakable riddle," and another poet suggested that perhaps he did not really exist at all.[38]

Pidan (a homophone of *pidan*, "thousand-year-old egg") is the web-name of the second poet to join the School of Rubbish, who became a member on March 18, 2003. He occasionally used the alternative ID Lao Tian, was co–forum moderator of *Beijing Review*, editor of the *School of Rubbish Webzine*, and responsible for penning influential School of Rubbish texts such as "On the School of Rubbish as a Movement" and the "School of Rubbish Synopsis."[39] According to the group's official records, a third poet named Zhi Feng joined the School of Rubbish on March 22, 2003. Unlike Old Man and Pidan, Zhi Feng kept a low profile, adopted a relatively humble and self-effacing tone in his communications, and primarily spent his time engaging in poetic discussion on *Beijing Review* and contributing poetry to the group's webzine.

In March 2005, on the second anniversary of the creation of the School of Rubbish and *Beijing Review*, Old Man finally ended the speculation surrounding his identity by posting a statement online admitting that he, Pidan, and Zhi Feng were in fact the same person.[40] He stated that Zhi Feng is his legal name, Old Man the original pseudonym he used for posting theoretical writings, and Pidan his preferred web-name for poetry authorship and forum participation. As for his reasons for adopting multiple identities, he explained, "using the web-name 'Old Man' was originally meant to facilitate the writing of poetry criticism online. The only more complicated reason I could possibly give was that I had truly hoped to become a hidden or virtual writer. Of course, I have now realized the difficulty of all of this." Such experiments with multiple identities can be understood within the context of the commodification of contemporary poethood, informed by China's powerful celebrity discourse and boosted by the liberties of anonymous and pseudonymous online interaction.[41]

Old Man's case clearly demonstrates how both the individual poet and the poetry group to which he or she belongs can exploit pseudonymity and multiple identities to help build individual reputations and form communal myths. Indeed, his "multiple selves" are a central symbol in the creation story and online activities of the School of Rubbish. Writing under a pen name is not new to Chinese literature; it has been practiced in print culture for centuries.[42] What is different about online communication is the way it enables poets to build a strong sense of intimacy with fellow writers and readers by engaging them in regular and direct interaction, while preserving almost absolute privacy regarding their offline existence. It allows Internet users to create new identities for themselves as poets, literary thinkers, and community leaders, opportunities that, because of practical and social limitations such as geographical location or educational background, may not have been possible in their offline lives. For the poets who rose to fame as members of the School of Rubbish, this is especially true.

RUBBISH POETICS

In addition to serving as a disembodied environment in which poets can engage in identity play and use multiple web-names to help with myth creation and group formation, Internet forums are also an important space for refining poetic views and articulating strategies for the writing and interpretation of poems. Rubbish poetry shows how these strategies can be as unconventional as poets wish: as Jay David Bolter points out, the Internet offers the paradigm of a writing system that molds to the needs of its readers and writers, rather than expecting that they change their habits to adhere to any preexisting standard or authority.[43] Once refined and articulated, strategies for reading and writing poetry act as a unifying force among larger communities of writers who already share basic understandings about the definition and aesthetic possibilities of poetry. For poets who joined the School of Rubbish in the mid-2000s, becoming part of an online poetry community, and through it a broader scene of Chinese poetry, involves a repeated process of writing, reading, commenting, debating, and, most important of all, demonstrating oneself to be an active and vocal participant in the live scenes of poetry that were controlled by the group.

The earliest theories to emerge from the group were all written by Old Man and published on *Beijing Review*, among which his ten "Poetry epistles" (Shi zha) were the first and symbolically the most important. This text, posted on March 15, 2003, is a collection of short commentaries on poets that Old Man had discovered online whose writings he believed broadly corresponded to his own poetic views. Interspersed throughout are statements pronouncing the establishment and basic poetics of the School of Rubbish, which later became the basis of another text, the "School of Rubbish Manifesto." The epistles commence with a declaration written in a humorous, quasi-classical style and a mixture of first- and third-person points of view, explaining the potential benefits of participating on *Beijing Review*:

> Using *Beijing Review* as his headquarters, Old Man will now come forward and play the lute. . . . To play the lute you need to have a score. Personally, I really don't know the score. So, *Beijing Review* has to lend me the score. Everything Old Man relies upon when writing these poetry epistles is on *Beijing Review*. No matter who you are, as long as you come forward, there is the possibility I will use you as my score. If I play out of tune then shout; if it makes you happy, then shout; if I'm careless and hurt you, then shout too.[44]

This declaration functions as an open invitation for interested poets to get involved on *Beijing Review*, with the enticing possibility of being noticed by the forum's creator and moderator.

The name of the poetry school created to advance the poetic values promoted in these "poetry epistles" is not mentioned until the fourth section, written about the poet Fa Qing. This section is worth reading in full, as it bears witness to the consolidation of Old Man's concept of Rubbish poetry and includes an early application of some of his core poetic principles. It also provides a good example of how the multiple identities of Old Man added credence to the

School of Rubbish in its earliest days when the "group" consisted solely of its creator.

> In his poem "I Caught a Big Fish" Fa Qing makes bold use of hyperbolic technique. "I spent twenty years preparing / my fishing equipment / my fishing line is made of thick rope thirty thousand meters long / the diameter of my hook is a hundred meters wide / on the end of my giant fish hook are hung / fifty-two live cows / I then drag my island-sized big boat / from the fishing village where my ancestors lived / down into the sea." A full twenty years later, "I finally caught / a big fish." I noticed on *Beijing Review* that Mr. Pidan recommended Fa Qing delete the last four lines of this poem: "ten million people / ate for a year / and still did not finish / this big fish." I guess Pidan was thinking that Fa Qing could write a poetry version of the famous novel "The Old Man and the Sea." So far, however, Fa Qing has not deleted these four lines. Why should he delete them? They form an important boundary for the poem: with these four lines, it is Rubbish; it is Rubbish Poetry. Finish eating the fish, and turn it into feces—this type of rubbish can only be transformed by going through the anus. If people who write this kind of poetry wanted to form a school, then that school would be the School of Rubbish. The USA had the Beat Generation, whose representative figure was Allen Ginsberg. After it was beat what became of it? The answer, of course, is rubbish. Therefore, if the Beat Generation had walked a beat further forward it would have become the School of Rubbish. If modernist poetry is to develop according to plan, it should have a School of Rubbish. Moreover, logically speaking, to compare the modernist School of Rubbish with the Beat Generation should be like comparing the philosophies of dialectical materialism and naïve materialism. In other words, the modernist poetry of the School of Rubbish should be one level higher than the Beat Generation.[45]

Here Old Man sets out the theoretical foundations of the newly named School of Rubbish, in doing so revealing his knowledge of previous poetic traditions, both Chinese (he later mentions the poets Liang Xiaobin, Han Dong, and the Lower Body group) and foreign. His reference to Allen Ginsberg and Beat poetics serves to position the School of Rubbish firmly within the avant-garde in the mold of the Beat Generation in 1950s and 1960s America. This subcultural identity is underlined through his use of words such as "anus" and "feces," an endorsement of bringing taboo bodily functions into poetry writing. The desire to "beat" the Beat Generation and thus make a contribution to global modernist poetry makes Old Man's Rubbish poetry an ambitious proposition. His comparison of dialectical and naïve materialism seems to imply, moreover, that Rubbish theory is not limited to poetry and is at the same time a philosophical mission based in Marx's philosophical materialism and Engels's dialectics.

The interpretive principles hinted at in this epistle are further clarified in a section posted twelve days later on March 27, 2003, that contains a culmination of Old Man and Fa Qing's subsequent forum-based debate on the definitions of Rubbish poetry. Old Man builds on his original suggestion of four theoretical principles, "return to the original, aim down, not-soul, not-flesh," to settle upon the following set of poetic values, known thereafter as the "Three Principles of the School of Rubbish":

> The first principle: return to the original, aim down, not-soul, not-flesh;
> [huanyuan, xiang xia, fei ling, fei rou]
> The second principle: separate and unified, contrary and common, no essence, no application;
> [lihe, fanchang, wu ti, wu yong]
> The third principle: crude, unrestrained, both dead and alive.
> [cucao, fanglang, fang si fang sheng]

He proceeds to elaborate on these principles, explaining that "not-soul" separates the School of Rubbish from China's agricultural poetic tradition, while "not-flesh" distinguishes it from the Lower Body school, who he thinks write primarily about sex and the reproductive organs. He notes that "no essence" and "no application" cannot be satisfactorily understood from the words alone, as the characters *ti* (body or essence) and *yong* (use or application) represent complex philosophical ideas from Chinese tradition.[46] Although Old Man does not explain the line "both dead and alive," readers might recognize it as a quotation from the chapter in the Daoist philosophical text *Zhuangzi* titled "On leveling things" (Qiwulun), translated by Eske Møllgaard as "just now it dies, just now it is born."[47] According to the *Zhuangzi*, life *is* death; birth marks the beginning of the end and thus human existence is spent in constant contradiction between the two. This phrase emphasizes the transcendental nature of all things, which may form part of the philosophical grounding for the school's emphasis on the end results (waste, rubbish, decay) or futility of all human activity.

In an amended version of the Three Principles, the "return to the original" of the first principle is replaced with "worship the low" (*chongdi*) to reflect a consolidation of the group's central poetic focus.

The phrase "worship the low" is designed to oppose the phenomenon of "worshiping the high" (*chonggao*), more commonly translated as lofty or sublime, seen by many poets as one of the fatal weaknesses of Misty poetry and much modern Chinese poetry before that. The School of Rubbish was by no means the first group to express their contempt for this tendency. "Oppose the lofty" had been a common battle cry among Third Generation poets in the 1980s, hand in hand with their rejection of the kind of poetic heroism that emanated from lines like "Let me tell you, world. / I—do—not—believe!" in Bei Dao's famously defiant 1972 poem "The Answer."[48] This position was epitomized in the poetics of the Sichuan poetry school "Not-Not," whose name itself is composed of the two epithets "not-lofty" (*fei chonggao*) and "not-rational" (*fei lixing*).[49]

Old Man posted the first official collection of Rubbish poetry on *Beijing Review* less than a week after announcing the founding of the school in his epistles. The collection, titled "Ten Representative Works and Commentary on China's School of Rubbish Poetry," consists of ten poems or poem series written and posted by ten individual poets on *Beijing Review* and includes a short commentary by Old Man at the end of each, in which he refers to the recently established Three Principles and clarifies the group's approach to online poetry literacy.[50] According to the first edition of the *School of Rubbish Webzine*, this text represents a milestone in the formation of the school. The poems selected by Old Man demonstrate what appear at first to be wildly divergent approaches toward the task of Rubbish poetry writing. In general, however, most adopt a light-hearted, irreverent tone, are written in colloquial language and slang, and make frequent allusions to bodily functions, the names of other famous poets, and aspects of traditional Chinese culture. All of these are features that were to become hallmarks of School of Rubbish poetry. Old Man's application of the interpretive strategies outlined in his Three Principles is observable both in his choice of poems and in the commentaries that follow them. Here is one short example:

> Poem no. 11: "Life" [Shenghuo]
> By Training Piglets to Fly in the Sky (Xunlian xiaozhu tianshang fei)
>
> Training piglets to fly in the sky
>
> Commentary on Training Piglets to Fly in the Sky's "Life":
>
> Is "Training piglets to fly in the sky" simply the name of a School of Rubbish poet? I've noticed that many heavyweight School of Rubbish

> poets have written poems of this name. Why might this be? It is not just the name of a School of Rubbish poet but, more importantly, a way of life; that so many poets have taken it as the title of their poems is also because it is not simply the name of a School of Rubbish poet, but also symbolizes a way of life. This life, in the eyes of School of Rubbish poets, is most definitely an extremely important one. "Misty" poet Bei Dao once wrote a poem entitled "Life" which consisted of only one word: "net." Times, after all, have progressed. If even piglets can fly up into the sky, then what can that net, seen as so oppressing by Bei Dao, really count for? From this we can see the School of Rubbish's surpassing of the previous generation. Perhaps taking a poem only one line long as a representative work is rather risky, but Bei Dao's "Life" was even shorter—only one character long; Gu Cheng's "Black Eyes" was not long either.[51]

As Old Man indicates, this short poem can be read as an answer to Bei Dao's canonical poem of the same name and represents the younger poet's (the author claims to have been born in 1982) irreverence toward both her poetic predecessors and a classic Misty poem. Like Bei Dao's single-word poem of the same title, "training piglets to fly in the sky" could be read as an expression of the futility or impossibilities of life, but the imagery is more flamboyant and humorous than that of Bei Dao's poem, whose "net" is usually taken as a metaphor for disillusionment or repression.[52] "Net" also takes on new connotations in the context of the Internet, a dual meaning that would most likely be picked up on by any readers of this poem at all informed about modern Chinese poetry.

The poem can also be taken as an example of self-reflexivity in poetry, as the phrase "training piglets to fly in the sky" is, regardless of any metaphorical implications, the author's chosen webname. Self-reflexivity "denotes the ability of the individuals of a social system to reflect on and evaluate both their conception of the system and their role in it."[53] By making the author's webname the entire contents of the poem, Training Piglets to Fly in the Sky implies that she plays a central role in the poetry group—and, given the title of the poem, a central role in "life." Referring to poets by name draws attention to the poem's constructedness and is among the favorite devices of School of Rubbish poets. Its functions include showing disrespect toward poetry foes and creating a sense of intimacy within a group of largely anonymous individuals who interact solely through the medium of the Internet. As such, it could be considered a way of coming to terms with what Glazier calls the "materiality" of the Internet, or a form of engagement with the medium.[54]

According to Norbert Bachleitner, self-reflexivity is everywhere in digital poetry. As the medium used to write and display poetry changes from printed page to screen, attention is drawn to the new possibilities afforded by the processing power of the computer and the effects that poetry can have on its readers.[55] More than just a fixed set of characteristics that belong to a particular object, materiality can be understood as encompassing the ways in which texts make meaning from the medium in which they are situated. It cannot, therefore, be decided in advance but instead develops through the interplay of the medium's physical characteristics and the signifying strategies of the poetic work in question.[56] In the case of online Chinese poetry in the 2000s, the physical characteristics of the Internet that have had the most observable effect on poetry literacy are the facelessness and immediacy of interpersonal communication and the rapid, multidirectional distribution of texts. This allows poets to preserve an element of anonymity in experimenting with their online identities, while engaging in dense textual interactions within forum-based communities. Poems that name-drop others can, thus, be considered an expression of poetry's online materiality. Faceless acquaintances made through online interaction are turned into more concrete realities by writing them into poetry; the community effectively "materializes" itself through writing, thus affirming the status of poetry as a social form. It can be viewed as a way of overcoming the distancing effects of communication in a disembodied medium in which poets rarely get to actually see and hear the person with whom they are interacting. Self-reflexivity and name-calling are strategies that have been adopted by both recognized and aspiring members of the group, as we shall see in the instances of intragroup gatekeeping behaviors examined next.

GATEKEEPING RUBBISH WANNABES

The boundaries of the School of Rubbish were decided by a combination of leadership activities by Old Man, the desires of individual poets to leave the group if and when they saw fit, and community-based gatekeeping practices in which existing members responded to poems written by would-be Rubbish poets and decided collectively whether the poet concerned had displayed adequate understanding of Rubbish poetics to be allowed entry into the group. This latter process is especially interesting, as it shows how the poetry group operated as a unified collection of voices to pass informal judgment on individual outsiders, in doing so deciding whether those individuals remained on the outside or were granted entry into the community. The following poem is an example of one such attempt to join the group. It was posted on *Beijing Review* on November 14, 2003, accompanied by a follow-up post from its author asking, "Would each friend see if I'm Rubbish or not?"

FOR THE SAKE OF RUBBISH I AM RUBBISH
[Wei le laji wo laji]

by Zhou Jun

For the sake of taking my seat I take my seat
for the sake of standing up I stand up
for the sake of standing up I take my seat
for the sake of taking my seat I stand up
for the sake of dying I die
for the sake of being born I am born
for the sake of being born I die
for the sake of dying I am born

The first *Beijing Review* participant to respond, just eight minutes later, used the web-name Poet Believes and described the poem as "not very Rubbish." Another poet named Thirst-Quenching (Jieke) replied two and a half hours later that the poem was "forced," upon which yet another, Fan Si, asked the post's author, Zhou Jun: "do you think all badly written poems are called Rubbish?" A poet called Shen Wu responded to Fan Si: "Old Fan, you fell into his trap, this is a famous poem used by this guy to make fun of us!" Although the last stanza of the poem does appear to have been copied from elsewhere, it is reasonable to assume that Zhou Jun's request for feedback from established forum members was made in earnest.[57]

The only poet to take Zhou's query seriously was Training Piglets to Fly in the Sky, who on November 20, 2003, posted her own interpretation of what constitutes Rubbish poetry to help explain to Zhou Jun where he might have gone wrong. In this longer post, titled "Rubbish poetry worships the low, the three standards of worshiping the low are . . . ," she rearticulates the basic interpretive strategies of Rubbish poetry as defined by Old Man and adds her own interpretation, which takes the form of another set of numbered slogans:

One opposition; three disposals; nine departures

One opposition: opposing "worshiping the high": facing down and infinitely descending.

> Three disposals: disposing of "truth, beauty, and goodness" and heading toward their opposites, the objective essences of "false, ugly, evil" which represent human existence in the world.
>
> Nine departures: departing from the deep-rooted and still existent "tradition, culture, justice, morality, civilization, nobility, law, order, fashion," thus reflecting upon the darkest and most truthful side of humanity and society.
>
> The "three disposals" are a division of the "one opposition"; the "nine departures" are an explanation and further elucidation of the "three disposals."

Yang Chunguang, an influential member of the School of Rubbish before his sudden death in late 2005 and advocate of "Post-Political Writing" (*hou zhengzhi xiezuo*), approved this theoretical explanation by stating that "this theory of Piglet's is the most clear-headed theory in the School of Rubbish, I recommend that all Rubbish poets get to grips with it." Zhou Jun responded, "Piglet, have a look at my poem, is it School of Rubbish?" Although "Piglet" did not answer, what does follow is a series of posts from her and other poets asking that "personal abuse" be deleted, suggesting that someone had posted a reply insulting her or someone else on the forum, which had since been deleted. Pidan's only intervention in all these exchanges was brief, promising to remove the offending post(s) immediately.

We can ascertain from the responses to Zhou Jun's poem that his attempt to join the School of Rubbish under this particular ID was unsuccessful. Although this name can be found responding to other posts around the same time, it stops appearing in late 2003, and Zhou was never listed as a member of the school. Despite his attempts to express a commitment to the school ("For the sake of rubbish I am rubbish") and the fact that the last two lines ("for the sake of being born / I die / for the sake of dying / I am born") could be said to echo the Daoist sentiments of the School of Rubbish principle "both dead and alive," the general consensus on *Beijing Review* was that he had failed to meet the criteria for membership in the community: successful application of the school's interpretive strategies. It may be that his attempt to come across as "Rubbish" was too self-conscious and lacked the necessary sense of natural spontaneity that characterizes the writing of School of Rubbish poets.

Other School of Rubbish hopefuls were even more unabashed in their attempts to join the school. On February 25, 2006, someone using the web-name A Feisty Pig (Yi tou xueqi fanggang de zhu) posted a series of three poems and a personal manifesto on *Beijing Review* under the heading "Going against the tide: I announce that from now on I have officially joined the School of Rubbish, so don't stop me!"[58] Here is the second poem in the series:

RUBBISH IMAGERY

(Laji yixiang)

I worry myself to death
because there really is
too little Rubbish imagery
where can I find things
with an ugly feeling?
I use my fingers to count
shit, feces,
anus, asshole
nostrils, maggots
menstruation, reproductive organs
bits and pieces on the human body
really are few and far between
god is truly unfair
giving us, the School of Rubbish,
such a tiny bit of imagery
oh, I forgot
the School of Rubbish doesn't believe in god
annihilate god
fuck him up the ass
then god in his
new mirror image
will appear
but it's still not enough
what should I do
I think so much I nearly lose hope
then suddenly I open my mind
and think of
Rubbish teacher
Comrade Pidan
what a fantastic image
strange that no one has used it
as Rubbish poets
we will never come across
a stroke of genius
more cool or more striking than
"annihilate Pidan
fuck Pidan up the ass"

The intentions behind this poem are plain to see. It is almost as though the poet has taken all the archetypal features of School of Rubbish poetry, mixed them together, and attempted to go one step further. The poem is highly self-reflexive, describing in short lines and colloquial language the mental processes of an aspiring Rubbish poet as he tries to come up with an original Rubbish image to use in his poetry. Its tone is irreverent, crass, and tongue-in-cheek, and the desecration of Pidan in its concluding slogan suggests an attempt to break new taboos and embody the predominant Rubbish spirit of opposition and destruction. Mentioning School of Rubbish members by name is also the ultimate demonstration of community membership. Usually practiced only by members of the group, it implies a cozy familiarity or intimacy with Pidan and thus with the group as a whole.

A Feisty Pig was more successful than Zhou Jun in his declaration of allegiance to the School of Rubbish: all eight of the individual responses to his post were positive. Among other replies, Blue Butterfly Lilac (Lanhudie zidingxiang) responded with "Ha ha! I support you"; someone else commented, "no one's stopping you"; Pidan simply posted "greetings, A Feisty Pig"; and School of Rubbish member ufo spelled out the consensus by announcing, "I agree: you are now a member of the School of Rubbish!" The entire thread was moved to the Information Archives section of *Beijing Review*, a sign of recognition reserved for poetry, criticism, and theory deemed to be of importance to the school as a whole.

Xu Xiangchou has made the following assertion regarding the nature of the School of Rubbish: "The 'School of Rubbish' are several brothers and buddies with basically unanimous artistic tendencies who have ended up together in order to facilitate mutual communication and learning. However, the 'School of Rubbish' is an open school of poetic art, and can take in new members at any time—you only need to be willing to explore with us, and to have already written works with rubbish tendencies."[59] This statement echoes Stanley Fish's description of the concept of interpretive communities. Connections are formed and individuals drawn together by shared poetic tendencies or interpretive strategies, creating a contingent network that regularly changes in size by accepting new members or saying goodbye to those whose tastes have changed. Most important, Xu confirms that community membership is ultimately demonstrated and validated through writing rather than just reading.[60]

Where the School of Rubbish differs from Fish's interpretive communities is the way in which it articulates the exact nature of its interpretive principles and strategies through the vast amounts of metatext it makes available on the Internet. Strategies are not only spelled out in manifestos, slogans, and theoretical essays but also actively demonstrated in a number of texts that include both poetry and commentary, particularly those written by School of Rubbish founder Old Man. All this means that people interested in joining the school have ample opportunity to clarify their understanding of Rubbish principles and, more important, to put them into practice through participating in poetry writing and evaluation on Internet forums and blogs. Furthermore, clear gatekeeping mechanisms exist for the confirmation of community membership. Rather than Fish's elusive "nod of recognition," would-be community members have their interpretive efforts picked to pieces by current members and if they are successful (like A Feisty Pig) are openly declared to be so: "you are now a member of the School of Rubbish!"

HISTORICIZING POETRY FROM "SEX" TO "SHIT"

At the same time as it endeavored to maintain the boundaries of its own community through online gatekeeping practices, the School of Rubbish was also keen to compare itself to preexisting poetry groups and to assert what it saw as its rightful place within current Chinese poetry scenes and the historical development of post-Mao avant-garde poetry. It did this mainly by commissioning literary criticism from sympathetic critics and engaging in conflict with other poetry communities, especially with Shen Haobo's Lower Body group. Online contention of this form is not simply a means of asserting one's own subjectivity and legitimacy as a poetry community; it also acknowledges the existence of rival groups, something that helps form and *perform* connections between communities. Luckily for the School of Rubbish, members of the Lower Body community were happy to oblige its desire for contention and for several months in 2003 participated in a battle of words that raged across several online poetry forums, including *Beijing Review* and *Poetry Rivers and Lakes.*

The Lower Body group is emblematic of the playfully competitive "rivers and lakes" approach to poetry activity that grew out of the prolonged fin-de-siècle Intellectual-Popular polemic. As Maghiel van Crevel has pointed out, although the Lower Body poets attempted to depict themselves as a new phenomenon on the Chinese poetry scene, their style of writing was in fact heavily influenced by the "post-colloquial" (*hou kouyu*) writing of older poets, in particular Xu Jiang and Yi Sha, both graduates of Beijing Normal University who were born in the mid-1960s and had been active in poetry circles since the 1980s.[61] The Lower Body poets also share an approach to topics such as knowledge, culture, and tradition with many Third Generation poets, especially Sichuan's "second world" poetry groups such as Macho Men and Not-Not that exhibited a staunchly antilyrical, anticultural approach to poetry in their writings.[62] In the Lower Body manifesto, published in the first of two unofficial print journals produced by the group in 2000 and 2001, Shen Haobo declared:

> So-called Lower Body writing pursues a palpable presence of the flesh. That is: of the flesh [*routi*] not the body [*shenti*]. . . . For externalia such as tradition, culture and knowledge have deeply alienated, polluted and defiled our bodies. Too many people have nothing like the flesh, only a weak cultural soma, no lower body like that of animal existence, only the upper body of a pitiful thing called "human being." But to return to the flesh and to pursue a palpable presence of the flesh means to let our experience go back to that of the essential, original animal flesh. We are each of us ourselves the flesh. As the flesh happens, so poetry happens, and as the flesh makes its presence felt, so poetry makes its presence felt. That's all.

The manifesto ends with the line, "We lay our lower body bare, the men their hilts and the women their holes. This is how bad it is, so what have we to be scared of?"[63]

Since it appeared in 1999, the Lower Body group has been primarily associated with writing in graphic terms about sex; several of Shen's pronouncements in the manifesto suggest that this is, indeed, a central preoccupation of the group's poetics. Poems such as Yin Lichuan's "Why Not Make It Feel Even Better?" (Wei shenme bu zai shufu yixie ne?), Nanren's "Viagra Gains Entry to the Chinese Market" (Weige zhun ru Zhongguo shichang), and many of those in Shen Haobo's poetry collections *A Handful of Tit* (Yi ba hao ru) and *A Great Evil Hidden in the Heart* (Xin cang da e) contain both direct and indirect references to sex and the sexualized body. They proclaim that rather than something to be hinted at with allusions and euphemisms, sex can be a source of pride, provocation, and in-your-face avant-garde positioning. At the same time, the lower body's function as the primary location of sexual (rather than intellectual) activity is also metaphorical, symbolizing the group's resistance to the moralizing tendencies of Chinese intellectuals on display in much modern Chinese literature. Their poems, too, go far beyond sex: as Van Crevel argues, they deal with the "trivial texture of everyday life" and incorporate every conceivable topic, especially "the troublesome, the hopeless, the awkward, the undignified."[64]

The theme of presence (*zaichang* and *zaichang gan*) that Shen repeatedly refers to in the manifesto relates closely to live-scene discourse, which first made an appearance in poetry criticism in the writings of Yu Jian in the early 1990s. In a 1993 essay titled "What are poets for?" (Shiren he wei?), Yu describes the predicament of poets living in the late twentieth-century market economy, whose personal motivations, intellectual goals, and social relevance were becoming less and less clear. Poets, he declares, must choose between two options: "Either accept responsibility and exist as a poet of the 'live scene.' Or refuse to 'be rejected,' continue to indulge in utopia's pessimistic cynicism, and, in the mind-set of a peasant farmer society, feel nostalgia for lost agricultural gods, demand asylum, continue spiritual masturbation in the utopian language of 'ifs' and 'thens,' and refuse the 'current moment,' 'live scenes' and the 'present at hand' [*shoubian*]."[65] Live scenes, in this understanding, symbolize a form of active engagement with the social realities of the here and now, something that Yu Jian as a representative of the Popular Standpoint values highly.

Shen Haobo also uses live-scene discourse to justify the appearance of his bodily poetics on the web. In a newspaper interview in 2007 he stated that "as a platform, the Internet has already become the true bodily live scene of contemporary Chinese poetry."[66] His usage here of "bodily live scene" is paradoxical in that there is something decidedly incorporeal about the Internet: communication takes place in a bodiless state where people can be present only in words and images. Associating the online world with a bodily live scene is a way of asserting a physical connection between poets and their writing, in the case of Shen and the Lower Body group exhibited to a large extent by writing *about* the body. In the same interview, he refers to the "flesh and blood" (*xuerou*) of the live scene that is *Poetry Rivers and Lakes*, contrasting it with the "relatively stable classics" that appear in print journals. In Lower Body poetics, the body is the greatest source of authenticity, the one indubitable fact of life. To speak of the "flesh and blood" of an Internet-based live scene is, therefore, to make a claim for the truth and immediacy of online poetry writing. It also reflects the gatekeeping implications of live-scene discourse: in Yu Jian's original formulation, "live scene" and "presence" represent a philosophical understanding of human existence itself; in Shen's understanding, they are used to refer to a site of poetry activity as specific as an individual online poetry forum, inhabited by a limited number of poets and readers. To be present on that forum is to understand contemporary poetry; to be absent will, therefore, inevitably result in misunderstanding and misrepresentation in other contexts.

The fact that the Lower Body group had already greatly expanded the limits of poetic possibility in the late 1990s and early 2000s meant that any poetry group that followed had to work especially hard to vie for recognition as the cutting-edge of Chinese avant-garde poetry. We have already seen how the School of Rubbish approached this task by "worshiping the low"; Pidan encapsulated the group's perception of the Lower Body school in the ninth of twenty-five School of Rubbish slogans (*kouhao*) with the words, "you only have to go one meter lower to get from enemy occupied territory (the Lower Body) to the liberated area (School of Rubbish)."[67] In the case of the Rubbish poet Xu Xiangchou and many of his imitators, going "one meter lower" meant writing not about sex and the reproductive organs but about "shit." Just as writing about the body for the Lower Body group functions as a way of expressing presence on the relatively disembodied medium of the Internet, so too can writing about bodily excretions be understood as a way of dealing with the materiality of the web. The scatological turn in School of Rubbish poetry was, in addition, a collective attempt to bring poetry back down to earth, with bodily excretions serving as a metaphor for poetry itself. According to this line of thinking poetry should ideally be free flowing, an honest reflection of the messy realities of human life, and unencumbered by the need to self-censor or be civilized and polite. Shit also functions as a great social equalizer: everyone does it, no matter how high their social position or professional rank or how deep the layers of civilizing behaviors that encompass them.

Xu, the second poet to join the school after Pidan/Old Man/Zhi Feng, is the most famous practitioner of what is known as "shit and piss writing" (*shiniao xiezuo*). According to Old Man, using "shit" as a symbol for worshiping the low is Xu's invention and has been a central influence on how outsiders view the School of Rubbish.[68] He has composed a whole set of poems titled "Shit Series" (Shi xilie), of which the following is an example:

INSIDE THE WALLS
[Zai yuanqiang de limian][69]

Inside the walls is a compound
inside the compound is a building
inside the building is a room
inside the room are some people
every person is wearing clothes
inside the clothes are bellies
inside the bellies are intestines
inside the intestines is shit

Poems like these have proved controversial even within the ranks of School of Rubbish poets and, according to Pidan, were responsible for one member deciding to quit the group less than a month after it was established. In his essay "On the School of Rubbish as metaphor" (Lun zuowei yinyu de laji pai), Pidan explains the importance of this type of poetry to the school's poetics:

> Shit poetry writing is a typical manifestation of the School of Rubbish's "shit and piss writing." The School of Rubbish often calls works that write about shit, piss, farts, and even pus "shit and piss writing." This is an important style of School of Rubbish writing. The difference between it and so-called "body writing" is that, if one looks at content, it normally writes about the excretions that have already been emitted—or are about to be emitted—from the human body, and not about actual flesh or whatever.

A number of sympathetic poetry critics adopted this theme of continuation and evolution to explain the group's "surpassing" of the Lower Body by shifting from writing about the body to writing about bodily excretions. Zhang Jiayan, for example, traces the protagonist in Chinese poetry all the way from Guo Moruo through to the School of Rubbish:

> The protagonist in Chinese poetry [has developed] from a mythical hero (Guo Moruo's phoenix and heavenly dog) to the battle hero (Ai Qing's trumpet player, Li Ji's Wang Gui), from political leaders to industrial, agricultural, and soldier paradigms (Mao Zedong, Lei Feng, etc.), turning into normal people, ordinary people, and common people; in the midst of this it once turned from empty language (a shell of a person) back to the search for "the individual"; maybe this happened in between the "Popular" and the "Intellectuals," and

> maybe the "Middle Generation" and "post-70s" are also searching for a new subject. However, the "Lower Body" finally caused the "person" in Chinese poetry to become crippled and incomplete and the "School of Rubbish" simply lets him fall to the ground, not only facing rubbish, but also turning him into "rubbish." Thus, Chinese poetry through these twists and turns has walked the "road downward" to its very end, and turned poetry's protagonist from a "person" into a "non-person"![70]

Zhang's rhetorical achievement here lies in portraying the transition from Lower Body to Rubbish poetry as smooth and inevitable, despite the notion of a linear path leading from one type of writing to the next being entirely a construct of the School of Rubbish.

Other discourse surrounding the appearance of Rubbish poetry and the challenge it posed to the Lower Body group focused less on continuation than on rupture. Xiao Yu'er portrays the moment of the school's appearance on the Internet as a scene of violent battle with the Lower Body group:

> As soon as they appeared they pointed their spears toward the Lower Body camp, igniting fires from all sides, engaging in all-out conflict, arguing frenziedly and accusing each other by name. Under the vicious cannon fire of the School of Rubbish, the Lower Body were caught unawares and hurriedly sought to fight back, but the School of Rubbish kept on creating new incidents, counterattacking, slandering Shen so-and-so, eluding attempts to block them, hacking forums, and recruiting supporters. Within a few noisy months, and despite all accusations and insults, the writing principles of the School of Rubbish spread their wings and found their way into the minds of passers-by . . . throughout all the disputes and complaining, people were made witness to the extreme self-publicizing [*chaozuo*] techniques of a new poetry school in the age of the Internet.[71]

According to Xu Xiangchou, the fuse that ignited the battle between the School of Rubbish and the Lower Body group was a statement posted on *Poetry Rivers and Lakes* on May 18, 2003, by a number of School of Rubbish members who had decided to quit the school, including Lao De, Fa Qing, Datou Yaya (Big Headed Ducky), and Jiangnan Buyi (Southern China Cloth).[72] Their statement announced that "after leaving the School of Rubbish, the School of Rubbish is no longer permitted to quote, edit, analyze, or criticize any of our poetry or theoretical essays in the name of the School. Any criticism or epistles about our poetry written in the name of the School of Rubbish before we quit the group must not be quoted or published after our departure in any form without prior consent." The reason they gave for quitting was that "we no longer agree with the wording and theory of the School of Rubbish. We never agreed with the 'Three Principles of the School of Rubbish.' We only want to write poems, nothing else."

Posting such a statement of dissent on *Poetry Rivers and Lakes*, home of the Lower Body group, was a premeditated move designed to take advantage of existing tensions between the Lower Body and the School of Rubbish. The gamble paid off when several Lower Body poets, to whom Xu disparagingly refers as the "Shen Haobos," took the opportunity to express admiration for the now ex-Rubbish poets. Xu proceeded to engage in a strongly worded series of one-on-one exchanges with Shen Haobo, in which Xu accused Shen of "opposing the avant-garde" and Shen called the School of Rubbish "ruffian proletariats" who had never produced a decent poem in their lives.[73] Later, Blue Butterfly Lilac summed up the attitude of the School of Rubbish as follows: "The 'Lower Body' has already completed its avant-garde mission; the arrival of the 'School of Rubbish' means the end for the 'Lower Body.'"[74] Such statements suggest that inter- and intragroup fighting is primarily a battle for discursive power; both sides attempt to attract attention within wider poetry scenes and thus establish themselves as prominent members of the contemporary poetic vanguard.

The School of Rubbish also attempted to extend its hold on literary history by becoming increasingly involved in offline literary production in the print and face-to-face spaces. Their webzine was also produced in an independently financed print version called the *School of Rubbish Journal* (Lajipai minkan). The first edition was published in July 2003, just four months after the group was established on *Beijing Review*. In addition, several members of the school have met in person and attended organized poetry events and get-togethers, thus bringing virtual relationships fostered through Internet communication further into the offline world.[75] From the limited and sporadic nature of the group's forays into print publishing and face-to-face activities, however, it is reasonable to conclude that the School of Rubbish remained a predominantly Internet-based poetry community. As Old Man put it in the 37th article of the "School of Rubbish Manifesto": "Without the Internet, there would be no Old Man; without the Internet, the School of Rubbish might have still happened, but it would have been something completely different, and [poets] would have been Rubbish in a far less Rubbish way, as if making a fuss over

Rubbish."[76] Since the deletion of the *Beijing Review* poetry forum in 2010, the group has lacked a central online space in which to congregate, and discussion of Rubbish poetics has gradually died down since 2008. By 2013, although several key Rubbish poets were still using their old web IDs to write blogs and weibo, the School of Rubbish as an organized online poetry group based around a central headquarters and producing regular textual offerings had, for all intents and purposes, ceased to exist.

CONCLUSION

As the textual interactions of the School of Rubbish attest, rather than immediately revolutionizing the content and form of modern Chinese poetry, certain dynamics of Internet-based communication have met the longstanding desires of Chinese poets to assert their poetic agency at the same time as they seek belonging in communities of like-minded poets, with the ultimate goals of asserting their poetry citizenship and being recognized as members of poetry scenes. Online poetry literacy is centered on an appreciation of modern Chinese poetry as a social form. For groups like the School of Rubbish, it involves declaring loyalty to the group by adhering to the group's interpretive strategies for "worshiping the low" and referring to group members by name in essays and poems. It also involves using those interpretive strategies to maintain the boundaries of the community: only poets who can write recognizable "Rubbish poems" are granted entry into the group. In this sense, the Internet seems to offer a distinctly social mode of learning, whereby aspiring poets do not achieve poetry citizenship through knowledge acquired by reading books but by participating in the real-time processes of poetry writing, critiquing, gatekeeping, and historicizing.[77]

Online poetry literacy also requires an understanding of the historical mission of the group, which in the case of the School of Rubbish was defined in direct relation to the poetry groups that had come before it, notably the Lower Body group and its preoccupation with the sexualized human body. This suggests that despite the importance of presence and real-time interaction in live scenes such as the online forum *Beijing Review* (a live-scene approach to literary activity that centers on the here and now), Internet-based poetry groups are also keenly aware of the discursive formation of literary history and their need to document and control narration of their poetic development. One aesthetic consequence of the contingency and immediacy of online communication has been an entrenchment of the kind of colloquial writing and antilofty poetics that emerged in the Third Generation poetry of the 1980s before being widely promoted under the banner of the Popular Standpoint in the late 1990s and 2000s. Although other poets use the Internet to share sophisticated poems that have been fine-tuned over lengthy periods of writing and rewriting, for many online groups the joy of the Internet lies in the speed with which poems can be produced and critiqued by fellow poet-citizens, thus facilitating connections between texts, poets, and communities. The result is a tendency toward an ever more free-flowing, chatty style of verse, or Pettitt's "lettered quasi-orality."

Another large part of the Internet's appeal for Chinese poets is found in the quality of being co-present with other human beings through the same technological medium. Geographic impracticalities and the relatively high costs and institutional barriers to print publication mean that many Internet-based poets will never have the opportunity to meet in person or see their works published on the printed page. The Internet gives them a way to create networks and nurture self-promoting animosities with others, as well as to seek acknowledgment as cultural producers and disseminate their texts. In this sense, early utopian expectations for the potential offered to poetry by the growth of the Internet have been realized, with one important caveat. Rather than resulting in significant amounts of technologically experimental poetry that makes use of the hypertext capabilities of the Internet to change the form of individual poems, as critics including Yang Xiaomin and Sang Ke suggested, the Internet and its relatively liberal communications environment have facilitated strategies for community-based interaction and activism that were previously impossible through print publication or face-to-face communication.

The School of Rubbish may not have forever altered the face of Chinese poetry or led to an irreversible shift in power relations within Chinese poetry scenes; in 2013, its name stood mostly as a reminder of the most active, contentious period in forum-based poetic interaction in the early to mid-2000s, as well as a landmark on poetry's progressive path "downward" from the Third Generation to the Lower Body to the Low Poetry Movement. To understand the group's historical significance, it may be necessary to look beyond the realm of poetry to consider how Rubbish poetry operates as an implied form of resistance against the sanitizing and individualizing efforts of the Chinese party-state. Considered in conjunction with the online behaviors of poetry communities such as the School of Rubbish, Hai Ren's argument that Chinese neoliberalism requires a process of individualization in distributing social values and norms takes on an interesting light.

From one perspective, the activities of individual poets such as the Rubbish poetry founder Old Man/Pidan/Zhi Feng can be understood as one example of what Ren terms the "DIY way of living," in which individuals become part of society by taking responsibility for the life-building process (even if, in this case, it involved highlighting the more destructive rather than constructive aspects of life). From another angle, however, online poetry communities demonstrate a level of collectivism and communal value-making that stand in contrast to the dominant processes of capitalist rationalization and socialization that are promoted by the Chinese party-state and promulgated though the media. Though they may not quite yearn for a return to the collectivist era of the work unit and the commune, poetry groups like the School of Rubbish suggest that community belonging and the ability to document one's own community-specific history remain instrumental to China's cultural producers. To extend this argument further, a strong sense of community may even serve, as Haomin Gong suggests in his discussion of migrant worker poetry, as a form of New Leftist intervention and a challenge to China's dominant neoliberal condition.[78]

In a discussion on *Beijing Review* on January 18, 2006, Old Man/Pidan wrote:

> History has provided two things for the rise [*jueqi*] of today's China: one is China itself, the other is China's School of Rubbish. The former is the principle architect of the rise, the latter is an emblem of the rise. If [China] cannot even contain a School of Rubbish, can it still be considered a rise? American people today, including Little Bush, understand China relatively well; if they also knew of the School of Rubbish I think this would be more important than anything else, as it would truly allow them to determine to what extent China has risen.[79]

Connecting China's "rise" to its ability to contain or (to quote a line from Xu Xiangchou's poetry) "give rise to a School of Rubbish" is an unusual proposition. In an era of global capitalism, it is economic growth and international influence, not modern poetry, that are usually taken as evidence of a country's success. Pidan's message, on the other hand, is one of tolerance and inclusion: the greatness of the nation depends on its ability to provide the conditions that enable the appearance and continued existence of controversial poetry groups like the School of Rubbish. Pidan implies that only such diversity can prove that the country has made progress beyond the days of cultural uniformity and absolute political repression. Unfortunately *Beijing Review*'s disappearance in 2010 might seem to suggest that China's ability to "contain" the School of Rubbish is not as strong as he had hoped. The group's theories and poetic writings, however, can still be found across the Internet, and even though they may no longer be operating as a close-knit community, its former members continue to propagate their ideas about Low Poetry through other forums, personal blogs, and weibo.

Online space has played a curious role within broader non-medium-specific poetry scenes. It has often been assumed that the Internet offers, at most, a platform from which aspiring cultural producers can launch themselves into the "real world," implying that success in the offline spaces of print and face-to-face poetry events is the ultimate decider of career longevity and individual reputation.[80] It is apparent, however, that many poets have become increasingly disinterested in and even disaffected by print media and that inclusion in web-based poetry selections and membership in online communities are often sufficient. Chang Shan alluded to this in a discussion of the School of Rubbish in 2004: "In the past, divisions and debates within the Chinese poetry arena, no matter whether they occurred between the 'Popular' and 'Intellectual' camps or within the ranks of Popular poetry, all took place in print publications and in reality. The School of Rubbish, on the other hand, has achieved its huge success through the virtual Internet. This means that Internet writing has officially entered the great halls of literature."[81] The poet and critic Xiao Yu'er made a similar point in 2003: "most Internet poets are no longer excited by the prospect of their poetry being published in journals and newspapers, unlike the older generation of poets."[82] When print publication of Internet-produced poetry does occur, it is often a means of documenting what has already happened in the online space, a more permanent record that has the potential benefit of introducing the group's or individual's interpretive strategies to a wider offline audience over the course of time.

Nonetheless, even in an age in which electronic means of producing and consuming literature are increasingly becoming the norm, it would be premature to declare an end to the age of print. Physical poetry publications retain a level of importance in the age of the Internet primarily because it is far harder to have one's works selected for publication in a journal, anthology, or individual poetry collection than it is to self-publish online via forums, webzines, and blogs. Print space remains fraught with poetry politics and gatekeeping practices in the early twenty-first century, offering multiple channels for the publication of poetry and involving collusions of interests and capital that are essential for the production of poetry on the printed page.

CHAPTER 2

Poetry in Print

1999, I was working for two magazines:
one called *Life Weekly*
one called *Works of Film.*
If I were to use a journalistic tone to describe this year to you
I would say: at the turn of the century
a clap of sky-born thunder rolled past an airplane window:
an old man on his way home
saw a flash of lightning.
And as for poetry—
poetry was being slowly written by me on a piece of paper

—YANG LI, "*I Want to Use the Manner of Poetry To . . .* " (Wo yao yong yizhong shige de fangshi . . .)

When we are very close to a particular era, it is easy for us to overlook its importance; this is something we can recognize only when time has passed. Contemporary things will become classics and enter tradition in the future; what is happening right now is just a live scene.

—YANG KE, interviewed in *Southern Metropolis Weekly*

Although the Internet has become the biggest and most versatile space for poetry production and interaction in the new millennium, printed texts have retained a unique ability to capture the imagination and stir the ambitions of Chinese poets. Poems that are first posted online are later sorted through and selected for inclusion in poetry journals, single-author collections, and anthologies. Less well-known poets make their work available in print through self-financed publications. Books and periodicals are distributed in person at poetry events, serving as gifts, badges of honor, and timely reminders of each writer's talents and enthusiasm. Although the space allotted to modern and contemporary poetry in China's bookstores is usually no more than two or three shelves—and even those are often dominated by collections of Mao's classical-style poetry—the print space of poetry in the early twenty-first century demands critical attention, not least because of Chinese poets' reluctance to abandon faith in the authority and permanence that surrounds the printed word.

In this chapter I investigate the functions of print media within poetry scenes and the kinds of planning, cooperation, and gatekeeping that go on behind the scenes of print. More specifically, I focus on the role played by multiple-author poetry publications in distributions of discursive power within China's poetry scenes. Throughout this book I borrow from Van Crevel a broad and non-medium-specific definition of publication as "the making public of a text beyond inner-circle audiences hand-picked by the author."[1] The key distinction of print publishing lies in the processes of material production: imprinting words onto paper, binding pages into books and journals, and distributing them across physical space to reach bookstores, libraries, offices, and homes. Official publication is defined as making print materials legally available for purchase through the acquisition of an ISSN or ISBN (*shuhao*). In China, it requires close cooperation with state-run publishing houses, printing presses, book agents, editors, censors, commercial distribution channels, bookstores, and the private agents who often provide the necessary capital.

Book publication thus stands as an interesting case study of the historical conjuncture at the beginning of China's twenty-first century. As part of the nation's broader cultural system reforms, publishing houses have been granted a greater degree of financial and operational independence than ever before but are still expected to follow censorship guidelines issued by the party-state. Money is a much bigger issue for print than for online publication, as each stage of the publishing process requires economic support and modern poetry is far from being the kind of best-selling literature that is profitable for its authors and publishers. Politics, too, are a more pressing concern in print publication, as China's differential system of media control means that poems that are published in print and available for sale legally through nationwide distribution networks are governed by far higher levels of self-censorship and pre- and post-publication scrutiny than those published on blogs and Internet forums.

Print publications play a distinctive role within poetry scenes not only because of the types of decision making and institutional gatekeeping involved in the material production of books and journals but also because of the symbolism associated with print collections of poems in the development of post-Mao poetry—and indeed, throughout the premodern and early modern history of poetry in China. Multiple-author anthologies exemplify the philosophy that the scarcer the opportunity for representation, the greater its symbolic value and, thus, the stronger the desire to be represented. To be selected as part of the "best" of Chinese poetry in a certain year or decade is a highly sought-after honor. This is not only because it acts as a public confirmation of literary achievements from peers and other gatekeepers in current poetry scenes but, perhaps even more important, because it poses the alluring possibility of inclusion in future literary canons. Being represented in print poetry anthologies, in other words, is seen as an essential step in what Hank Lazer has called the "competitive and snarly nature of making literary history."[2]

The "best" elements of a cultural scene are not necessarily those that make it into the public eye, become famous, or are translated into other languages; similarly, the category of "good poetry" is both highly subjective and historically determined according to multiple factors (aesthetic, ideological, economic, and social). The trajectories that poems follow from writer to reader can be torturous. On the way to short-term recognition and long-term preservation and canonization, they must withstand a chain of value judgments, media dynamics, random occurrences, and gatekeeping controls, which, when working together, are likely to relegate all but the most fortunate works to obscurity. In light of this, the analysis that follows will pay as much attention to publication logistics as to the discourses and ideologies that affect attitudes toward poetry in print in an attempt to reveal some of the complexities of print culture in early twenty-first-century China. Most of this chapter is based on interviews I conducted with editors and publishers in Guangdong and elsewhere in China, as well as on their written recollections included as prefaces and postscripts to books or published on the Internet.[3]

I focus on the production processes of a long-running series of poetry yearbooks known as the *Chinese New Poetry Almanac* (or in its self-translated English title, the *China New Poem Almanac*), which were published primarily in Guangdong between 1999 and 2011. As its editorial committee hoped, the *Almanac* stirred up much contention among poets and readers. Its journey began with the publication of the inaugural 1998 edition in February 1999, designed to serve as a counteranthology to Cheng Guangwei's *Portrait of Years Gone By*, which many poets outside of Beijing believed had given preferential treatment to proponents of

Intellectual Writing in the capital. By promoting the Popular Standpoint and being produced in the south of China, the *Chinese New Poetry Almanac* offered a contrasting representation of current poetry writing that selected poets from across the country and from a range of groups, generations, and isms. The fact that its editors conceived of the anthology as an act of resistance against the discursive power of Intellectual Writing became clear at the Panfeng Meeting of April 1999 when Yang Ke provoked the Beijing-based poets and critics into a fiery battle of words by boasting of the *Almanac*'s commercial success in China's book market.

The *Almanac*'s initial understanding of the Popular as outlined by poets such as Yu Jian and Han Dong was intended as an alternative to the perceived emphasis on knowledge, history, and authority displayed by poetry publications dominated by Intellectual poets in the north of the country and embodied in the discourse of the poetry arena. Instead the *Almanac* offered a vision of the Popular as a timeless and authentic source of "good poetry," free from the grip of China's intellectual and political elites and connected to such concepts as memory, independence, and tradition.[4] Representing a Popular Standpoint did not simply mean selecting a more diverse array of poems and poets than was typical of multiple-author poetry publications in the 1990s, although this was an important part of the *Almanac*'s mission. It also involved experimenting with new editorial strategies such as committee-based voting and the executive editor system, as well as with documenting live scenes of poetry by selecting poems from more contingent spaces such as unofficial print journals and the Internet. This live-scene approach incorporated innovative techniques for representing the here and now of poetry activity, for example, by including reports on poetry polemics and lists of the biggest incidents to have hit poetry scenes that year. As such, it communicated the idea that poetry is not just poems but also possesses a social life that can offer entertainment value to poets and non-poetry-reading publics alike.

However, the *Almanac*'s attempts to counter the discursive power of the poetry arena's predominantly Beijing-based gatekeepers were brought into doubt as time went by and it became seen as a source of gatekeeping authority in its own right. By examining the issues of contention that surrounded the *Almanac* throughout its publication history in the 2000s, we can observe how such print poetry publications, like the online poetry groups explored in the previous chapter, embody the tension between the discourse of the poetry arena and that of live scenes, filtering poetry scenes according to their own terms at the same time as they attempt to lay claim to an aura of immediacy and authenticity as less mediated documentations of the here and now of modern Chinese poetry. One could argue that dissatisfaction regarding the contents and editing of the *Chinese New Poetry Almanac* was inevitable, as such an ambitious print publication could not possibly exist for so long without capitulating to the political and economic demands placed on modern poetry in China and without sacrificing its Popular spirit of inclusion and anti-authoritarian resistance along the way. The contention that accompanied the publication of the *Almanac* in later years also relates to the conflicting media dynamics of print publication and the online space: as we shall see, much of the anger directed at Yang Ke and his editorial team was expressed in forum-based communication on the Internet, a space that by the mid-2000s had grown accustomed to a much more interactive, contingent mode of poetry production.

CHANNELS OF PUBLICATION

Print publishing in China can be loosely divided into three channels, the distinctions between which are not always entirely clear: official, semi-official, and unofficial. Official publications, which are sometimes referred to as the first or primary publishing channel, are either commissioned by publishing houses themselves or are connected to national and regional government organizations such as the Writers' Association. In order to be sold legally they must have a book number or periodical number, and they are mostly distributed through state-run bookstores and, in the case of journals, China's post office system. Whereas official journals are distinguished by their affiliation with branches of the Writers' Association and institutions of higher education, officially published books are a more ambiguous category and in many cases overlap with second-channel publications.

Semi-official publication, more commonly known as the second or secondary channel (*di er qudao*), refers to the practice of editors and/or book agents purchasing book numbers from state-run publishing houses in order to sell and distribute their books on the market. Second-channel book production involves a series of cooperative publishing arrangements (*xiezuo chuban*) among writers, editors, book agents or dealers (*shushang*), printing presses, private distributors, and publishers. Originally intended to facilitate the publication of scholarly books by financially and managerially inefficient state publishing houses, the second channel has, over the past two decades, produced books that span a wide range of genres, subject matter, and intended audiences.[5] By the end of the 1990s there were ten times as many private book dealers in China as official publishing houses, and by midway through the following decade second-channel publications accounted for about 20 percent (around twenty thousand) of book titles published in China each year.[6]

Unofficial publication refers to the production and distribution of any print materials that cannot be legally sold in bookstores or elsewhere because they do not carry a book or periodical number. Such materials are produced using private funds and often relatively basic, small-scale printing technologies before being distributed through noncommercial channels. This typically means sending publications by mail or delivering them by hand to reach an audience of other writers, critics, and friends. Unofficial publications need not undergo any sort of censorship process as they do not require cooperation with state-run publishing houses. As such, they tend to include writings that conform less to the ideological and aesthetic "mainstream" of state-approved culture. Categories of unofficial publications include individual poetry collections, journals or periodicals, and multiple-author anthologies.[7]

PUBLISHING ATTITUDES

In a survey on attitudes toward poetry activity that I circulated among Chinese poets in 2006, I asked what print publication meant for them personally.[8] The results should be understood in light of the fact that the survey was distributed via email, online forums, and blogs and are therefore weighted toward the experiences of Internet-active poets. Nevertheless, they suggest some interesting trends. Of the forty-five poets who completed the survey, 35 percent stated that the primary benefit of print publication is distribution and communication, or allowing more people to read their work; 31 percent said they valued the affirmation and recognition that print publishing brings; 18 percent identified the preservation of texts to be the main advantage; and another 16 percent claimed print publishing to be of little or no importance to them.

A number of the poets' comments touched upon the issue of reputation or poetry citizenship: in order to be taken seriously as poets, writers need to have print publications of their work to distribute at poetry events. One respondent wrote, "On certain occasions, if you haven't published a poetry collection you can feel embarrassed, like a good person caught in difficult circumstances; other people might start to doubt your identity as a poet, and at the very least you might make them think that there are problems with your writing output." The implication here is not just of the importance of print publication to individual reputation but also of its function of summarizing or distilling the best of a poet's writing over a period of time. This is the first level of gatekeeping implicit in the print space of poetry: before being chosen by others for inclusion in books and journals, poets carry out their own process of selection and rejection, deciding which poems are worth making public.

That over a quarter of survey participants indicated personal recognition to be a major benefit of print publication is further evidence that poets are keenly aware of the next level of poetry gatekeeping: selection by others. Having one's works chosen for inclusion in journals and anthologies is a sign of having made it as a poet, and poets' biographies often include a list of print publications in which the poet's works have been featured. This serves a publicly oriented vision of poetry citizenship: the greater the poet's number of publications and other public accolades, the more respected and successful he or she must be. Being selected for publication by the gatekeepers of print suggests that a poet has achieved a level of recognition from peers (fellow poets, critics, and editors) within the poetry community, awarded independently of any financial or political concerns. Inclusion in official journals, anthologies, or educational textbooks may, nonetheless, require submission to external demands such as censorship practices or commercial pressures.

ANTHOLOGIES

China has a long and much-studied history of producing literary anthologies, often seen as the first step in the formation of canons.[9] Literary anthologies share a number of interrelated goals that include valorization or preserving someone's notion of "the best of a kind," propagation, canonization, and literary interpretation, often by including the editor's commentaries alongside the texts themselves.[10] Anthologies have been regarded as works of history in their own right, a facet noted by the eighteenth-century writer Yuan Mei in a letter to Shen Deqian when he states that "the ways of selecting poems and of writing history are the same."[11] The task of writing poetry history by selecting some poems (*cai shi*) and deleting others (*shan shi*) is thought to have begun with Confucius's compiling of the *Book of Songs* in the sixth century BC. The Han dynasty historian Sima Qian wrote that Confucius "eliminated those [poems] that duplicated others and took those that could enact propriety and righteousness,"[12] thus reducing a collection of three thousand poems to one a tenth of its size.

Throughout the following centuries, generations of scholars and editors have taken it upon themselves to compile and recompile collections of Chinese literature. In doing so, they have both determined generic parameters and asserted what were often highly contentious views of who and what should be read, studied, and emulated in years to come.[13] Regardless of when and where they are produced, literary anthologies reflect changing strategies of valorization that are inevitably shaped by the historical circumstances and movements of the time such as reforms, revolutions, and revivals.[14] In the post-Mao era, the development and valorization of modern Chinese poetry have taken place in the midst of conjunctures marked, in turn, by market reforms and intermittent political crackdowns, cultural fever, high-speed economic growth, and media revolution. The process of compiling collections of the "best" or more representative poems written during this period began in the 1980s and continues to the present day, motivated by the need to make sense of the many changes taking place both within poetry writing itself and within the broader social and medial contexts in which poetry is written, published, and consumed. As we will see in the case of the *China New Poetry Almanac*, print poetry anthologizing is as much about asserting authority over literary history as it is about representing poetry scenes to a wider, unpredictable audience.

CHINESE NEW POETRY ALMANAC

Eleven editions of the *Almanac* were published between 1999 and 2011, covering the years 1998, 1999, 2000, 2001, 2002–3, 2004–5, 2006, 2007, 2008, and 2009–10, as well as a ten-year retrospective anthology of works from the first nine volumes published in 2010. Each edition was published in the year following the time period it represents. The chief editor of the series is Yang Ke, a

Guangzhou-based poet, university lecturer, blogger, and deputy editor of the Guangdong Writers' Association journal *Literary Works* (Zuopin). The various editions of the *Almanac* were mostly financed, edited, printed, and published in Guangdong. The 1998 edition of the anthology is famous for having represented the Popular side of the Panfeng Polemic; the front cover displayed the slogan "In art we adhere to the true, eternal, Popular Standpoint" (*yishu shang women bingcheng: zhenzheng de yongheng de minjian lichang*). The anthology also prides itself on having achieved a number of firsts: the first entirely privately funded yet officially published poetry yearbook; the first officially published anthology to select poems from unofficial journals, self-published manuscripts, and the Internet; the first official publication to feature Bei Dao's poetry since it had been banned ten years earlier (eleven of his poems were featured in the 1998 edition); and, perhaps most significant, the first commercially available annual literary anthology to be produced and published outside the capital with the word "China" in the title. According to Yang Ke, prior to this point all collections claiming to represent "Chinese poetry" had been published in Beijing.

The *1998 Chinese New Poetry Almanac* was one of a number of poetry yearbooks published in 1999 that attempted to counteract the dearth of public interest in modern poetry during the 1990s and represent poetic writings of that decade to a broader audience. April saw the release of the *1998 Modern Chinese Poetry Almanac* (1998 nian xiandai hanshi nianjian), edited by Beijing-based poetry critic Tang Xiaodu and published in Beijing by the China Federation of Literature and Art Circles Publishing Corporation. In July, Liaoning People's Publishing House released *The Best Chinese Poetry of 1998* (1998 nian Zhongguo zui jia shige), edited by Peking University professor and Middle Generation poet Zang Di. Finally, the *1999 Chinese Poetry Yearbook* (1999 Zhongguo shi nianxuan), edited by Chongqing poet He Xiaozhu, was published in December by Shaanxi Normal University Press. In their accompanying commentaries, all four editors allude to the goal of bringing modern poetry back into the public eye. Of the four, however, only the *Chinese New Poetry Almanac* continued to be published over the following decade.

Publishing Processes of the Chinese New Poetry Almanac

Yang Ke first conceived of the idea to publish a yearbook of avant-garde contemporary poetry in 1998 with a man named Li Mingpeng, a poet and real estate entrepreneur.[15] They were soon joined by a writer and book agent from Hubei named Yang Maodong, who volunteered to provide financial sponsorship for the publication. As chief editor of the anthology, Yang Ke described his intentions thus: "for the benefit of this era of rapid change, to preserve texts of value: texts that suggest historical continuity with the past eighty years of Chinese new poetry, and which are the true distillation of Chinese contemporary poetry"; "to break through obstacles in the way of communication between poets and readers"; and to ensure "poetry fulfills its hematopoietic [*zaoxue*, or blood-creating] function, and not just a blood-transfusing function"; in other words, to ensure that the *Almanac* would not lose them money.[16]

Finances and Distribution

For the first four editions, Yang Maodong was both the sole private sponsor of the *Almanac* and a book agent with the experience necessary to negotiate the purchase of a book number from a state-owned publishing house. According to Yang Ke's records, up to several hundred thousand renminbi are required to finance each edition of the *Almanac*, depending on the number of copies printed. Of this, ¥15,000 (US$2,500) is required to buy a book number from a state-run publishing house. Printing costs are in the region of ¥8.5 (US$1.40) per book. For example, the 1998 edition, with a print run of 20,000, cost ¥170,000 (US$27,750) to produce. Design and typesetting costs add up to several thousand renminbi, depending on the amount charged by individual designers. Another several thousand goes toward mailing free copies of the *Almanac* to poets, critics, libraries, and foreign researchers. The market price of the almanac is ¥28 per copy (US$4.60), of which half (¥14, US$2.30) is profit; with the exception of the ten-year anthology published in January 2010, which sold for ¥38, the price remained fixed for each edition; Yang Ke claimed to be wary of alienating readers by making it more expensive. Bookstores that sell the *Almanac* keep a further 20–30 percent of gross revenue.[17]

Key to the early planning of the *Almanac* was the hope that the finances of the publication would not just break even but might even make a profit, thus fulfilling the "hematopoietic function" of book publishing. The unusually large print run of 20,000 copies for the 1998 edition and the establishment of a Chinese New Poetry Almanac Fund reflected this confidence. The fund was intended to amass all profits made through sales of the anthology and use them to finance editorial meetings and dinners, as well as provide a small amount of compensation to the editors. Yang Ke's hope was that the fund would one day be sufficient to enable the *Almanac* to sponsor a range of poetry-related activities and events. At the beginning the situation looked hopeful. All 20,000 copies of the 1998 edition were distributed within months, mostly from commercial sales but a number were given away. Both it and the 1999 edition of the *Almanac* made a profit, allowing its editors to stage a small number of face-to-face poetry events, including the Longmai Poetry Meeting (Longmai shihui) in November 1999 and a large-scale poetry event in Guangzhou in early 2000, to which over 160 young poets were invited.[18] Editorial meetings were also among the *Almanac*'s biggest expenses, requiring funds to cover the committee's food, accommodation, and transportation costs.

The primary means of commercial distribution for this anthology, as is the case for most modern poetry publications, was not through Xinhua (China's national book distribution network) but through smaller, privately owned specialist bookstores such as the Beijing bookstores Forest Song (Feng Ru Song) and All Sages (Wansheng Shuyuan) located in the city's northwestern university district. This distribution channel is not without its hazards. Bookshops that are willing to risk stocking niche publications often go bankrupt in the process, leaving their owners unable to pay suppliers for copies of books already sold. The option of sending an employee to chase after any outstanding sums of money is unrealistic, as the cost of transportation is usually far greater than the amount of profit likely to be recovered.[19]

Underlying the distribution tactics that Yang Ke adopted for the *Almanac* was a fundamental awareness that circulation was to be essential to its success, not so much in an economic sense but in terms of the anthology's influence within Chinese poetry scenes and the broader literary world. This is why Yang sent free copies of each edition of the *Almanac* to individuals and institutions both in China and overseas, in the hope that the anthology would not become yet another cliquish publication of limited reach. According to Yang, he gave away over one thousand copies, or roughly ¥30,000 (US$4,900) worth of books, a sum that directly impacted the *Almanac*'s profits. Yang also had to cover all postage costs himself, which ranged from just a few renminbi for domestic mail to an average of ¥35 (US$5.70) for international packages—more than the price of the book itself.[20]

The upshot of all this was that revenue proved extremely hard to come by. According to Yang Ke, only the 1998 and 1999 editions of the *Almanac* made a profit; all later editions either broke even (in the case of the 2002–3 edition, the only edition since the 1998 edition to be distributed through the Xinhua bookstore system) or posted a loss. The print run of each edition also steadily diminished from a peak of 20,000 copies of the 1998 and 1999 editions down to as few as 3,000 copies of the 2006 edition. Yang admits that few people would be willing to "serve" contemporary poetry if it is going to continually lose them money. The only compensation for the financial losses incurred by the *Almanac* is its widespread influence throughout the 2000s. As he explained, its impact on Chinese poetry scenes can be credited to his strategy of giving copies away for free and not to commercial distribution. The key to power and profit within the publishing industry, as Yang acknowledges here, lies primarily with cultural distribution rather than production.[21]

PUBLISHING POLITICS

The 1998 edition of the *Almanac* was published by Flower City Publishing House (Huacheng Chubanshe), a Guangzhou-based publisher established in 1981. That compromise and negotiation were going to be defining features of the *Almanac*'s publication process was clear from the start when Flower City expressed doubts over the phrase chosen to adorn the front cover of the book: "The true, everlasting Popular Standpoint." A senior staff member contacted Yang Ke to explain that printing this sentence in such a prominent position on the cover was likely to invite "political annoyances." Yang responded by inviting staff from Flower City to dinner and offering to add an additional clause: "*In art we adhere to* the true, everlasting Popular Standpoint." It was agreed that this was enough to assuage the concerns of censors and distract readers from the political implications of a Popular Standpoint, placing the emphasis instead on the artistic side of the *Almanac*'s cause.

The political sensitivities surrounding the word "popular" (*minjian*) might seem surprising. In economics, *minjian* can be used to describe privately owned enterprises (*minjian qiye*), which, despite their distinction from state-owned organizations, are nonetheless a product of the market economy and thus part of the Chinese government's grander vision of domestic economic development.[22] Since the latter half of the 1990s, *minjian* has also been used to describe a particular type of popular or unofficial intellectual (*minjian zhishifenzi*) who is not employed by the state and who expresses opinions on contemporary affairs that diverge from official discourse.[23] This is a relatively new type of social identity that still views the system (*tizhi*) as its antithesis and takes detachment from the system as its primary moral justification and source of self-worth, thus ensuring its connection with that very same system.[24] It is not surprising, given the anti-establishment connotations of the word *minjian*, that Flower City Publishing House found reason to delay the publication of the *Almanac.*

Aside from complaints about the contents of the anthology from "old-timers" (*lao qianbei*) who regularly sent letters to the publishers to express their dissatisfaction with individual poems, the *Almanac*'s biggest complications arose in 2003 when Shen Haobo was acting as joint executive editor. While Yang Ke was in the midst of discussions with Haifeng Publishing House, which had published the 2001 edition and had indicated it would be willing to continue publishing the *Almanac*, Haifeng's employees learned that Shen, whom they knew as the founder of the notorious Lower Body poetry group, was to be coeditor. Shen himself was in the middle of negotiating a deal with Dalian Publishing House to release his first officially published poetry collection, *A Great Evil Hidden in the Heart.*

Although Haifeng could not have known of this in 2003, Shen would run into trouble in early 2004 when Dalian Publishing House discovered that the version of his collection that they had just printed was not the same as the edition he had submitted for prepublication approval. As a result, they had unwittingly published a number of poems considered too sexually risqué for official publication (as had, in fact, been Shen's intention). Upon discovering what had happened, government censors took immediate action. *A Great Evil Hidden in the Heart* was accused of containing an "evil plot" and possessing "an extremely bad social influence." On charges of illegally buying and selling book numbers and publishing "prohibited content of a sexually explicit nature,"

Dalian Publishing House was ordered to shut down for six months and to destroy all existing copies of Shen's poetry collection. The director of the publishing house was fired; other people involved in the book's production were either dismissed or put on record as having committed a serious offense.[25] Shen himself went into hiding for several months. By the time he returned to Beijing the affair had blown over and he appeared to have escaped further retribution.

Even before all this had taken place, Shen Haobo's existing reputation and involvement as coeditor of the 2002 edition of the *Almanac* prompted the responsible editor from Haifeng to withdraw from publishing negotiations with Yang Ke and refuse to publish the *Almanac*. With no choice but to start looking once again for a publisher willing to sell him a book number, Yang eventually reached an agreement with the Tianjin Academy of Social Sciences Press, a small academic press of the kind that is often granted greater ideological leeway in China's differentiated censorship system.[26] This last-minute change resulted in a delay of the publication of the 2002 *Almanac*; it consequently became a two-year edition, covering both 2002 and 2003. It was finally published in June 2004, after Shen Haobo had run into trouble with his own poetry collection. The 2002–3 *Almanac* was considered to be the most contentious edition published so far as it contained a large number of risqué poems by younger poets born in the 1970s, many associated with the Lower Body school. Shen's name, printed on the front cover, also ended up attracting unwelcome attention from more conservative readers. According to Yang Ke, one wrote directly to the General Administration of Press and Publication (GAPP) to lodge a complaint about a poem by Ma Fei titled "The People Stink" (Renmin chouhonghong). The poem reads:

> Hadn't been on the bus for ages
> the taxi took so long to come
> that the bus got here first
> squeezing my way on
> I found myself among the people
> and noticed the people stink
> from mouths nostrils anuses
> stinky gas
> endlessly seeps out
> there's simply no hope of blocking it out

This unflattering portrayal of "the people," a term that is heavy with political and historical connotations in the PRC, was evidently too blatant for this reader to ignore. GAPP responded by sending an employee from Beijing to conduct a thorough inspection of the book. His conclusion was that "the problem was not all that serious," but he recommended nonetheless that an old-timer from Beijing's literary circles be asked to provide a second opinion.

To the relief of the editorial committee, the old-timer declared that the poet's only crime was one of being "insufficiently elegant," but seeing as any rude or sexually explicit content had been presented in the name of artistic experimentation, this was forgivable. This criticism circulated internally and was not made public, unlike in the case of Shen Haobo and the Dalian Publishing House (which was reported on the Internet), but the following year's *Chinese New Poetry Almanac* felt its ramifications nonetheless. Having witnessed the commercial successes of early editions of the *Almanac*, Chongqing Publishing House had contacted Yang Ke to express an interest in publishing and fully financing the 2004 edition. After learning of the censorship issues experienced by the 2002–3 edition and Shen Haobo's own publishing problems, however, the editors felt compelled to conduct an extra-careful review of the 2004 manuscript. When they pointed out several poems that might prove problematic, Yang Ke attempted to compromise by offering to move them to a less prominent position in the book or even to swap them for less "sensitive" poems. This strategy had been successful in the past, but it was not to work this time. After delaying publication for several months, Chongqing Publishing House finally pulled out altogether, leaving the *Almanac* once again without a publisher. At this point, Ruan Qingquan, sponsor of the 2002–3 edition, offered to provide full financial backing and again called upon Haifeng Publishing House to purchase a book number. By this time it was already several months into 2006, and so the 2004 edition, like its predecessor, turned into a double-year publication that covered 2004 and 2005 and was finally sent to the printing press in April 2006. Having encountered so many obstacles in recent editions, the producers of the *Almanac* decided that in the future they would only approach publishing houses to purchase a book number at the last minute when the book was ready for publication.

Top-down censorship is only one type of censorship regularly practiced in PRC literary production since the end of the Cultural Revolution.[27] Equally if not more significant is the practice of self-censorship by authors and editors, the latter of which is known euphemistically as the "responsible editor" (*zeren bianji*) system.[28] Zhang Qinghua, compiler of *The Best Chinese Poetry of 2001* (2001 nian Zhongguo zui jia shige), once confessed,

> Each time I have compiled a collection I have had this experience of "having no choice but to give up," of having to delete the most shocking representative works of poets, even though they might be most capable of representing contemporary poetry's historical reflections and critiques of reality, and even though they might contain the boldest, most unusual thinking and artistic aspirations. This inevitably turns anthologizing into "crippled anthologizing" [*canque de bianxuan*], because the process of filtering and selection is not just a case of "discarding the dross and selecting the essential," but also a process of compromise and of conforming to norms. There is no choice but to obey the autocracy of public aesthetic experience: that which looks healthy, elegant, progressive, and harmonious has always, in fact, avoided truth and depth.[29]

The publishing processes encountered by the *Chinese New Poetry Almanac* tell us several things about the state of print poetry publishing in China today. First, the guidelines that apply to producing a poetry anthology with access to the book market are far stricter than those in place for online poetry production: put simply, not all poetry disseminated on the Internet can make it into print. Yang Ke told me that he had originally hoped to include poetry by the School of Rubbish in one edition of the *Almanac* but had to abandon this plan because of his fears of censorship reprisals. Official gatekeeping mechanisms, whereby texts are read according to the ideological guidelines of the CCP and deleted or edited as necessary, are present at multiple stages in the publication process, including auditing (*shencha* or *jiancha*) by in-house editors and changes made to future editions of a book or journal as a result of readers' complaints post-publication. The latter also affect editors' self-censorship practices, as problems in the past are likely to lead to closer scrutiny in the future.

Despite these government-imposed and public-enforced censorship processes, there is still far greater freedom in print publishing than ever before in post-1949 mainland China. The poems that have caused problems for the *Chinese New Poetry Almanac* have been brought to the attention of censors primarily via readers' complaints. It is impossible to know exactly what motivates them; perhaps deeply ingrained political conformism, literary nostalgia, or even jealousy.[30] Some of the challenges experienced by the *Almanac* were also a result of its being such a large-scale and long-running second-channel print publication. Not only did individual editions run to over five hundred pages each, thereby increasing the likelihood of individual poems invoking negative reactions, but its publication and distribution involved the collaboration of a large array of people, including its editorial committee, authors, sponsors, publishers, distributors, and bookstore owners. Many of the bumps in the road were, accordingly, due less to political strictures than to logistics. It was, in fact, the *pre*-scriptive expectations of poets and of members of the editorial committee that had the biggest impact on the contents of the anthology. In other words, poetry anthologies such as the *Chinese New Poetry Almanac* are governed far more by internal questions of design and content—physical, poetic, and poetry-political—than by external, *pro*-scriptive controls.

REPRESENTING THE POPULAR

Central to the foundation of the *Chinese New Poetry Almanac* was the desire to restore some level of equity to distributions of discursive power within China's poetry scenes. A similar ambition had already been vociferously stated prior to the publication of the *Almanac* in the writings of certain Popular Standpoint poets and critics, accusing their Intellectual nemeses of obstructing access to or distorting representations of poetry writing in the 1990s; as we have seen, these accusations provided much of the rhetorical heat that triggered and prolonged the Panfeng Polemic that began in 1999.[31] As chief editor of a nationwide compilation of contemporary poetry and thus aware of the need to appear diplomatic, Yang Ke showed restraint in his early comments regarding the disparities in China's poetry arena. In the "Work notes" to the first edition, he writes that it is "not an anthology that selects whoever happens to be famous and always attempts to play for safety. It represents, rather, the Popular and demonstrates our way of viewing poetry. Poetry writing should not become a vassal for knowledge [*zhishi*] and it is certainly not the case that the only good poems are those that can be subsumed within Western value systems—poetry should be able to represent itself independently, to point directly to people's hearts, and to call upon each reader's artistic intuition."[32]

A more aggressive version of these views was put forward by Yu Jian in his essay "In lieu of a preface," published in the same edition and subtitled "The light of poetry, cutting through the Chinese language" (Chuanyue hanyu de shige zhi guang). This lengthy piece, first written in 1988 and updated for inclusion in the *Almanac* in 1998, amounts to no less than what Van Crevel calls a "declaration of war" toward Intellectual Writing.[33] Yu's denunciation of Intellectual poets and all that they stand for suggests that his attitude is not just anti–Intellectual Writing but also anti-intellectual in a broader sense, in places even taking on overtones of Cultural Revolution–era Maoist discourse.[34] In one often-quoted paragraph Yu declares, "1990s 'Intellectual Writing' is a total betrayal of the poetic spirit, its Achilles heel lying in having caused Chinese poetry to become a vassal for Western 'linguistic resources' and 'intellectual systems.'"[35] He accuses Intellectual poets of lacking, among other things, independence, creativity, talent, respect for Chinese-language poetry, freedom, and appreciation of life.[36]

All of these, by way of Yu's typically dichotomous logic, can be found instead in the Popular. Yu declares, "Good poetry is found in the Popular: this is an indisputable fact of contemporary poetry and also a great tradition of Chinese poetry. Popular refers to an independent quality. The spirit of Popular poetry lies in its refusal to adhere to any big beasts [*pangran dawu*]—it only exists for the purposes of poetry itself."[37] His understanding of the Popular does not just appeal to concepts such as presence, tradition, originality, and everyday life, all hallmarks of poetry published in the unofficial journals he mentions such as *Them*, *Today*, *Tropic of Cancer* (Beihui guixian), and *Poetry Reference* (Shi cankao). It also, by implication, excludes Intellectual poets, especially those featured in Cheng's *A Portrait of Years Gone By*, published in February 1998.[38] In this sense, Yu's definition of the Popular is also an attempt to refilter the broader sphere of current poetry production, in the same vein as Cheng and others' poetry publications of the late 1990s, which were seen as having a strong Northern and Intellectual bias in their anthologizing decisions.[39]

Yu's invective against Intellectual Writing was taken up by, among others, Xie Youshun, at the time a critic known mostly for his writings on fiction. In his essay "The inner true face of poetry" (Neizai de shige zhenxiang), featured in the April 2, 1999, edition of the newspaper *Southern Weekend* and one of the first nationally published articles to discuss the *Chinese New Poetry Almanac*,[40] Xie begins by praising the *Almanac* for directing attention toward important poets left out of Cheng Guangwei's anthology, such as Han Dong, Yu

Jian, Wang Xiaoni, Yang Ke, and Zhou Lunyou. He accuses Cheng's anthology of being a "concentrated reflection of certain small groups' narrow-minded psyches" and points to the *Almanac*'s successes in "fighting against the restrictions of choosing people according to qualifications and seniority and overemphasizing poetry-within-the-system." According to Xie, "the current poetry order is extremely unreliable and most likely conceals the truest and most valuable parts of poetry. That China has so many unofficial poetry societies speaks, from a different perspective, to many poets' despair toward the public, systematized poetry order."[41]

Despite pleading for a more inclusive approach toward poetry anthologizing that does not simply select members of the poetry arena and those already recognized by "the system" and "the current poetry order," Xie makes his own gatekeeping ambitions clear in the next paragraph: "the broad Popular might also contain a mixture of good and evil. If this is the case, then we can only ask that more people cleanse the scene of the current state of poetry, in order to let readers understand what the true poetic spirit really is . . . the *1998 Chinese New Poetry Almanac*, adherent of the 'true, eternal Popular Standpoint,' rather than simply upholding a 'belief in good poetry' . . . has in fact cleansed the scene of the current state of poetry and allowed contradictions that have long persisted inside of poetry to float to the surface."[42] Xie's use of the phrase "cleanse the scene" (*qingchang*) proved controversial among China's more Intellectually minded poets. To ask that a scene be cleansed is, in effect, a plea for a more ruthless form of gatekeeping that removes the "evil" elements of China's poetry scenes and leaves behind only the "good" bits. As the bulk of his essay points out, these are namely the poets left out of Cheng's *A Portrait of Years Gone By*. In other words, Xie's desire is not to witness a fairer or more inclusive representation of poetry scenes but simply a different representation, filtered according to the terms of the Popular.

Yang Ke has often adopted live-scene discourse to depict an institutionally and demographically broader understanding of poetry activity in China than that suggested by the discourse of the poetry arena. He explains the *Almanac*'s editorial committee's choice to select poems from unofficial journals and the Internet as being "related to live scenes of poetry," specifically the tendency of contemporary poets to avoid publishing solely in official poetry journals. By selecting works from a wider range of sources, Yang and his fellow editors hoped that the poems included within the *Almanac* would be "more objective, more real, and more diverse."[43] Whereas the original conceptualization of the Popular Standpoint was born from a desire to increase the visibility of primarily Southern China–based poets, the implications of the term "Popular" became increasingly narrow in subsequent years, to the point that Yang Ke felt obliged to step in and remind poets of the original connotations of Popular poetry.

> That good poetry is found in the Popular has become common knowledge, and this has clearly had a facilitating effect on the subsequent rise of the "post-70" poetry generation and on the burgeoning of Internet poetry. At the same time, however, we must admit that the word "Popular" is easily misunderstood. In my opinion, it naturally belongs first of all to the poetry groups who have "worked for" the concept's establishment, but at the same time it also belongs to "Intellectual" writing or any kind of writing under a particular "flag"; even more so, it belongs to the broad masses of "anonymous" writers. It is precisely the clashes between poets that have energized and enriched the connotations of the "Popular" and caused everyone to be subsumed within the "larger Popular."[44]

Yang Ke's comments underline the point that there exists both an institutional notion of the Popular (poetry activity that takes place mostly outside of government control) and a poetry-political one, the latter specific to the efforts of poets who spoke on behalf of the Popular Standpoint during the Panfeng Polemic. His tone is conciliatory, almost admitting that narrower definitions of the Popular have ended up mediating too much in representations of poetry scenes. Judging by the contentious reception of later editions of the *Chinese New Poetry Almanac* that took place on the Internet, the editors were, themselves, by no means immune from suspicions of overly zealous poetry scene gatekeeping.

DOCUMENTING LIVE SCENES

Mediating poetry scenes extends beyond attempts to define the standpoint represented by individual anthologies and includes the design and layout of the books as physical objects intended to stand the test of time. The design of the *Chinese New Poetry Almanac* was, from an early stage, a matter of contention among its editorial committee. There were disagreements over whether the 1998 edition should attempt to appeal to the "ordinary reader" (*yiban duzhe*) or whether it should be marketed as a more high-end cultural product. The initial plan had been to base the book's design upon German scholarly publications with plain black covers, which the editors perceived to be a more avant-garde style.[45] Two factors led them to change their mind. First, Fu Mahuo pointed out that the cover of the book had to be bold enough to catch the reader's eye in a bookshop or on a list of new books published in a newspaper. Second, the anthology was due to be published around the Chinese New Year in 1999, and black would have been considered inauspicious. The recently published *Them Ten-Year Poetry Selection* (Tamen shinian shixuan), coedited by Yang Ke and Xiao Hai, had used a black cover with an image of a skull, and as a result many bookstores had refused to stock it.

In the end, a compromise of black and red was settled upon, and white lettering used for the book's title and the names of the chief editor and publishing house. The spine, back cover, and top quarter of the front cover are black, but the lower three panels on the front are bright red, thus appealing to the color's auspicious associations around the Chinese New Year. The book's slogan, "In art we adhere to the true, everlasting Popular Standpoint," is printed in small red letters along the very top of the front cover, as well as on the inside of the first page of the book. On the front cover is a reproduction of an oil painting by the contemporary artist Luan Xiaojie of a thin, shirtless man with an elongated neck, dressed in nothing but a pair of jeans, striding barefoot across a red landscape.

Few adjustments were made to the external design of the *Almanac* throughout the first five years of its publication. From the 1998 to the 2002–3 editions, the size, paper quality, and fonts remained unchanged, and the only differences were in the color of the lettering, the color of the front and back covers, and the image used to adorn the front cover. The first major changes occurred with the 2004–5 edition. Noticing that sales figures had begun to dwindle, Yang Ke decided a more consumer-oriented approach was needed. Fu Mahuo, who was responsible for the Internet-inspired design of his commercially successful poetry anthology *Poetry Rivers and Lakes: Avant-Garde Poetry Files* (Shi jianghu: Wangluo shige dang'an),[46] volunteered to conduct market research in Guangdong to determine what customers were looking for when browsing for books. He stood by the entrance of the Sanlian Bookshop in Guangzhou for two hours, asking customers who had just purchased a book their reasons for buying it. Of the small number of people who had purchased a book of poetry, most admitted that they had done so because they thought that the book was well designed or because they were curious to know what current poetry was like.

Fu's market research and his recommendation that the overall design of the *Almanac* be overhauled brought about several changes to its cover design, contents, and layout. The most obvious change was in the size of the book, which grew from 19 by 14 centimeters to 22 by 18 centimeters; it was also printed on thicker, high-quality paper. The design of the book's title on the cover underwent a makeover as well; it was incorporated into a red seal, tilted at an angle near the top of the page as though drawn haphazardly by hand, with the date printed directly below in black ink. Upon opening the front cover, further changes are apparent. Rather than beginning with a list of contents or preface, the first section is comprised of two pages of black-and-white photographs of thirty contemporary poets, titled "Faces of Chinese Poetry" (Zhongguo shige de lian). These were taken by the photographer Song Zuifa and were soon to feature, along with several hundred unofficial poetry journals, in a high-profile exhibition in Guangzhou in August 2006. This was the first time the *Almanac* had featured photos anywhere other than on the front cover. The trend continues inside: photographs also accompany the seven poets featured at the front of the book, are interspersed throughout the poetry events from 2004 and 2005, and are used in a section at the back of the book summarizing poetry publications from those two years.

Photographic images of poets, poetry events, websites, and poetry publications testify to the representational power of images in the media age. John Hartley describes pictures as a conjunction of symbolic imagination, individual identities, and collective social actions, and "the nexus between culture and politics." [47] The choice to employ them within a publication that had up to this point contained nothing but words demonstrates how the sense of reality implied by such images can be exploited as currency within China's contemporary image culture.[48] It also reflects the curiosity of readers about the poet-behind-the-poem, similar to what Yeh labels a "cult of poetry" and what Van Crevel suggests is very much a "cult of poet-*hood*."[49] Chinese readers, moreover, might be especially inclined to search for evidence of authorial personality in the poems they read. As Hockx proposes, this can be explained by traditional notions of poetry writing as a sincere means of expressing personality.[50] Being able to link the written word to the physical image of the poet is at once an important substantiation of poetry as a social form and "a strategic exercise in image-(re) building in order to sustain readership."[51]

One of Fu Mahuo's suggestions for attracting new, non-poet readers to the *Almanac* was to increase the volume of "non-poem content." Photographs, descriptions of face-to-face and print-based poetry activities, summaries of recent writing trends, and increased amounts of biographical information all appeal to curiosity about poets and poetry scenes, and less so about the texts of poems themselves. The overall effect was to turn the *Almanac* into something more akin to a documentation of China's poetry scenes than simply an anthology of poems and to enhance the function of the *Almanac* as a poetry scene spectacle. Subtle changes also occurred in other parts of the book, which had grown to include six new sections: "Poet laureate of the year," "Budding poets of the year," "Top ten poetry events of the year," "Chronicle," "Most original poetic form of the year," and "Recommendations of the year." The "Top ten poetry events of the year" range from a nationwide exhibition of contemporary poetry titled "Jia Shen Storm Twenty-First Century Chinese Poetry Grand Exhibition" (Jiashen fengbao ershiyi shiji Zhongguo shige dazhan)[52] to the death of post-1970 poet Ma Hua in a jeep accident in Yunnan, and from a poetry recital by Duoduo to the First Chinese Blog Poetry Awards.

In the postscript to the 2004–5 edition, Yang Ke claimed that the *Almanac*'s redesign continued its tradition of embodying "originality, an avant-garde essence, and the feeling of live scenes." The new version, however, was also "more alive," contained more information, and had incorporated "lively, contemporary, uncertain, fresh elements," making it "better looking" and more attractive to readers, and ensuring the poetry contained within "possesses more possibilities."[53] This appeared to be an attempt not just to increase the book's spectacular appeal to "ordinary readers" but also to capture some of the contingency and effervescence of the face-to-face and online spaces of poetry, both hybrid agoras of oral and print communication dynamics. Despite Yang's optimism about the commercial appeal of such a live-scene approach to poetry, however, many reactions to the new-look *Almanac* that emerged on poetry forums and blogs in 2006 were negative, describing it as "tacky" (*yongsu*) and echoing Xi Du's earlier portrayals of Yang Ke as a book agent putting commercial interests before poetic concerns.[54] Yang responded by stressing the importance of the changes: "People's tastes in books have temporal characteristics. That is precisely why this year's *Almanac* has changed in size and packaging. But if we look beneath the surface, the 'new' almanac is in fact extremely serious. For example, the additional photographs are by no means simply there to 'ingratiate' ourselves with reading 'fashions' but rather because they are also a part of live scenes of poetry."[55] In a newspaper review of the latest *Almanac*, Xie Youshun supported Yang, reporting that the new features had "reinforced . . . the feeling of live scenes and the editors' intentions." The latter, according to Xie, are of particular importance: "As live scenes of poetry have become bigger and more complex to the extent that no one is able to fully grasp them, the primary means by which most people now understand poetry is by relying on the trustworthy efforts of editors who categorize and sort through large volumes of poetic works and poetry events."[56]

Yang's and Xie's comments inadvertently reveal one of the key tensions inherent in the print publication of a book like the *Chinese New Poetry Almanac*. On the one hand, there is a desire to reflect and represent in as authentic a manner possible the "true" live scenes of poetry. This involves documenting not just poems but also the scenes in which they are produced and the discourses and ideologies that shape those scenes; in short, the multiple functions of poetry as a social form. In 2000 in the postscript to the first edition of his journal *Document* (Xianchang), Wu Wenguang laid out a similar approach to that adopted by the *Almanac*: "Choosing 'Document' [live scene] as the name of this book implies 'present tense' and 'on-the-scene presence' [*zaichang*]. . . . As for these 'people present' [*zaichangzhe*] whom I have documented, the first thing I have done is reveal in as detailed a manner possible their texts, information, background, and live-scene photographs, and then, through relying upon interviews, reveal the many relationships between the person and the background to his or her piece of work, the environment in which it was produced, and the live scenes of the time."[57] Documented in this way, culture becomes more than simply a series of recognized texts but also a life spectacle of the kind that Hai Ren argues is increasingly important in communicating the meanings of everyday life in the Chinese media and that is closely tied to the transformation of "cultural institutions" into "cultural enterprises."[58]

The emphasis in both instances of "live-scene" publishing strategies is on the supposedly unmediated, authentic nature of the publication: the editors document and "reveal," relying upon indisputable evidence such as the texts themselves, biographical data, interviews, and photographs, in doing so illuminating the conjuncture defined by the works of art, their producers, audiences, and the broader social context in which they are produced and disseminated. If these editors' strategy is to rely upon the function of print books as commercial spectacles, the primary ideology to which they appeal is one of authenticity. Being "live," the cultural scenes that are the objects of documentation are intended to embody this authenticity through their relative lack of mediation, temporal, ideological, or otherwise. Half of the editorial intentions of the *Almanac* is, as the character *jian* in almanac (*nianjian*) implies, to be a mirror, reflecting both poetry writing produced each year and the processes and contexts that surrounded its production. At the same time, however, the processes of publishing a book like the *Almanac*, no matter how authentic, unmediated, or "live" its attempts at self-presentation, depend upon the ideology of the text and the associated values of authority, permanence, and control. As Xie explains, the importance of the book's editors—and thus by extension the *Almanac* as a whole—lies precisely in their role as gatekeepers, categorizing and sorting through the vast quantities of raw materials that populate live scenes of poetry.

THE POETRY POLITICS OF BOOK EDITING

Part of the live-scene approach to poetry anthologizing adopted by the *Almanac* involved selecting poems from a wider range of sources than is typical for officially published poetry anthologies. For the inaugural 1998 edition, the editorial committee did not just browse through official literary journals, newspapers, and other single- and multiple-author poetry collections; they also consulted unofficial poetry journals and self-printed or handwritten manuscripts. Their focus was on poetry written in 1998, but they also considered earlier works that had recently reappeared in the public eye. Their inclusion of Bei Dao's poems reflected their desire to bring suppressed voices from the unofficial world of poetry to the fore. Once the poems had been printed out and gathered together, the editorial committee met several times to decide which poems to publish. The editorial process was intended to be democratic; each editor voted for his preferred poems and the poems that won the most votes were selected for inclusion. Differences of opinion were inevitable. In some cases poems were selected that only a single editor had recommended, provided the editor could justify his choice on poetic grounds. The procedure for the 1999 edition was much the same, with the addition of editorial meetings held in Guilin and Beijing in November.

For the 2000 edition of the *Almanac* Yang Ke widened the net; this time he not only posted notices in mainland Chinese poetry journals inviting poets to submit their work but also wrote letters to active poets both in China and abroad and asked for recommendations from more senior poets and critics. The Misty poet Shu Ting was among those who offered their services, putting forward the names of promising young poets from Fujian. Others recommended works from Shanxi, Hong Kong, Macau, and Taiwan.[59] By October 2000 the editors had finished gathering poems for selection and the Guangzhou-based members of the editorial committee (which had grown to include more representatives of the Popular Standpoint including Shen Qi, Hou Ma, Zhang Ning, Yi Sha, and Shen Haobo) completed a preliminary sorting. In November the entire editorial committee met for the first time to discuss in person which poems should be published. Again the decision process was intentionally democratic; each editor selected around one hundred poems.

The difficulties with this system did not become apparent until Yang Ke began to sort through the results of the ballot. He discovered that the most "ordinary" (*putong*) poets had received by far the highest number of votes, whereas the poets and poems he considered truly "edgy" (*jianrui*) and that represented divergent poetry aesthetics had received just a few votes each. Although this situation could equally be attributed to differences in opinion between Yang Ke and the rest of the editorial committee regarding what constitutes an "edgy" poem, Yang's explanation was that because of the stringency of their personal poetic views, they had only been able to select a limited number of poems that they really liked and had chosen the rest because they were "so-so." It just so happened that they all agreed on which poems were so-so but less on which poems were outstanding, hence the large number of votes awarded to the "ordinary" poets.

At this point Yang and the editorial committee decided that the democratic mode of poetry selection was no longer working. With the committee's increase in size, a greater range of poetic views was now being represented and it was practically impossible for everyone to reach a consensus as to which poets and poems should be included in each edition. The first attempt at an alternative editorial system was made for the compilation of the 2001 edition, when Yang Ke was studying at Peking University as a visiting scholar. Yang informally handed over the job of executive editor to the poet Song Xiaoxian, who had joined the editorial committee that year. Song compiled and selected all the poems in that year's *Almanac*; the only significant adjustment Yang made was to move Xu Jiang from somewhere in the middle to nearer the front of the book.

The following year Yang Ke went one step further and invited two other members of the editorial committee, Shen Haobo and Xie Youshun, to act as official executive editors (*niandu zhixing zhubian*). Shen was put in charge of selecting poetry and Xie made responsible for editing the sections of poetry theory and criticism. For the 2004–5 edition, Yang Ke gave the same positions, respectively, to Xiao Yin, editor of the unofficial journal *Or* (Huozhe), and post-1980 poet A Fei. Yang Ke explained his rationale behind adopting the new rotating-editor system as follows: "The *Almanac* is a 'public vessel' of the poetry world, and not the tool of any individual poet: as I see it, determining the 'rules of the game' is often more important than one's taste in selecting poetry. . . . Bold, individual, even somewhat prejudiced or ambiguous choices will ensure the *Almanac's* unique, edgy character; letting various people of different artistic styles and ideas carry out their artistic ambitions will guarantee a balance between artistic pursuits of differing orientations. I believe that this change will be of benefit to the development of the *Almanac* and of Chinese new poetry."[60] This was, by Yang's admission, a major reversal in the *Almanac*'s anthologizing principles. Instead of trying to arrive at some sort of democratic consensus among a large group of editors and finding artistic differences a hindrance rather than a help, the new system would relish those differences. Up until this point, calls for diversity were supposed to have been answered within each separate edition, brought about by the differing poetic tastes of the editorial committee. From 2004 onward, however, the diversity of the poetry world was to be highlighted through the unique literary preferences of the executive editors from one edition to the next.

It was not until 2007 that complications with the rotating-editor system began to surface. Keeping his promise to select different editors for each edition, Yang Ke had invited the poets Shucai and Yin Lichuan to act as executive editors for the 2006 volume. Shucai is a member of the Third Way (Di san tiao daolu), a poetry collective established at the end of 1999. Yin is most famous within literary circles as a figurehead of the Lower Body poetry group. The two thus represent quite different positions on the poetic spectrum; as a proponent of the Third Way, Shucai's views on poetry are set intentionally apart from both Intellectual Writing and the Popular Standpoint, whereas Yin Lichuan has been closely associated with the Popular Standpoint since she began to write and publish poetry in the late 1990s.

Problems with this editorial pairing soon became apparent. A number of poems Yin Lichuan selected for inclusion in the *Almanac* "mysteriously" failed to find their way into Yang Ke's email inbox, and Shucai was so swamped by the tasks of sorting through submissions and searching poetry journals for outstanding works that he was forced to repeatedly delay submission of the manuscript. He explained to Yang Ke that reading tens of thousands of poems had "ruined his appetite for poetry," leaving him incapable of distinguishing good writing from bad. Upon Yang's insistence, Shucai finally sent him a draft of the manuscript in April 2007. Assuming expectations were so high that poets would be unable to wait a few more months to find out what and who had been selected, Yang decided to take the unusual step of posting the table of contents online, which at this point consisted of a list of names: two executive editors, the editorial committee, and the poets whose works were to be published.[61] With the regular publishing of the *Almanac* by now a major event in Chinese poetry scenes, this table of contents was copied onto hundreds of poetry websites all over the Internet and the names subjected to close scrutiny by the more than 1,400 poets who had submitted their works.

Comments immediately began appearing on poetry forums and blogs; poets either proudly reacted to having been selected or made angry statements like "a *Chinese New Poetry Almanac* without XXX and XXX is like a Chinese Communist Party without Mao Zedong and Deng Xiaoping!"[62] After the contents were posted on *Poetry Rivers and Lakes* on May 5, 2007, poets noticed that certain names were missing, of which the most glaring were thought to be Xu Jiang, Yang Li, and Hou Ma.[63] Xu, editor of the unofficial poetry journal *Sunflower* (Kui), had been included in every edition of the *Almanac* up until this point and was considered a key representative of the Popular Standpoint and a dominant voice on the *Poetry Rivers and Lakes* forum. He reacted by leaving a post on May 7 that read, "the truth is: Yang Ke has finally expelled himself and the *Almanac* from the Popular! He has returned to the matrix of his poetic taste: the Writers' Association form! Ah, the immortal heart of the system, ha ha ha!"

Xu followed this up on May 22 with a post containing an essay of over seven thousand characters titled "On the fake popular" (Lun wei minjian).[64] He uses the *2006 Chinese New Poetry Almanac* as a "case study of degeneration" in putting forward his opinion that the term "Popular" has lost its true meaning, degenerating into the "fake Popular." This degeneration can, Xu argues, be traced back to the 2004–5 edition of the *Almanac*, which had already "exposed an overwhelmingly official journal-type of mediocre style, lost its personality, used a *Spring and Autumn Annals*-style of editing, and revealed an intentional rewriting of the truth of many poetry arena activities (just like 'Intellectual Writing' did back in the day)."[65] Xu claims that any personal offense resulting from his omission was due to having been considered, out of the 1,400-plus poets who submitted their works, to lie somewhere between number 231 (a record number of 230 poets were selected for inclusion that year) and number 1,400. This could only mean, he added with heavy sarcasm, that recent standards in modern Chinese poetry had risen at an astonishing rate.

On June 3, Yin Lichuan left a post on *Poetry Rivers and Lakes* titled "A statement regarding my withdrawal from the editorial committee of the '2006 Chinese New Poetry Almanac,'" in which she revealed that not a single poem she recommended to Yang Ke for inclusion in the *Almanac* had been published. Even worse, neither Yang nor Shucai had consulted her before finalizing and publicizing the table of contents. Her response was to declare that "The 2006 *Chinese New Poetry Almanac* is turning into a hodgepodge with no clear poetic views, with 'poetry' but no 'new,' with 'year' but no 'mirror.' . . . If you [Yang Ke] don't approve of my selections, then you should have said so earlier! Because I have to withdraw! Because I'm no longer an executive editor but have become nothing but one of your tools! Please do not use my name in vain! Please don't turn me into a representative of 'the Popular'! To say nothing of the fact I didn't get to represent anything!"

Shen Haobo also weighed in with criticism of his own, expressing his dismay at this most recent edition of the *Almanac* and accusing Yang Ke of paying more attention to personal relations than good poetry:

> The *Chinese New Poetry Almanac*, this brand that we once defended with our pens as guns, has lately deteriorated into a fairground of fake poetry. Have a look at those idiots in the list of contents, those mediocre nobodies, those totally soul-less poems . . . you and that no-good Shucai have wiped out all the great achievements of Chinese

> avant-garde poetry in recent years, you've got rid of its edgy power, the very soul of Chinese poetry! You've wiped out the results of Panfeng, which have been realized in each outstanding poet—you have betrayed Panfeng. After you became one of those with a vested interest in Panfeng, you wanted to turn *Chinese New Poetry Almanac* into your own private gift—what is it you wish to gain, by giving it away all over the place? . . . You have insulted my friend! You have insulted my poetic standpoint! You have insulted the "Popular Standpoint," that we once cried out so loudly!

Shen's outburst culminated with an ultimatum to poets who work "within the system" for various branches of the Writers' Association, giving them the choice of "choosing poetry or the Great Hall of the People." The best option, he suggested, would be to "go be a People's Representative poet" (*renmin daibiao shiren*) and "stop pretending to be avant-garde and [to represent] the Popular Standpoint!"[66]

While many of these criticisms of the 2006 *Almanac* boiled down to personal insults stemming from bruised egos and damaged personal relationships, they also had potential implications for the publication of the book, which eventually appeared in October 2007. Yin Lichuan and Yi Sha had made it clear they no longer wished to have their names associated with the *Almanac* and thus were removed from the list of editors. That the *Almanac* had been criticized from within by editors past and present and by ardent supporters of the Popular Standpoint also pointed to more serious problems underlying the pretext and logistics of the anthology's publication. By publicly questioning Yang Ke's motivations as chief editor and associating him and the *Almanac* with the ideological control of the Writers' Association and the "system," it appeared that they had fatally undermined Yang's ability to represent the Popular and document live scenes of poetry.

Dissatisfaction with the 2006 edition had been largely divided along two lines, one accusing it of trying too hard to be fair and inclusive in its selection of poets, resulting in the presence of a large number of "mediocre nobodies," the other blaming it for using subtle, underhanded means to express the editors' own subjective opinions. In other words, it was criticized for not being authoritative enough *and* for being too heavy-handed in its gatekeeping of poetry. Both, according to *Poetry Rivers and Lakes* stalwarts Yi Sha, Shen Haobo, Yin Lichuan, Xu Jiang, and others, had the ultimate effect of divorcing the *Almanac* from its roots: Popular poetry. It was its advocacy of the Popular Standpoint and its defense of anti-Intellectual writers that had provided the anthology with its original raison d'être. Now, by not selecting some of those writers, they argued, it had turned its back on its original mission and core base of support. Despite these poets' claims to be focusing more on the quality of poetry and not on its authors, statements such as "you can't flaunt 'China' and 'the Popular' without us three [Xu Jiang, Yang Li, and Hou Ma]" made it clear that it was ultimately poetry politics, the *who* and not the *what*, that was at stake. Yang Ke's position in the Guangdong Writers' Association was seen as further evidence that he had taken power, diplomacy, and "poetry arena harmony" (*shitan hexie*) to heart more than the future of Chinese avant-garde poetry.[67]

CONCLUSION

It is easy for anyone who contests the contents of print anthologies like the *Chinese New Poetry Almanac* to overlook the wider conjuncture in which their battles are situated. Any symbolic struggle that takes as its pretext the concept of national recognition and canonization has at its heart a concern over the relevance of that canon to the general population and its place within the wider sphere of contemporary culture. Writing about the late 1980s "canon wars" in the United States over literary textbooks and anthologies, John Guillory points out that the debate represented a crisis in the category of "literature" as a form of cultural capital. During a time when the centrality of literature to the U.S. educational system was less certain than in the past, the issue of canonicity, or who and what should be included in the canon, was in fact secondary to the more general crisis in literature's historical value, as it was the gradual decline in the cultural capital of literature that had given rise to the canon wars in the first place.[68] Similarly, contention over forms of representation in post-2000 Chinese poetry scenes can be understood in light of poets' fear of marginalization and their recognition that "serious" literature has lost ground to more readily commercialized forms of culture. If the cultural activity in which you participate already possesses a limited audience and social reach, all the more reason to ensure you are included in its more widely available representations.

This brings us to an important related point: representation in itself is not enough to ensure canonization if it is not accompanied by institutional support and, most crucially, effective distribution mechanisms. As Guillory points out, unless they are made in an institutional context that allows for the reproduction of literary works and their repeated reintroduction to new audiences over time, individual judgments of aesthetic greatness count for very little.[69] For modern Chinese poetry, this means that poems need to be continually reproduced through the various poetry websites, print publications, and face-to-face events that shape and comprise poetry scenes. In his role as chief editor, Yang Ke was well aware of the effects of successful distribution on the influence of the *Almanac*, hence his willingness to invest large amounts of money in DIY distribution channels. Only when enough people have access to the *Almanac* can it possibly hope to achieve its goals. This is the same for any poetry publication, whether produced unofficially without access to the book market, through the second channel, or through official production and distribution channels.

The types of representation analyzed in this chapter point to differing goals inherent in the production of print collections of contemporary poetry, as well as a gradual shift in the positioning of the *Chinese New Poetry Almanac* from a textual space of resistance against the discursive power of the Beijing-dominated poetry arena to a dominant source of power and a poetry scene spectacle in its own right. The first objective is to convey live scenes of poetry by recommending certain poets and their texts and by fleshing out critical and interpersonal contexts for members of the public less familiar with contemporary poetry. This is at the same time a poetry-political aspiration intended to "even out" representations of the poetry scene through gatekeeping efforts—a task that inevitably requires elevating the position of some poets and relegating that of others—and to carve out space for new faces and differing tastes. Documenting live scenes in both their graphic and poetry-political senses can be understood as a desire to contribute toward the creation of a public space for contemporary poetry, a kind of imagined community as described by Benedict Anderson, whose participants may "never know most of their fellow-members, meet them, or even hear of them, yet in the minds of each lives the image of their communion."[70] This documentary drive also acknowledges the status of books as life spectacles that possess entertainment value, communicating the value of poetry scenes as part of everyday life to a wider (potentially non-poetry-reading) public.

While this impulse certainly has one eye firmly on the present, the other wanders forward in time. To assert a particular representation of contemporary poetry is also an attempt to mediate the present as the history of the future, to have a say in who and what should be remembered in years to come. Throughout its twelve-year publication history, the *Almanac* displayed a strong sense of historical consciousness, starting with its attempt to wrestle discursive power away from Beijing-based poet-intellectuals and their supposedly biased understanding of "1990s poetry" and proceeding through the various mechanisms through which the *Almanac* endeavored to document live scenes of poetry in the 2000s. Many of the contents and design considerations of the *Almanac* reflect the belief that, as Yang Ke put it, "what is happening now is just a live scene." This statement is at once honest in its acknowledgment of the limitations of contemporary anthologizing and astute in its appeals to the discourse of lives scenes. Prioritizing the values of immediacy and authenticity, Yang insinuates, can help counteract the high levels of mediation and gatekeeping inherent in any textual representation.

Producers of print publications like the *Almanac* are, indeed, highly conscious of the influence they have over distributions of discursive power within poetry scenes. Yang Ke has pointed out on several occasions that the poets selected for inclusion in the *Almanac* have gone on to great things. The first volume of the 1999 edition included for the first time in a commercially published poetry collection the writings of a large number of poets born in the 1970s, including Lower Body representatives Shen Haobo, Li Hongqi, Duoyu, Wu Ang, Sheng Xing, and Yan Jun, many of whom have since become prominent voices within China's poetry scenes. The 2004–5 edition featured female poet Zheng Xiaoqiong as one of the "Budding Poets of the Year." Zheng, born in 1980, was at the time employed as a manual worker in a metals factory in Dongguan, Guangdong. Although she had already published a number of poems in official literary journals, her inclusion in the *Almanac* seemed to anticipate further success: in May 2007 she was awarded the prestigious People's Literature Award (Renmin wenxuejiang) for her prose writings, and she has since been written about widely in English-language as well as Chinese news reports as a major representative of Migrant Worker Poetry (Dagong Shige).[71]

The challenge for print publications such as the *Chinese New Poetry Almanac* is to assert the value of its particular literary representation in the context of increasingly decentralized arenas of position-taking and canon formation and the growing commercialization of the publishing industry as part of the country's cultural system reforms. It is no longer a contest between academic and nonacademic, official and unofficial literary compilations or histories, as was the case for much of the 1990s. Since the turn of the millennium, all print publications have become increasingly subsumed within the broader environment of China's cultural industries, in which financial independence is accompanied by a differentiated system of censorship and media control. Although they possess a greater degree of ideological freedom than ever before, as an important part of China's broader communications infrastructure print publications are still expected, to varying degrees, to help communicate the values and ideologies of the party-state. This combination of privatization, commercialization, and differentiated ideological control explains the fine line that the producers of the *Almanac* had to tread in using second-channel publishing mechanisms to expand representations of Chinese poetry scenes without landing themselves in hot water. It also explains, in part, why representatives of the Popular Standpoint on *Poetry Rivers and Lakes* were so furious with Yang Ke for his later editorial decisions: Yang was thought to be acting not just on behalf of contemporary poetry but, more damagingly, as a proponent of "the system," of "poetry arena harmony," and of the conspiracies between poetry, money, and power that they imply.

At the same time as they attempt to survive in the gray areas between ideological control and commercialization, print poetry publications are now competing against texts circulated through new media, such as the hundreds and thousands of forums, blogs, microblogs, and e-zines that defy the traditional gatekeeping authority of the poetry arena and present their own dynamic, interactive approaches to cultural hierarchies. A book like the *Almanac* has to somehow subscribe to the ideology of the text by stressing its relative permanence and authority as an officially published print product, all the time staying sensitive toward the rules of the game offered by new media: a preference for mass participation over individual authority, for contingency over editorial control, for contextualization and networking, and for documenting the present in its ever-changing state as the history of the future. The contention that surrounded later editions of the *Almanac* is not just a reminder of the limited space available for representations of modern poetry in the broader cultural realm and of the strong historical consciousness of Chinese poets and critics but also a sign of how clashes between media dynamics, discourses, and ideologies help enliven and give shape to the country's poetry scenes.

CHAPTER 3

Poetry on the Stage

I'm not a poet whose recitation
can move a room to tears
but I can use my words
to move these blue walls that surround me
when I step upon the stage, black birds
are my listeners, wings settled upon
open pages of red-skinned notebooks and handkerchiefs
I see this each morning
so thank you all
thank you all the winter still loves a poet

—WANG YIN, "*Recitation*" (Langsong)

The microphone grasped between my hands is like the head of an erect penis, covered in a metal web that glints darkly. I find myself confused: can I use it to rape the world? Will it heed my every word with rapt attention? Who am I? A professor, a president, a politician, a TV presenter?

—YU JIAN, "*Recitation*" (Langsong)

Activities that take place face-to-face and "in the flesh" have played a central role in the development of post-Mao modern poetry in mainland China. From the salons and open-air recitals organized by the Today group in the late 1970s and early 1980s to the proliferation of poetry recitals held in cafés and bars in the 1990s and turn-of-the-millennium large-scale gatherings like the Panfeng Meeting, face-to-face poetry events (*huodong*) are a mainstay in the lives and careers of contemporary Chinese poets. They have a powerful effect on the dynamics of poetry scenes, giving geographic shape to poetry communities and generating aesthetic developments, one-off incidents, and long-running sources of contention that have in some cases irrevocably changed the course of contemporary poetry and helped further—or set back—the reputations of poetry scene participants. Chinese terms used to denote face-to-face poetry events include meetings (*huiyi* or simply *hui*), recitals (*langsonghui*), festivals (*jie*), ceremonies (*yishi*), conferences (*yantaohui* or *xueshuhui*), summits (*fenghui*), salons (*shalong*), and gatherings (*juhui*). Although some are scheduled to take place on an annual or more frequent basis, many are one-off occasions held to mark a specific poetry-related, cultural, or national incident such as a poet's death, an ongoing poetry polemic, or a national disaster.

Communicating face-to-face is the oldest and most basic means of sharing poetry, traceable to the days when poetry was not written down or recorded using technological means but transmitted using nothing but memorization, repetition, and the human voice.[1] In Chinese, this medium of transmission is built into the word "poetry," which is comprised of the characters for poem (*shi*, a combination of "speech" [*yan*] and "temple" [*si*]) and song (*ge*). What Foley terms the arena of oral tradition or oAgora is in theory the most open of the three media spaces examined in this book; although it is subject to rules imposed by the group in question, access to the oAgora is open to any qualified person who wishes to take part. Foley notes that while some oral traditions discriminate according to factors such as age, gender, or ethnicity, most involve "open-ended, diverse audiences as participating, present partners."[2] Successfully navigating the oAgora requires fluency in its language, which in the case of contemporary Chinese poetry events is not just standard Chinese (Mandarin), the language usually used for reciting poetry and public speaking, but also the behavioral codes that determine when and how to assert one's poetry citizenship through face-to-face interactions.

Face-to-face events are characterized by a high level of contingency, defined by Foley as "an evolving reality" that depends on events and conditions that have not yet been established. Foley identifies five trademark contingencies that characterize business in both the oAgora and the eAgora (the Internet): the very next option; the performance; the network; meaning; and authorship. In the oAgora, agency is only partially in the hands of the person navigating the oral network: it also relies on other people who have paved the way by putting together networks of contingencies that can support any number of specific outcomes or configurations.[3] The oAgora, in short, has much in common with China's discourse of live scenes, which are also understood in terms of presence, process, and participation in the here and now and are thought to be open to whoever happens to be on the scene during the unfolding of the cultural event. The face-to-face space of contemporary poetry activity is also, however, shaped discursively by the history of the poetry arena and those who have come before.

As with the media spaces explored in the previous two chapters, the face-to-face space is a hybrid agora, affected by the ideology of the text as much as it is by the contingencies of oral or online communication. The openness that Foley ascribes to the arena of oral tradition is also mitigated by a variety of gatekeeping strategies that shape the planning, unfolding, and interpretation of face-to-face poetry events. Attending these events is often taken as a sign of membership of the poetry arena, and many of the big-name poets who are regularly invited to events like those analyzed in this chapter are associated more with official and institutional uses of poetry than with "live scenes." In contemporary China, moreover, attitudes toward the face-to-face space of poetry are complicated by political factors as well as by the more recent mobilization of poetry recitation events by economic forces, guided by the logic of the cultural economy. Yu Jian's apparent identity confusion in this chapter's epigraph is in part a performative expression of his distaste for the elitist and official implications of poetry recitation as public culture in twentieth- and twenty-first-century China.

Some scholars have already begun investigating the sociocultural implications of face-to-face poetry events in contemporary China. Van Crevel describes a 2002 poetry recitation event featuring female poets and artists from the viewpoint of poetry's marginalization, invoking Oscar Wilde's famous adage that "the only thing worse than being talked about is not being talked about" to emphasize the importance of such events in forging a sense of community among poets. Crespi takes a historical perspective, analyzing poetry recitals in the 2000s within the context of modern Chinese poetry's quest for a national voice and seeing them as one example of the "flourishing social practice of the cultural event," an elusive category of cultural activity that has come to supplement and replace the paradigm of movements and mass campaigns (*yundong*).[4] In this chapter I examine face-to-face poetry events on their own terms, considering the media dynamics and logistical concerns that impact the ways that poetry is made meaningful within this space. I situate these sites of poetry activity within the framework of media dynamics, poetry scene discourses, and the broader conjuncture defined in part by the growth of China's cultural industries and the changing functions of media and culture in contemporary China.

My ethnographic research and textual analysis have revealed that the face-to-face space of poetry in the early twenty-first century offers an opportunity for poets to assert their poetry citizenship and membership in poetry scenes at the same time as it shows signs of being incorporated into China's cultural economy. Under the mantra of "using culture to promote business," poetry's high-culture allure is used to help sell real estate developments, strengthen a city's brand image, or enhance the reputation of individual cultural brokers or entrepreneurs. This is happening within a broader media and communications environment that has witnessed the transformation of culture from the intellectual connotations of "literature and the arts" into a site for the pursuit of economic profits and entertainment. Poetry has been affected by these developments in unexpected ways. The media, for example, have proven willing to report on poetry events as long as doing so benefits the event sponsors and conveys the more dramatic and spectacular aspects of poetry scenes. Media coverage can, in turn, highlight the "eventfulness" of poetry activities and affect distributions of discursive power within poetry scenes, for example by publicizing the ideas and writings of certain poets over others. While operating according to the party-state's preferred use of communication technologies for guiding public opinion and negotiating ideological messages, the media also meet the desires of poets to convey to a broader audience the fact that, contrary to assumptions of its marginalization and imminent "death," poetry as a social form is in rude health in China today.

POETRY RECITATION AS PUBLIC SPEECH

In an essay titled "Langsong" (Recitation) published in the newspaper *Southern Weekend* in February 2005, Yu Jian opens an impassioned tirade against practices of poetry recital in contemporary China with the following barrage of questions:

> Can it really be true that writers spend their whole lives writing, hidden inside the deepest room, simply in order to end up here, facing a microphone whose job it is to turn your language into sound? As you stand there on wobbly legs as though awaiting sentence, in front of you lies a giant cave, built with the rocks of so-called readers—do poets really spend their whole lives hidden in the darkness just

> to show their faces in front of this cave, a bag of coal heaved upon their backs? The microphone grasped between my hands is like the head of an erect penis, covered in a metal web that glints darkly. I find myself confused: can I use it to rape the world? Will it heed my every word with rapt attention? Who am I? A professor, a president, a politician, a TV presenter? I inadvertently abandon my native language, my tongue stiffening, suspecting that this metal penis will only respond to standard Chinese—does anyone speak to it using their local dialect?

In this (melo)dramatic reenactment of the moment of public judgment that occurs when written poetry becomes sound, Yu Jian presents himself as simultaneously terrified and aroused, wobbly and stiff. For him, the poetry reading on which he is set to embark is a formidable moment of public sentencing, one that requires a masculine authority more commonly associated with professing, ruling, politicking, and television presenting, but definitely not being a poet. One underlying cause of his oral petrifaction emerges at the end of the paragraph: he assumes he is required to speak in standard Chinese, the official or "ordinary" (*putong*) language of China, rather than his local Yunnan dialect. His grievances become clearer still later in the essay:

> As soon as they are faced with a microphone, writers unwittingly fall into a trap, wearing themselves hoarse in order to "recite" their work. From this we can witness the appearance of an "era of recital." If a poem cannot be recited, then it has no right to exist. Some poets have sensed the danger of reciting, sensed that recital is in fact the guillotine of poetry, that as soon as poetry is accompanied by that kind of sound—for example, the voice of a television announcer—it becomes a corpse under the shroud of sound. Poetry is soundless but the era of recital has affected poets so that they, too, will turn their work into poetry with sound and imagine some kind of sound of the era for their poetry. This sound is completely divorced from the poet's flesh, like the noise of some giant. In some cases, the sounds imagined by the reader are completely different from the voice of the writer, and thus when the writer appears in front of the microphone, the audience will be greatly disappointed. Sound can change, and even completely destroy, poetry.

Yu's revelation here that sound can "destroy" poetry might come as a surprise to millennia of poets and audiences across the world for whom oral performance was the primary if not sole means by which poetry was composed, shared, and enjoyed. His repeated assertions that "poetry is soundless" and "poetry is not for recital" sketch a poetics in which the modern written word is wholly detached from the noises it produces when read aloud. Despite making a brief reference to the classical tradition of chanting (*yinyong*) poetry, Yu states that this has nothing to do with the modern custom of poetry recitation (*langsong*), arguing instead that "recitation is the product of twentieth-century revolution."

Here, Yu Jian has a point. Modern poetry recitation has a long history of involvement in twentieth-century Chinese politics and the politics of revolution in particular. Starting around the time of the 1911 Republican revolution, Chinese writers and intellectuals increasingly came to understand poetry as a "literary representation of nationhood" and, over the following decades, sought different ways of using poetry to extol the virtues of the Chinese nation as it grew more conscious of its place in the world. An iteration of this goal was put forward in 1932 by the China Poetry Society (Zhongguo Shige Hui), a branch of the League of Left-Wing Writers (Zuoyi Zuojia Lianmeng), who proposed that poetry be "taken among the popular masses and recited."[5] By the end of the 1930s, regular poetry recitation events held in major cities like Wuhan, Shanghai, Guilin, and Chongqing to aid in the War of Resistance against Japan had helped consolidate what Crespi describes as a recognizable "recitational aesthetic" that, though hotly debated by poets and critics, focused on the need for poets to express emotions such as grief, anger, and indignation and to communicate with and impact the subjectivity of their audiences.[6]

In bemoaning the association between the sounds of poetry and China's revolutionary history, Yu Jian's concerns are likely to lie less with early twentieth-century experiments with nationalistic uses of poetry recitation and more with its later subjugation to the hegemony of the CCP during the second half of the twentieth century. The popularity of public poetry recitation peaked in the early 1960s, by which time it had turned into "a mass-performance art, a state-sanctioned cultural form aimed at engaging and placing on public display the revolutionary passions of China's urban populace."[7] Poetry recitations were part of Mao's blueprint for ideological programming, for piercing popular psyches with the values of communist revolution. They were made more challenging, as Crespi suggests, by the need to simultaneously embody the values of the lyrical and the theatric: poets were expected to move their audiences with genuine, heartfelt emotion while also paying conscious attention to physical and oral modes of theatrical expression such as vocal phrasing, enunciation, movement about the stage, and hand gestures. Such expectations did not immediately fade away with the end of the Cultural Revolution in 1976 but helped shape the poetics of younger generations of writers who had come of age during the 1960s and 1970s. Hence the fervent tone of Bei Dao's most frequently recited poem, "The Answer" (Huida), with the eminently recitable lines "Let me tell you world, / I—do—not—believe!"[8] Although the message might be different from the revolutionary optimism expressed in Mao-era poetry, in their declarative style and repetitive lines, Bei Dao's poems of the late 1970s were arguably caught under the spell of an earlier "era of recital."

Placed in this historical context, Yu Jian's discontents make more sense. His displeasure with contemporary practices of poetry recitation do not simply reflect an understanding that poetry is best appreciated in silence and not spoken aloud; this seems unlikely given the fact that Yu has willingly recited his poetry countless times in his career. The connections he draws between the act of enunciating, China's political, intellectual, and media elites as represented by professors, politicians, presidents, and TV presenters, and the sexualized human body as reflected in the metaphor of the microphone as penis and recitation as "rape" suggest that poetry, the body, and power have become mutually implicated in a way that undermines the freedom and integrity of poetry. "Sound," rather than simply denoting the noises made when a poet opens his or her mouth to speak, operates here as a metaphor for the political appropriation of the human body and speech. Given Yu's longstanding emphasis on the vitality of China's Popular poetry tradition and the anti-Intellectual bias he expresses in his writings, this appropriation is especially problematic. For Yu, the body of the poet as he grasps the phallic microphone represents what Xiaobing Tang describes as "a material semiotic component for ordering everyday reality and signifying the power of the body politic"; the politicized body thus becomes "public enunciation" and "the unmediated site for the exercise and demonstration of power."[9] It is precisely this spectacle of poetry-as-power to which Yu Jian so strongly objects.

Yu Jian's other gripe relates more directly to the question of language. He is not alone in his attentiveness toward the problems associated with an insufficient command of Mandarin Chinese and the resultant fear of public speaking; many poets whose first language is not Mandarin share these sentiments. At each poetry recitation event I attended in China from 2005 to 2010, at least one poet would preface a reading with an onstage apology for his or her "bad" or nonstandard Chinese. These apologies became part of the performance, a way of drawing attention to the problematic nature of language, the tenuous links between signifier and signified, and, ultimately, the difficulties of achieving transparent communication between poet and audience. Approaches to dealing with this perceived handicap include requesting that another poet with superior standard Chinese or recitation skills perform the work, or choosing to read the work in the poet's native dialect in an act of linguistic defiance that is often greeted by the audience with a mix of encouraging yells of "Great!" scornful guffaws, and embarrassed giggles, as though the poet had chosen to recite stark naked.[10]

Language or dialect is a significant factor in shaping attitudes toward poetry recital and public speaking in China more generally. Responding to a question in my poetry survey about the advantages and disadvantages of poetry recitation, several poets mentioned the issues of language and sound; one suggested that "Recitation allows the pleasure of poetry to be expressed, as poetry has the ability to produce pleasure. Sounds allow poetry to enter people's hearts . . . if upon listening you have no reaction, that is a sign of a bad poem." Another shifted the responsibility of linguistic competency from the poet to the audience: "if others don't understand my Yunnan dialect, that's their fault for not preparing their ears properly." A different Yunnan poet wrote, "my poetry is only suited to being read in a dialect from the area of Yunnan close to Sichuan. If it was read in standard Chinese, that would be like Mei Lanfang playing the part of Li Da or Liu Dehua [Andy Lau] playing the part of Chiang Kai-shek: it may well turn into a 'parody,' because many of my poems have only a visual sense of pleasure."[11] Local languages, therefore, can be seen as a source of authenticity as well as a potential handicap in the public culture of enunciation; for many poets, writing poetry involves heeding its sounds as they are formed in the poet's own native tongue.

The inflammatory statements contained in Yu Jian's essay did not go unnoticed and sparked a noisy debate in newspapers, journals, and poetry websites for a period of time in 2005 and 2006. Numerous poets and critics joined in with their own spirited defenses of poetry recital. Shen Haobo began a brief blog post on the topic by stating simply, "recitation is a part of poetry," and confessed that he saw nothing wrong with recitation containing performative elements.[12] The poet Pang Qingming suggested that the true reason behind Yu's dislike of poetry recitation is his lifelong "hatred" of standard Chinese and criticized him for using public forums to propagate a "betrayal of the poetic spirit."[13] Poetry critic Zhang Taozhou also took issue with Yu in an article commissioned by the newspaper *Southern Weekend* to present the other side of the argument, published later the same month alongside excerpts from Yu's essay.[14]

The apparent contradiction between the widely accepted need to use Mandarin in poetry recital and an equally widespread distaste for such linguistic supremacy can be understood within the context of the enduring dichotomy between official and unofficial culture, or between state-sponsored, poetry activity and the self-professed avant-garde. It also relates to a tension inherent in Chinese poetry scenes. On the one hand, there is what many depict as a cliquishness to contemporary poetry activity, with only recognized poet-citizens gaining access to publications and events. At the same time, a pervasive sense of readership crisis has prompted some to attempt to open poetry up to a wider audience, as demonstrated by the organizers of the two poetry events I turn to next, the 2006 Big Square Poetry Festival in Beijing and Lushan Famous Poets Summit in Changsha. Reciting in Mandarin rather than the poet's native language can be seen as a practical means of ensuring that poetry is heard and understood by the greatest number of people possible. The question becomes one of whether contemporary poets really desire to be appreciated by that large an audience or whether recognition from peers is the definitive motivating factor in organizing and attending poetry events.

THE CONTINGENCIES OF FACE-TO-FACE EVENTS

As public occasions centered around the genre of contemporary poetry and requiring the physical presence of poets, poetry events provide a unique opportunity to observe the treatment of poetic text in the arena of oral tradition, as well as the social behaviors of participants and audiences who meet face-to-face. The reading or recitation of poetry is, as Yu Jian's comments suggest, often treated as a chore or necessary evil, a reminder that the event is, after all, *supposed* to be about poems and a ritualized practice capable of stirring up a range of performer and audience reactions that include excuse-making, embarrassment, and ridicule. The "additional" activities that comprise face-to-face events, that is, those not directly related to the oral performance or discussion of poems, extend poetry's social and cultural meanings and reinforce the fact that poems are but one element of the social form that is poetry.

Agreeing to attend a poetry event in China often requires not just reciting poetry in public but also engaging in a variety of activities such as commenting on the quality of a poet's writings in that same poet's presence, interacting with cultural and business entrepreneurs, hanging out at tourist destinations, getting drunk with members of local governmental organizations, and being constantly observed, photographed, and talked about by other participants and event sponsors. It also involves making oneself susceptible to the contingencies of face-to-face interaction, in which meanings, networks, and performances evolve in real time, shaped by the surrounding context and the collaborations of people and forces that are necessary for the staging of poetry events. Despite their organizers' best efforts to act in a gatekeeping capacity by deciding who should be invited to poetry events and what the purpose or theme of the event should be, what ends up happening and the reasons poetry events are remembered and written into history are beyond anyone's total control. One reason for this, as we will see, is that poetry events are the product of the contemporary conjuncture in which economic forces, political interests, and cultural production come together in what might appear to be synergistic harmony but which always contains the potential for tension and contention owing to the differing ambitions and ideologies of those involved.

The unexpected consequences of poetry events could be observed at the Big Square Poetry Festival (Dachang shige jie) that took place in the Jianwai SOHO complex of Beijing's Central Business District on the evening of June 18, 2006. Part of Beijing's "Together with Migrants" (in Chinese, *women zai yiqi*, literally "we are together") festival organized by UNESCO and sponsored by the chair of SOHO China, Pan Shiyi, and its CEO, Zhang Xin (who is also Pan's wife), the Big Square Poetry Festival was the second poetry recitation event of its kind to have been held since 2004. It was intended to enhance the cultural life of Beijing's migrant workers as well as to experiment with "boundary crossing" (*kuajie*) in contemporary poetry; aside from recitations by a large number of poets from across the poetic spectrum and from all living generations of poets (Misty through to post-1980 poets), the event incorporated live performances of rock and folk music designed to make poetry recitation more "entertaining" for its audience. In an interview with *Beijing News*, one of the organizers explained the hope that this approach would "provide a new path for the renaissance of poetry, as this kind of event has to be more interesting than watching a talent show."[15]

Pan Shiyi and Zhang Xin, who launched their real estate empire in 2001, have long been aware of the benefits of associating themselves and their business with the arts. In addition to poetry, they have been involved with film, magazines, and contemporary art and have won prizes for their contributions to Chinese architectural design.[16] Real estate developers like SOHO China have "cast a spell on every Chinese city through the enchanting siren sound of speedy development and the magic wand of architecture."[17] The company's involvement in the arts can be considered a strategic public relations exercise as much as a contribution to Beijing's cultural scenes, especially in light of the Chinese real estate industry's reputation for corruption.[18] News articles and blog posts written in the days before the Big Square recital focused less on the real estate credentials of its sponsors, however, than on the "open" nature of the event and the need to bring poetry back into the public sphere (*gonggong lingyu*) or, in the words of poet and co-organizer Hu Jiujiu, to let poetry "walk onto the streets, walk into residential areas, and walk onto the square."[19]

The timing of the event posed two immediate challenges. Its organizers described the anticipated four-hour duration, from 8:00 pm till midnight, as an experiment or piece of performance art designed to test how long the audience could endure nonstop poetry recitation. To make matters more challenging, poetry found itself in a real-time battle for audience attention with two World Cup soccer matches that were being broadcast on television the same evening, as well as an open-air screening of Jia Zhangke's recent film *The World* (Shijie) in an adjacent square within the SOHO complex. Although the audience diminished in size as the evening wore on, there were still a hundred or so people present right to the very end. Such tenacity could be explained in part by the presence of Pan Shiyi and a number of famous cultural figures, including the poets Shu Ting, Xi Chuan, and Shi Zhi, who had reportedly just checked out of a psychiatric hospital, the musicians Confucius Sez (Zi yue) and Zhou Yunpeng, and theater director Zhang Guangtian.

Another reason so many people stayed to the end was that the evening gave rise to several unscripted incidents that highlighted the contingency of face-to-face poetry events and the challenges involved in attempting to bridge the divide between modern poetry, migrant workers, media personalities, and big businesses. The most memorable of these occurred when it was time for the hosts (Hu Xudong, Shen Haobo, and me) to invite Shu Ting, television anchorman Ma Bin, and Pan Shiyi onto the stage to present Shu Ting's poetry. As Shu Ting rarely agrees to recite her work in public, it had been arranged that Ma would do so on her behalf, to the disappointment of the throng of excitable Shu Ting fans gathered directly below the stage. Having quietly apologized to the audience that her standard Chinese was not good enough to recite her own poems, Shu Ting then handed the microphone back to me, and I passed it to Ma so that he could recite her famous poem "To the Oak Tree" (Zhi xiangshu). No sooner had Ma taken his place center stage than he realized he had lost the recital program. This prompted him to start shouting angrily at the offstage volunteers to find him a copy of "the words" (*shi ci'er*), as though this were a dramatic performance being held up by a substandard stage crew.

While the hosts waited in the wings observing the growing mayhem, Pan Shiyi, from his position on the far side of the stage, found another microphone and began reciting "To the Oak Tree" in his own less-than-standard Mandarin while Shu Ting stood beside him, steadying the program in his shaking hands. Shu's proximity to Pan and her two-handed grasp of the program throughout the reading symbolized her ownership of the poem she had declined to recite, a work which, because of its inclusion in countless poetry anthologies and school textbooks since the early 1980s, had long since become part of China's modern literary canon and of the public's cultural memory of modern poetry. Meanwhile, Ma Bin, unimpressed by the fact that Pan had stolen the limelight, located another copy of "the words" and without seeking permission or waiting for Pan to finish began to recite the equally famous 1968 poem "Believe in the Future" by Shi Zhi, using the typically booming, authoritative voice of a CCTV television presenter. Ma's performance elicited audible groans and scornful laughter from the square below and prompted one spectator to charge up to the stage shouting, "Let *me* read it!" This led to even more shouts and laughter from the audience, and it took several minutes to restore order and get the recitation program back on track.

Although the entertainment this incident created was probably not the kind hoped for by the festival's organizers, it did in a roundabout way validate their decision to stage the event in an open-air urban space within the SOHO building complex. This choice of location was intended to be conducive to attracting a diverse audience of migrant workers and casual passersby (as it happened, this translated into a few white-collar professionals and a larger group of students, journalists, and musicians, as well as one or two foreign researchers) in addition to the usual crowd of writers and critics. In press interviews, the organizers had spoken of their desire to encourage interaction and exchange (*jiaoliu*) between poets and audience members. The chaos and hilarity that emerged during Shu Ting's portion of the recitation could be taken as a sign of success in this regard. Rather than distracting from the more important act of listening to and appreciating the poems, the audience's reaction to the onstage power struggle between Shu Ting, Pan Shiyi, and Ma Bin became a part of the event itself, a moment of communal participation that can only happen contingently on a live scene of poetry.

In his history of contemporary poetry readings in the U.K. and United States, Peter Middleton suggests that audiences are formed during (rather than prior to) the performance event, creating a network of subjectivities that has the potential to become part of the poem itself.[20] The audience, in other words, is not a static phenomenon but a performance in its own right, whose participation in the listening process makes them part of what Middleton terms the "intersubjective drama." Similarly, the migrant workers, students, poets, and musicians in attendance at the Big Square Poetry Festival, rather than passively consuming Pan and Ma's recitals through silent listening, actively staged their own reception of poems like "To the Oak Tree" and "Believe in the Future" by becoming subjectively, vocally, and physically involved in the recitations. Ultimately it was this moment of interaction and unscripted (yet entertaining) conflict that came to define the whole event as a well-intentioned but ineffective attempt at interclass and intergroup boundary crossing, as Hu Xudong suggested in a blog post written after the festival.

Indeed, at the same time as it brought people together in communal spectatorship and shared affective response, the reason the Ma-Pan-Shu incident produced such awkwardness and amusement was because of the stark differences in its participants' social backgrounds, identities, and poetic tastes; even the event's theme, "Together with Migrants," was built on the assumption of difference. Ma Bin's formalized poetry recital aesthetics contrasted with the predominantly casual and naturalistic reading voices adopted by the majority of the poets who took part and marked him out as a representative of China's media elites. It differed, too, from the high-energy performances of younger poets like Hu Jiujiu, who in half reading, half roaring his poems gave off a sense of joyful abandon and avant-garde "edge" that was completely missing from Ma's recitation. The poet-audience's audible dissatisfaction with Ma's reading style was their way of drawing attention to his lack of authenticity as a poetry scene participant and thus their own more authentic knowledge of contemporary poetry aesthetics. Not only is Ma a television presenter and representative of the state-run media, he also publicly violated poetry recitation etiquette by interrupting an ongoing reading and performing the work of a living legend, Shi Zhi, in his presence, without seeking permission beforehand. Pan Shiyi hardly fared any better, demonstrating a naïve eagerness to recite on Shu Ting's behalf despite the fact that his Chinese was demonstrably no more standard than that of the poet, whom he professed to be one of his biggest idols.

Having already spent time being photographed by the artist Han Bing and invited to take part in several performance art installations earlier in the day, the migrant workers in whose name the event was being held could be seen wandering in and out of the square throughout the evening looking alternately bored and bemused by the events taking place onstage. Their physical appearance marked them out among the more affluently dressed poets and musicians who occupied much of the square's seating. As part of UNESCO's broader program on international migration aimed at promoting the human rights of migrants and contributing to their "peaceful integration" into society, the festival was intended to make Chinese migrant workers feel more included in the cultural life of the city they were currently helping construct.[21]

But the incongruous presence of these migrant workers within the already completed parts of the SOHO complex and the absence of any interaction between them and the other attendees mostly served to accentuate the challenges of surmounting the socioeconomic divide between Beijing's "haves" and "have-nots." To suggest that inviting these workers to a four-hour reading of contemporary poetry in an orchestrated demonstration of interclass solidarity would improve their quality of life could be considered hopeful at best, condescending at worst. As Hai Ren suggests in an analysis of the "affective work" performed by migrant workers present at the Chinese Ethnic Culture Park in Beijing, their job is not just one of "producing" tourists as "middle-class bodies" (or highlighting class differences to the benefit of the wealthier visitors to the park) but also of "being framed as subjects of charity in their employer's philanthropic enterprise."[22] One might note, furthermore, that reciting poetry to a captive audience of nearby construction workers was likewise a ploy in audience-maximization designed to profit the marginal social group that is contemporary Chinese poets. Such a strategy could, from one perspective, only strengthen the impression that poetry events tend to have a hard time finding a public as enthusiastic about modern poetry as their poet-attendees and organizers.

At the same time, however, the Big Square Poetry Festival's attempted mobilization of China's disenfranchised classes and reliance upon synergistic convergence with real estate entrepreneurs reflected the reality of poetry activity in early twenty-first-century China, in which poetry's relative invisibility within mainstream culture has meant that poets have been forced to adopt an entrepreneurial approach of their own toward staging poetry events, navigating the often treacherous terrain that straddles the culture industry, poetry as high culture, and the individual and collective ambitions of poets as participants in China's poetry scenes. The complexity of this task and its relationship to the conjuncture of early twenty-first-century China will become clearer in the following analysis of an even bigger poetry event that took place earlier in the same month in the Hunan capital of Changsha: the Lushan Famous Poets Summit.

THE LUSHAN FAMOUS POETS SUMMIT

The pervasiveness across China of large-scale poetry festivals, conventions, and summits has been a notable phenomenon in the face-to-face space of poetry since the turn of the millennium. Most are organized by individuals known as poetry activists, some of whom are returning to poetry scenes after a period of absence developing their non-poetry professional careers. The rest of this chapter focuses on an ethnographic survey of just such an event, held in Changsha on June 9–11, 2006, and organized by the Hunan poet, architect, and urban planner Tan Kexiu. Officially titled the First Lushan New Century Famous Poets Summit (Shoujie Lushan xin shiji shige mingjia fenghui), it was typical in several ways of the kinds of large-scale activities that have punctuated poetry calendars since the Panfeng Meeting of 1999.

My aim in describing in detail my experience of this event as a participant-observer is to draw attention to individual roles and microprocesses that usually go unnoticed but that reveal much about the synergistic collaborations that underpin the organization and cultural meanings of such poetry events, as well as their relationship to poetry politics and discourse. Like the Big Square Poetry Festival, the Lushan Famous Poets Summit involved the cooperation of a diverse range of sponsors and participants, including representatives from the world of real estate. And, like so many examples of poetry activity that take place on the Internet, in print, and face-to-face, the Lushan Summit gave rise to contention within poetry scenes around issues that were as ideological and poetry-political as they were related to poetry writing and aesthetics. Close examination of the components of individual poetry events highlights the functioning of poetry scenes as historically conditioned, loosely affiliated networks of people and institutions who come together in the service of the social form of poetry and whose contingent interactions on individual sites of poetry activity not only give the scene its sense of effervescence and liveliness but also give rise to unpredictable outcomes that affect distributions of discursive power within poetry scenes.

The Organizers

Tan Kexiu was born in 1971 in rural Longhui county, Hunan, and after graduating from the Xi'an University of Architecture and Technology in 1995 moved to Changsha to embark on a career in urban planning. He is well-known in the city both as a literary figure and as an architect, and holds various professional positions that include vice secretary of the Changsha Municipal Urban Planning Association and chief designer and CEO of the Hunan Fangyuan Construction Project Design Agency. He is also vice chairman of the Hunan Poetry Committee and was most famous in the mid-2000s for his role as editor in chief of the poetry journal *Tomorrow* (Mingtian), the name of which was chosen to position the journal as the rightful successor to the post-Mao avant-garde tradition begun in the late 1970s by *Today*. Two editions of the journal were published as books via second-channel cooperation with Hunan Arts Publishing House in 2003 and 2005, and a third with Changjiang Literature and Arts Publishing House in 2012. The Tomorrow poetry group is also responsible for organizing the poetry festivals known as the Tomorrow E'erguna Chinese Poetry Biennial Exhibition (Mingtian E'erguna Zhongguo shige shuangnian zhan) and its concomitant biennial poetry awards held in the town of E'erguna, Inner Mongolia, in September 2004 and January 2007, sponsored by the E'erguna government and local tourism bureau. After a gap of five years, a third exhibition was held in Hibiscus Town, Hunan, in April 2012 to mark the publication of the third edition of *Tomorrow*.

The primary financial sponsor of the 2006 Lushan Summit was the real estate company Lushan Villas (Lushan Bieshu), a subsidiary of Hunan Kaida Financial Investment Corporation Limited (Hunan Kaida Caixin Touzi Youxian Zeren Gongsi), which specializes in land development. Lushan Villas is a luxury property development located amid mountainside scenery about six miles outside the city of Changsha. Aside from the Tomorrow poetry group, the event's sponsors included the Changsha Houtian Planning Consultancy Company Limited (Changsha Houtian Cehua Guwen Youxian Gongsi, a company that specializes in Internet consultancy services); the Changsha High-Tech Bocai Experimental School (Changsha Gaoxin Bocai Shiyan Xuexiao); the poetry committee of the Hunan Writers' Association; and the local paper *Xiaoxiang Morning News* (Xiaoxiang chenbao). The summit was organized by a hierarchical committee consisting of seven consultants, a director, five deputy directors, one secretary-general, three vice secretaries, and an office director. The seven consultants included the poet Han Zuorong, editor of the official literary journal *People's Literature*; Tan Zhongchi, the mayor of Changsha and president of the Hunan poetry committee; the eighty-six-year-old poet Peng Yanjiao, a former member of the Civil War–era literary society the July Group (Qiyue pai); and the poets Lin Mang and Yu Jian.[23] As their credentials suggest, many of the organizers had a foot in the poetry world as well as in China's halls of political power.

The Activities

Saturday, June 9, 2006, Grand Sun City Hotel, Changsha Summit delegates began gathering at this five-star hotel in the morning, arriving by air and train from across China. After registering in the hotel lobby, each received a plastic bag containing a program of events, several poetry books donated by participating poets, and a copy of the poetry collection that was to accompany the following evening's poetry recital. I had been invited to attend the summit by the School of Rubbish poet Yudu (Residual Poison), a young man in his early twenties and an employee of Tan Kexiu's architectural design company who knew of me through my online communications with School of Rubbish creator Pidan; he had suggested to Tan that it might be "beneficial" to have a foreign researcher in attendance.

Shortly after arriving at the hotel I ran into Shen Haobo, who invited me to join him, Yang Ke, and Guangdong poet Lu Weiping for lunch at a small restaurant on the banks of the Xiang River. Topics of conversation included other poets in attendance, the contents of the latest (2004–5) edition of Yang Ke's *Chinese New Poetry Almanac*, Tan Kexiu's decision not to invite female poets to the summit for fear of gossip regarding interpoet romantic liaisons dominating the summit, and other recent poetry scene news. At 5:00 pm a press conference was convened in the hotel ballroom, immediately followed by a formal banquet. Tan Kexiu, Lushan Villas' managing director Yue Gencheng, Tan Zhongchi, and Chen Zhongyi each gave an address, with Tan Kexiu introducing each of the committee members and the seventy-odd poets and critics in attendance. In his opening address, Yue Gencheng explained the motivations behind Lushan Villas' involvement as follows:

> Following poetry's deepening inroads into life, we have organized the First Lushan New Century Famous Poets Summit event. Our goal is to bring the most important poets of the Chinese poetry arena together in Changsha for the first time so that they might sum up the achievements of contemporary poetry, discuss poetic standards, investigate the current situation and future possibilities of post–Third Generation poetry, and so they can walk into life and walk into Lushan Villas. This is the most meaningful permutation of poetry and architecture and the best means of creating a refined cultural residence in the Hunan area and nourishing an atmosphere of humanism. It is also a manifestation of poetry's extension into the finer points of life. By developing this event, we really hope to turn Lushan Villas into a refined "poetic residence" and "place of poetic residence": Lushan Villas is going to become a classic image in people's minds.[24]

Even before the summit's main program had begun, Yue's speech foreshadowed what were going to be its main themes, including the importance of "life" and humanism to contemporary poetry and the fruitful connections to be forged between poetry and real estate.

In a last-minute change to the program, delegates were reassembled after dinner for a book release ceremony and forum to discuss Tan Kexiu's recently published poetry collection *Trio* (Sanchongzou), held in a small, airless meeting room on an upper floor of the hotel. After a slow start, assessments of Tan's collection grew increasingly uninhibited, and several poets, Yu Jian and Mo Mo included, criticized Tan's poetry (in his presence) for lacking artistic sensibility. The initial format of one person offering their thoughts while others listened quickly gave way to multiple debates and disagreements taking place simultaneously and at loud volume around the table. Yi Sha, who had already been a focus of attention since the summit began owing to his recent dramatic weight loss, in typical fashion was outspoken in his comments; the Hangzhou poet Pan Wei even asked him, "Yi Sha, do you think you might sometimes use your ears?" The discussion continued until close to midnight, by which time the meeting room was so hot and clouded with cigarette smoke that it had become impossible to continue.

Sunday, June 10, 9:00–11:30 am, Grand Sun City Hotel: The First Lushan New Century Famous Poets Summit Forum This forum took place in a large conference hall on the top floor of the hotel. After a series of presentations from poets and critics including Li Shaojun, Shen Qi, Chen Zhongyi, and Xiao Ying (one of three female poets and critics, not including myself, who managed to evade Tan Kexiu's prohibition on women), the floor was declared open to the seventy or so poets present. Shen Haobo was among the first to take to the stage, announcing that he had been reconsidering the avant-garde poetics of the Lower Body group and had discovered a newfound admiration for the writings of the *Today* poets. China in 2006 was, he declared, completely different from the China of several years ago. Then, the Lower Body group was writing in opposition to the mainstreams of culture, civilization, and "the classics." Now, the "free spirit" of the Internet meant that anyone with a computer could go online and become famous through writing "appealing" essays. Under such circumstances, Shen posited, "that so-called free spirit, so-called creativity, so-called liveliness, and that so-called resistance or disgust toward culture, civilization, and the classics have become cheapened, have become extremely trashy; under such conditions, how should we understand the avant-garde?" His answer was to "uphold the glory of poetry, uphold the meaning of the classics, and uphold the spirit of the noble classes." A "truly avant-garde poet," Shen declared to much surprise, "should be a member of the noble class, and we should rediscover China's avant-garde poetic tradition: Misty Poetry."[25]

This unexpected about-face may have been prompted by interpoet conflicts in recent years on Internet forums like *Poetry Rivers and Lakes* that, as discussed in Chapter 1, had witnessed newer groups like the School of Rubbish attempting to wrestle the mantle of "true" avant-gardism from the Lower Body group. It led to a number of other poets stepping onto the stage to elaborate on their own understandings of avant-garde poetry and its importance to Chinese culture and civilization. Other delegates seemed disappointed by Shen Haobo's rejection of his previous, more rebellious approach to poetry. Zhu Ziqing joined in from his seat in the audience by shouting out, to great amusement, "Why not make Shen Haobo feel even better?" (Wei shenme bu rang Shen Haobo zai shufu yi xie ne?), a playful reference to the sexual overtones of Yin Lichuan's famous Lower Body poem "Why not make it feel even better?"

June 10, 2:30–4:00 pm, Lushan Villas: The Post–Third Generation Poetry Forum Shortly after lunch, delegates were shuttled in two buses to Lushan Villas, where young cheongsam-clad employees of Kaida Financial Investment greeted them. After signing their autographs on a large red banner erected outside the Lushan Villas sales center, they were directed to take their places in assigned seats laid out in tiers within the spacious entrance hall. This was the scene of the summit's second forum, the Post–Third Generation Poetry Forum (Di san dai hou shige zhuanti taolunhui). Chaired by Li Shaojun, editor of the Hainan official literary journal *Horizons* (Tianya), it was described as an opportunity for poets and critics who had not had the chance to speak earlier in the day to offer their perspectives on the topic of "Post–Third Generation Poetry," that is, poetry written by people born since the latter half of the 1960s and published in the previous two decades.

The main talking point of the forum came from a speech given by Tan Kexiu in which he fought back against the criticisms of artistic failure leveled at his poetry the previous night by launching an attack on what he called "petty literati poetry" (*xiao wenren shige*). Such poetry, Tan claimed, is written by poets who lead a "traditional literati-style life," "deaf to all that goes on beyond their windows . . . spending every day inside their offices, in front of piles of paper and computers, producing poetry that deals only with the self and is completely divorced from reality and the masses." He went on: "Petty literati poetry does not focus on questions of reality but rather on so-called poetic technique, including issues related to linguistic, rhetorical, and stylistic method. This type of poet and writing has no relevance to the current era. If one were to situate such prattling petty literati poetry within a larger historical perspective it would be revealed to be ineffectual writing."[26] Li Shaojun took up this question of technique versus content in his comments. He identified Tan's proposal that poets "throw themselves into real life" as typical of New Critical Realist Poetry (Xin Pipan Xianshi Zhuyi Shige), a recent and decidedly New Leftist literary phenomenon that explains the positive reception of Migrant Worker Poetry as well as a general intensification of social consciousness among many avant-garde poets.

June 10, 4:00–6:00 pm, Lushan Villas: Folk-Song Collecting After the forum ended, attendees were invited to partake in an activity enigmatically described as "live scene folk-song collecting at the poetic residence" (*shiyi jusuo xianchang caifeng*). This consisted of an hour or so in which we strolled around the manicured gardens of the Lushan Villas complex, mingling with summit delegates and employees of the sponsoring businesses and offering ample photo and video opportunities for the media representatives in attendance. In a culminating ceremony, Yu Jian, Mo Mo, Han Zuorong, and Yue Gencheng were asked to pull back a piece of red velvet cloth to reveal a commemorative stone plaque engraved with the words "Lushan Tomorrow Poetry Wall Foundation Ceremony" and the date, June 10, 2006.

June 10, 8:00–10:00 pm, Tian Han Grand Theater: Lushan Tomorrow Poetry Recital One final event was scheduled for later that day: the Lushan Tomorrow Poetry Recital, held in the music hall of the Tian Han Grand Theater in central Changsha. This recital was organized in conjunction with the Changsha High-Tech Bocai Experimental School and featured performances by students and staff from the school as well as the poets in attendance. Large billboards had been on display for several days in prominent locations in downtown Changsha, emblazoned with the names of the event's sponsors and the slogan, "Working hard for the renaissance of the people's poetry" (wei minzu shige fuxing er nuli). Interest in the recital was high: the event was sold out, and people lined up outside the theater to inquire where copies of the program could be purchased. Several poets wondered out loud how Tan Kexiu had managed to drum up so much public enthusiasm for modern Chinese poetry.

The recital itself was emblematic of the sort of cultural clash that occurs when avant-garde poetry is appropriated by official literary establishments and manipulated to serve commercial ends. By the time we arrived at the theater, staff of the High-Tech Bocai Experimental School had already set up the stage. A grand piano stood left of center and next to it a solitary microphone stand. At the back of the stage hung a large red poster emblazoned with the title of the event and its various sponsors. Most of the evening's recitals were accompanied either by music performed live by a pianist from the school or by a recording of classical music broadcast over the theater's built-in sound system. This arrangement seemed best suited to the performance styles of the students and teachers, who wore formal evening attire and recited their chosen poems in an expressive, theatrical style. Other performances included song-and-dance numbers put on by primary school students dressed as a frog, a snail, and a yellow chick. The poet VIPs were given no opportunity to prepare before being called by the female emcee onto the stage to recite the poem that had been selected for recital by the summit's organizing committee.

A few participants requested that the music be stopped for the duration of their time onstage. Most recitals, however, were marked by a jarring conflict between the gentle melodies of the Chinese and Western-style classical music and the avant-garde poetics and candid sociocultural concerns expressed in the poems. Music and poetry recitation, as Van Crevel observed after attending a recitation event in 2002, "are a potentially powerful combination, as long as they match."[27] For the majority of performances at the Lushan Tomorrow Poetry Recital, they definitely did not, and the resulting disparities gave the occasion a surreal atmosphere. Of the readings given by invited poets, the Changsha audience was most receptive to Zhu Ziqing's rendition of "Song of the Storm-Petrel" (Haiyan zhi ge) by the Russian proletarian poet Maxim Gorky, a poem included in Chinese middle-school textbooks. Zhu made use of his impressive vocal range and recited the poem by heart, placing the microphone back in its stand and gesturing dramatically with both arms as the poem reached its climax. This was met with enthusiastic applause from the Changsha audience and whoops of approval from his poet friends seated below. Yu Jian, by contrast, sat in silence in the first row while another poet recited his long, appropriately passively titled poem "Watching the Ocean" (Kan hai) on his behalf. The recital was taking place not long after his essay "Recitation" had been published and Yu was evidently sticking to his guns by resisting the opportunity to take part in another "unsophisticated assassination" of poetry.

Other participants, sensing a palpable gap between their own poetic sensibilities and those of the student- and teacher-dominated audience, relished the opportunity to push the boundaries of acceptability. After a number of unenthusiastic and unembellished readings, Yi Sha's rendition of his poem "Spring's Breast Plunder" (Chuntian de rufang jie) roused the audience by refocusing their attention on the poetic content at hand. The poem is written in the voice of a husband addressing his wife who is about to undergo surgery for a possible double mastectomy to treat breast cancer. It employs everyday language and a simple linear narrative form to describe the husband's emotional reactions upon being asked to give medical permission for the operation. Yi Sha's poetry of the late 1990s and early 2000s usually renders bodily imagery in a sexual and humorous manner, which is partly why he was such a source of inspiration for the Lower Body group and other poets connected with *Poetry Rivers and Lakes*. "Spring's Breast Plunder," on the other hand, conveys serious subject matter in a far more somber tone. Yi Sha's oral delivery was appropriately subdued, pausing in between stanzas and adopting a tender voice when the narrator tells his wife that he is psychologically prepared for the potential outcome of the surgery:

> My darling, in fact
> yesterday afternoon, before
> you went to book your appointment
> when the door to the doctor's room swung open
> I caught a glimpse of two
> women who had had both breasts removed
> the doctor was changing their dressings
> I thought they were both still very beautiful
> and so I was already prepared

While awaiting news about his wife's operation, the narrator is approached by an illiterate farmer who has just learned that his wife has to have a double mastectomy and who asks the narrator to sign his name on his behalf to give legal permission for the surgery. This topic of the socially disadvantaged masses echoed the forum debates on the topic of petty literati poetry and the need expressed by Tan and others to represent a broad spectrum of social experience in their writing. Yang Ke continued this theme, reciting "The People" (Renmin), a poem that consists of little more than a list of pastimes and professions from injured workers and young female hair salon employees (a euphemism for prostitutes) to students, drunks, gambling addicts, teachers, and secretaries. These people, as the title provocatively implies, are the true faces of contemporary Chinese society, no matter how unsavory their lifestyles or arduous their careers.

The most riveting performance was Shen Haobo's reading of his poem "The Actual Fact of Ma Heling" (Shishishang de Ma Heling), one of a series of poems titled "Records of Wenlou Village" (Wenloucun jishi) that Shen composed after visiting the "AIDS village" of Wenlou, Henan, in May 2004. The poem consists of forty-three lines, of which twenty-five begin with the phrase "in actual fact" (*shishishang*). Read aloud, the alliteration and repetition form an insistently rhythmic effect that, combined with Shen's angry tone of voice, contributed to a growing sense of urgency, injustice, and psychological distress. The first nine lines of the poem read as follows:

> In actual fact she's already waiting to die
> just like the other hundreds and thousands of people waiting to die in this village
> in actual fact her husband is already dead
> just like everyone else who has already died in this village
> in actual fact she's not at all willing to just wait to die like this
> in actual fact she remarried less than a year after her husband died
> in actual fact the man who married her had also just lost his wife
> in actual fact Ma Heling is already over fifty years old
> but still appears plump and normal

The poem proceeds to explain in sympathetic terms how the spread of AIDS in the village was perpetuated by the villagers' unwillingness to use contraception. Like Yi Sha's "Spring's Breast Plunder," it subverts the topics of sexuality and the body from a life-giving source of fun and pleasure into one of tragedy and death. Again, this social topicality tied in neatly with the themes of New Critical Realist Poetry and a seemingly New Leftist poetic concern for the current era that had been debated earlier in the day. The poem's explicit language seemed less appropriate for an audience consisting of a large number of young children, but Shen Haobo's heartfelt delivery, coming at the end of a long evening of slick performances and lackluster readings, gained him the loudest cheers of the night. After the recital ended, students and other audience members surrounded the poets, requesting their autographs on copies of the recital program.

Monday, June 11, 10:30 am–12:00 pm: Changsha High-Tech Bocai Experimental School After a brief tourist trip to Changsha's Yuelu Academy earlier in the morning, conference attendees were shuttled in minibuses to the High-Tech Bocai Experimental School. Upon disembarking and being informed of the plan for the morning's activities, several poets were set to make a hasty escape but were tracked down by Tan Kexiu who insisted that everyone put in an appearance to "give the school face." We were led inside a large classroom filled with excited elementary school students. Each poet was introduced as an important famous guest, with Tan Kexiu in particular treated like a local celebrity. The main activity involved the students pulling poets' names at random out of a hat, upon which they were asked to choose a poem to recite from memory. Another consisted of the children, some as young as seven, reciting their own poems and requesting feedback from the visiting "experts."

It became apparent that the school had an unusually keen interest in modern poetry; one of the teachers was an aspiring poet, and the school had made a concerted effort to educate students in aspects of poetic creation such as free verse, random association, abstract imagery, and the importance of covering a wide range of subject matter. The "experts" claimed to be impressed by the writing standards on display and seemed to enjoy—perhaps with a dose of irony—the opportunity to interact with their "fans" and share their approaches to poetic writing with an especially youthful audience. This was the final planned activity of the Lushan Summit. Delegates spent the remainder of the day checking out of the conference hotel, saying good-bye, and traveling to the Changsha train station and airport to begin their journeys home.

It can be difficult to do descriptive or analytical justice to such an eclectic grouping of activities as comprised the Lushan Summit, as they cover a range of concerns, activities, and cultural impulses that are worthy of detailed research in their own right, including academic poetry discussions, real estate promotion, collusions of poetry and tourism, public poetry performance, and the place of modern poetry in China's education system. Face-to-face poetry activity is not limited to any one of these concerns and, in the case of large-scale events like the Lushan Summit, can involve a combination of them all. To narrow the focus of discussion to a single subcategory would be to overlook the larger significance of face-to-face poetry events, which are in many ways defined by the diverse nature of the people and institutions of which they are constituted.

Certain themes and patterns can, however, be singled out for discussion as epitomizing modern poetry's conjuncture in the early twenty-first century. They include the role played by individual poetry activists like Tan Kexiu, the synergy between poetry and real estate, and the role of the media in publicizing poetry events and turning them into newsworthy "incidents" that also reflect poetry's status as a social form and potential for creating entertaining spectacles of poetry's interventions in everyday life. In particular, the Lushan Summit stirred up contention within poetry scenes around the topic of petty literati poetry, a concept coined by Tan after his poetry was criticized for its artistic failures on the first day of the summit. The debate, which continued in print publications and on the Internet, reflected tensions between a neoliberal emphasis on individualization and New Leftist appeals to community and intellectual intervention in the socioeconomic injustices that characterize life for many disadvantaged social groups in present-day China.

POETRY ACTIVISTS AND THE CULTURAL ECONOMY

The key figure at the center of the Lushan Famous Poets Summit was Tan Kexiu. Tan conceived the event, negotiated sponsorship from Changsha-based businesses, schools, and literary and media organizations, secured the venues in which the different activities were held, and persuaded the seventy-odd well-known poets, critics, and academics from across the country to attend. Crucial to his ability to do so were his multiple identities as poet, architect, and urban planner. These experiences gave him the practical knowledge and professional connections required to handle the logistics of a three-day poetry event that aimed to make a splash in national poetry scenes while simultaneously contributing to the cultural life of the city of Changsha, its businesses, and inhabitants.

Poetry activists are individuals who are able and willing to invest large amounts of their own time, effort, and money into organizing poetry events. They can be thought of as a subcategory of cultural brokers, prominent figures in contemporary Chinese cultural life who, as Yomi Braester asserts, function as influential middlemen (they are, more often than not, male) by mediating between groups of differing cultural backgrounds.[28] They also encapsulate the ability of individuals to embrace the DIY way of life or, as Hai Ren puts it, "learn about, calculate, and cope with the new possibilities, uncertainties, risks and consequences" brought about by the "brave new way of living" under neoliberal conditions.[29] Among the paragons of cultural brokering who have benefited from the growing collusions between real estate development and the arts in twenty-first-century China are Pan Shiyi and Zhang Xin; other examples include Chen Jiagang and Deng Hong in Chengdu, and Zhang Baoquan in Beijing.[30] As Braester shows, there are also a number of contemporary filmmakers in China who have adopted a similar mode of cultural brokerage, ranging from the independent (Ning Ying and Wu Wenguang) to the more mainstream and commercially successful (Zhang Yimou and Feng Xiaogang). All of these directors have found ways to promote their work through links to big businesses without having to sacrifice their aesthetic independence or ideological concerns; Braester describes the resulting collusion between cinema and commerce as a creative mix of cultural identification, image making, and market strategies.[31]

Aside from promoting modern poetry within media and society and facilitating a cross-generational gathering of poets, an important motivation for Tan in organizing the summit was the chance to bolster his personal stature within national Chinese poetry scenes, an opportunity that proved as risky as it was empowering. It was for this more self-serving reason that Tan decided to convene a book release ceremony and forum discussion on the evening of June 9 for his volume of poetry, *Trio*. This act of self-promotion fueled the criticisms directed at him during the forum and in the debates that followed the summit; poets accused him of exhibiting nauseating "celebrity-like behavior" and of mobilizing professional resources to curry favor with famous poets.[32] By placing his own poetry on the agenda, Tan succeeded in making himself an object of attention but in a way that he did not anticipate or much enjoy. Although Tan's efforts to gain credibility as a writer seemed to have partly backfired, in organizing various face-to-face poetry events and in publishing three volumes of the poetry publication *Tomorrow*, Tan did succeed in elevating his fame within the Changsha and national Chinese poetry scenes. He also provided an opportunity to the poets he invited to his events to affirm their membership in poetry scenes. Receiving invitations to attend face-to-face events like the Lushan Summit is a small yet key step in achieving recognition as poet-citizens and requires that poets actively join in the activities that take place during the event and behave in a manner that is expected of them.

Although individual poetry activists or cultural brokers like Tan might be the most visible sign of the collusions that take place between poetry and big business in the staging of face-to-face poetry events, this relationship goes much deeper and can be considered a defining characteristic of the changing meanings of culture in China today, whereby the traditional elitist goals of education and enlightenment are being supplemented, if not replaced, with the notions of culture as entertainment and as a site for profit-making.[33] A brief glance at the list of sponsors of the Lushan Summit reveals that the significance of these occasions far exceeds the opportunity they provide for attendees to affirm their membership in poetry communities. Under the logic of the cultural economy, any high-culture allure (alluded to by Yue Gencheng with words such as "refined," "meaningful," "classic," and "humanism") that businesses acquire through sponsoring literary activities and events can be converted into economic capital in the marketplace.

Poetry is particularly conducive to this treatment. With its rich historical lineage, associations with high culture, the education system, and social refinement, and its avoidance—voluntary or otherwise—of the moral contamination associated with a market-driven production approach, poetry is perceived by image-conscious enterprises as "pure" and culturally esteemed. It thus acquires a symbolic value in inverse proportion to its low-level economic status: as Crespi puts it, "where the cash nexus tends to be regarded as dirty, calculating, lowbrow, and crude, poetry is perceived as elegant, pure, disinterested, and culturally prestigious."[34] In lending its name to the Lushan Summit and providing it with financial sponsorship and venues for poetry-related activities, Lushan Villas hoped that potential customers would come to associate the company's name with these positive values, which would then feed into its hoped-for brand image as the kind of "place of poetic residence" in which Changsha residents might aspire to live.

Perhaps the most well-known example of a cultural broker who has successfully exploited the synergy between poetry and big business is the billionaire entrepreneur and CEO of Beijing Zhongkun Investment Group (Beijing Zhongkun Touzi Jituan), Huang Nubo.

Huang, who also publishes poetry under the pen name Luo Ying and made headlines around the world in the early 2010s for his attempts to build a golf resort in Iceland,[35] donated ¥30 million to various poetry institutions in China in 2006. This enabled the establishment of the New Poetry Research Institute (Xin shi Yanjiusuo) at Huang's alma mater, Peking University, which is responsible for publishing a number of poetry-related academic manuscripts, journals, and poetry collections each year, as well as for organizing conferences and poetry recitals. Poet-tycoons like Huang are part of a group of writers sometimes known as the "returnees" (*guilaizhe*), absent from much of 1990s poetry activity but now back with renewed enthusiasm. In patronizing the arts they are said to be supplementing the dryness of their careers as businessmen with the spiritual rewards of literary creation and interaction. Another explanation is that this not only allows entry into the ranks of China's cultural elite but also helps deflect attention away from their huge wealth, something that can still be looked on with disdain in a nominally socialist society and that, in the past, has often been viewed with suspicion by the Communist government.[36] Being "cultured" has long been considered a worthy trait in Chinese society, in contrast to the distaste with which merchants and moneymaking endeavors were held in the traditional Confucian worldview.

INCIDENTIZATION AND THE ROLE OF THE MEDIA

Media were central to the pre-event planning and publicizing and postevent processing and evaluation of the Lushan Summit, helping not only to attract local and national attention to the event itself and its sponsors but also to convert it into a newsworthy spectacle or "incident" via a process known as "incidentization" (*shijianhua*). From the perspective of the event's organizers, the advantages of incidentization are primarily economic. Converting symbolic capital accrued through association with elite cultural activities into economic gains via the logic of the cultural economy is often a lengthy process that is unlikely to result in fast profit for the businesses concerned. Media publicity that accompanies events such as the Lushan Summit is, on the other hand, of more direct benefit.[37] Aside from the posters that festooned Changsha throughout the duration of the Lushan Summit, the bulk of its publicity came in the form of media reports written after the event, published in local and national newspapers and magazines as well as on websites. Each mention of the event in print and online media served as a public relations opportunity for Lushan Villas, whose name became indelibly connected to this particular chapter in poetry history.

The media's willingness to report on face-to-face poetry events, ostensibly of marginal interest to the non-poetry-reading majority of their audience, can be attributed in part to the methods of media courting practiced by organizers of cultural events, which relates in turn to the shift in China from a propaganda to a public relations model of communication.[38] Media coverage is rarely free; it must be earned by offering perks and payments to the journalists who are invited, if not actively wooed, to attend. If the event stretches over more than one day, journalists and photographers stay in the same hotel as the poet VIPs, are wined and dined at opening and closing banquets, and generally treated as guests of honor. Even in the case of one-day recitals or poetry forums in their own city, journalists are presented with envelopes containing money for "travel expenses" (*chema fei*). This is in effect an unofficial form of compensation, as the amount is usually significantly more than the cost of traveling to the event.[39]

Reports that simply state that a particular poetry event is about to be held or has just concluded barely qualify as newsworthy. To make them more appealing to readers, journalists highlight discord, controversy, and any unexpected occurrences that might enliven their accounts; focusing on contingency and contention undoubtedly helps increase the spectacular appeal of poetry events. In the case of the Lushan Summit, the most dramatic and unexpected incident that occurred was the debate between Tan Kexiu and other attendees on the topic of petty literati poetry. Here is an excerpt from a subsequent news report published in the August 23, 2006, edition of the *Hunan Daily News*:

> Since the Post–Third Generation Sharp Poetry Discussion was held in June this year at the Lushan Poetry Meeting, the topic of "Petty Literati Poetry" has swept like a bomb through the poetry arena. The sounds of a polemical battle began resounding in Changsha, with fiery-hearted people of the poetry world quick to respond, launching a heated debate from their bases in a variety of newspapers and web media. The poetry arena, which has laid low and lonesome over the past twenty years, has suddenly started sharpening its swords once more. With all cannons firing, this scorching summer is set to get even hotter.[40]

To understand the violent rhetoric of this report and its patently inaccurate claim that nothing had happened in the poetry arena for twenty years, we need to look at what happened since the conclusion of the Lushan Summit on June 11, 2006, and consider the differences implied by the Chinese terms *huodong*, which usually translates as "event" or "activity," and *shijian*, which can be translated as either "event" or "incident."

Crespi offers a definition of the former as "a collective pursuit of leisure, entertainment, socializing, networking, self-improvement, and/or publicity that frames a certain time, space, and participatory sphere outside the flow of everyday life and labor."[41] In general, a *huodong* can be reported on in a descriptive fashion and publicized beforehand as something out of the ordinary or "outside the flow," but unless something unexpected or shocking happens during the event, its newsworthiness is short-lived. Incidentization requires the collusion of poets and the media. First, poets must behave in a way that is of potential interest to the general public and usually do something more than just write and recite their poetry. Second, the media must describe and document these developments in a manner that demonstrates their significance as "unexpected events" in live scenes of poetry as well as their wider sociocultural relevance and spectacular appeal to Chinese audiences.

In the case of the Lushan Summit, the raw material for incidentization and documentation was the protracted debate triggered during the conference around the topic of petty literati poetry, which evolved into a renewed interest in the value to modern poetry of a transparent and committed approach to everyday reality. Shortly after the summit ended, a number of poets and critics who had been present in Changsha published essays on this topic, which circulated on the Internet between June and August 2006. Essays written in support of Tan Kexiu and his denouncement of petty literati poetry included Shen Haobo's "Can poets face up to the times?" (Shiren nengfou zhimian shidai?) and Tan's own definitive essay, "Petty literati poetry on the road to suicide" (Zisha lushang de xiao wenren shige). In his essay, Shen Haobo questioned contemporary poets' collective inability to respond to an era of great change in Chinese society and criticized their tendency to focus on the individual, art, and linguistic freedom. These are qualities that had been essential for the ideological liberation of modern poetry in the early post-Mao years, he conceded, but had since been overemphasized to the extent that poets were now neglecting the social realities in which they were situated. His comments took on strongly New Leftist overtones, concluding, "this era is constituted by all of us and our souls are naturally aware of everything around us, so why should we give up, hide in our studies, hide within language, and hide within art?"

Other poets disputed the importance most of Tan's supporters attached to poetic reflections on "the era" (*shidai*) and the implied dominance of social realism (life) over poetic technique (art). The former Lower Body poet Duoyu responded with a series of essays that included "Can poets face up to themselves?" (Shiren nengfou miandui ziji?) and the provocatively (and self-defeatingly) titled "I'll say it again: Poetry criticism is essentially talking to itself" (Zai lun shige piping jibenshang shi yi zhong zishuo zihua). He responded directly to Shen's essay by arguing that "facing up to the era" was precisely what Intellectual poets of the 1990s had been attempting to do by wrestling with difficult concepts such as "narrative" (*xushi*), "bearing [responsibility]" (*chengdan*), "conscience" (*liangxin*), and "integration [with the world]" (*jiegui*). His other point echoed Yu Jian's earlier commentary on the politics of poetry recitation and the ideological implications of enunciating on a public stage. The question of whether poets can face up to the era is, he argued, a false one: "this is a mode of thinking that faces outward, defining poets as people who face the streets, the square, the countryside, the masses, the lower rungs, the margins, incidents big and small, and who speak out [*fayan*] on all the trivialities of this world. This is a type of 'enunciation.' In today's era, poets do not have a microphone, so should they try to grab one? If they manage to grab hold of a microphone, can they guarantee that they will not lose their voices when trying to speak out?"[42]

Media reports mostly ignored the wider historical and ideological implications of this debate, instead tracing its origins to the Lushan Summit, more specifically to the late-night "book launch" for Tan Kexiu's *Trio*. On July 1, the Guangzhou newspaper *Yangcheng Evening News* published a series of articles titled "Sharp poets harshly criticize 'petty literati poetry'" (Xinrui shiren menglie pengji "xiao wenren shige"). The article consisted of a summary of the different viewpoints put forward during the summit followed by a full reproduction of the essays written by Tan, Shen, and others. On July 7, the cultural section of *Southern Weekend* offered support for Tan's side of the debate by publishing a brief biography of him alongside his poem "Empty" (Kongkongdangdang) from *Trio* and including a mention of the Lushan Summit. The August 23 *Hunan Daily News* article was one of the last published on this topic. Its language is clearly intended to appeal to a public fascination with conflict of any kind while perpetuating the misconception that nothing much has happened to Chinese poetry scenes since the mid-1980s, the last time most Chinese people over a certain age had any meaningful contact with modern poetry.

In concluding the debate, it suggested that what may be most important in reporting on poetry is not so much the question of who gains the discursive advantage in such interpoet debates or which poets might be declared the "winners" but *how* these discussions occur. "Any comments beneficial to poetry's progress should be respected," it told its readers; "What people need to remember is the process that has led to such deep thinking." Poetry activity, in other words, has an important role to play in contemporary China, if only as one example of culture's inroads into everyday life. Although it seemed unlikely that the specific processes of the Lushan Summit would be remembered for too many years to come, the media's coverage of face-to-face poetry events at the very least helps reinforce the historical value of contemporary poetry activity and strengthen public awareness that China's poets are far from a dying breed. Instead they are busy doing what poets have always done: meeting, drinking, gossiping, reciting, and debating every last detail of their art, regardless of who is listening.

CONCLUSION

Face-to-face poetry events are about far more than just poems, even though they are created in the name of poetry, they are dominated by poets, and many of their participants do appear to have poetry's best interests at heart. Events like the Lushan Summit are made possible through the cooperation of a variety of interest groups, including poets, commercial sponsors, local government institutions, and the media, many of whom are operating under the synergistic logic of the cultural economy and the knowledge that supporting Chinese culture and courting the media make good commercial and political sense. In particular, the promotion of local culture and businesses on a national stage is a central organizational tenet that makes it possible to bring together groups that otherwise seem to possess entirely disparate needs and ambitions.

While poets use poetry events as a way of networking with other poets and critics, familiarizing themselves with and helping create the latest developments within poetry scenes, and generally publicizing their poetry citizenship within a larger community of writers, non-poet individuals and groups responsible for the financial and logistical support of such events have quite different reasons for investing in their success. For local government officials and business figures, staging face-to-face poetry activity in one's city or province is seen as a way of contributing to China's creative cultural industries, which have been described as interconnected industry clusters that use creation and innovation to provide cultural experiences to the public, centered on the basic need to produce new cultural content and trade in intellectual property.[43]

Poetry events thus have a role to play in enhancing the image of the host city as a location of elite cultural activity and source of productive synergy among culture, businesses, and the state. Individuals like Tan Kexiu who occupy multiple roles within their cities of residence are instrumental in forging connections between culture and local business and political elites, producing spectacular cultural occasions that draw in members of the public and rally cultural producers around the theme of the event. In the case of the Lushan Famous Poets Summit, one central theme was "life," indicated by Lushan CEO Yue Gencheng's wish that poets might "walk into life and walk into Lushan Villas." This theme has clear overlaps with the concept of "life spectacles," an aestheticization of everyday life that is central to the government's construction of the middle class but that nonetheless contains ambiguities and unresolved tensions.[44] The Lushan real estate complex was clearly positioning itself as an appealing lifestyle choice for the middle class of Hunan province, in the hope that they would elect to live in a "refined poetic residence" in the outskirts of Changsha.

As a contingent event in the oral arena, the unfolding of the Lushan Summit brought the ambiguities and tensions of life spectacles to the fore in unpredictable ways, providing an opportunity for poets to reconsider what exactly it might mean to "walk into life" or, as it was rephrased in the subsequent debates, face up to the era. The criticism of petty literati poetry and praise for what Li Shaojun termed New Critical Realist Poetry harked back to longstanding debates over the importance of realism to modern Chinese literature and related questions of whether poetry should be written for poetry's sake (*wei shige de shige*) or for life's sake (*wei shenghuo de shige*).[45] The latter position has long been associated with the May Fourth goals of national renewal as well as with the submission of culture to politics in communist China. Mao's exhortations that writers and artists should "observe, experience, study, and analyze all the different kinds of people, all the classes and all the masses, all the vivid patterns of life and struggle"[46] became national law after 1949 and dictated the direction taken by Chinese culture for at least the next three decades. As Shen Haobo suggested in his contribution to the petty literati debate, much of the post-Mao history of modern Chinese poetry has been about trying to move beyond the ideological demand that literature "serve" the masses.

The reemergence of realism in the form of a more socially conscious, publicly oriented approach to culture encapsulated by concepts such as New Leftism, the lower rungs (*diceng*), and the "grassroots" must be understood in light of the Chinese party-state's decision in the Reform era to prioritize economic growth and market reforms over the welfare of the nation's rural and less affluent classes. As Ban Wang and Jie Lu propose, the New Left does not just demonstrate a preference for engaging aesthetically with everyday life issues among disadvantaged populations, as some of the poems recited at the Lushan Summit implied, but can be understood as a broad social movement that connects intellectuals and artists with grassroots representatives such as factory workers, migrant workers, peasants, and volunteers in resisting the deepening exploitation and oppression brought about by China's neoliberal model of economic development.[47] Marston Anderson's suggestion that "the real" be viewed as "an effect of the fiction" holds true for many New Leftist works of culture in the early twenty-first century: by not shying away from the less positive sides of life in contemporary China, they effectively create a new reality to counter the image of "harmonious society" put forward by the Chinese party-state.[48] In a similar vein, just as realist literature during the May Fourth era was a reaction to the "purposelessness" of entertainment fiction and the threat it posed to the authority of China's elite intellectual class,[49] a turn toward a more realist or New Leftist mode of writing within poetry scenes could also be understood as an attempt to reassert poetry's aura—and the authenticity of poets as cultural producers—during a time in which the relevance of modern poetry to contemporary society has been gravely brought into doubt.

There is a clear overlap between the kind of New Left–inspired grassroots or New Critical Realist Poetry advocated by individuals like Li Shaojun and Shen Haobo and the mode of documentary realism explored in the previous chapters of this book in connection to live-scene discourse. When applied to the creation of artistic works such as documentary films and poems, live scenes imply more than simply a focus on the contemporary spirit or here and now of cultural activity; they also represent, as Zhen Zhang suggests, a kind of "edgy realism" that attempts to capture the contingencies of everyday life. While poets have employed live-scene discourse to various ends such as asserting the value of the Internet as the most happening site of poetry activity and attempting to turn print publications into commercial spectacles that tap into the energy and authenticity of online and unofficial poetry production, underlying the documentary urge is a basic understanding that there exists some form of "reality" that can be encapsulated through presence and participation on the scene. This is also a historical mission fueled by poets' desire to master their own creative destinies and leave their mark on literary history.

The ambiguities and ambivalences that emerge in the face-to-face space of poetry are determined in part by the contemporary conjuncture of the early twenty-first century. Among its defining characteristics are the political and economic appropriations of culture indicated by the collusions between big businesses, local government organizations, and poetry activists. Another is the growing sense that cultural system reforms are serving to create a new entrepreneurial class of cultural elites who are able to navigate the complicated sociopolitical and economic relationships that exist between the various involved parties. These elites, while appearing to serve their chosen area of culture, also benefit both economically and personally from occupying multiple roles within Chinese society.

This new entrepreneurial class is also highly adept at manipulating the media to act in a marketing capacity for their cultural and business needs, while at the same time responding to the party-state's newfound understanding of the media as a public relations tool for shaping and negotiating ideological messages. Tan Kexiu, for example, maintains connections with the Hunan newspapers that helped publicize the Lushan Summit, writes several blogs and microblogs, preserves his poetry citizenship by publishing his writings in both official and unofficial poetry journals, and serves as editor for the second-channel publication *Tomorrow*. In this light, the criticisms that Tan's poems are not "artistic" enough, put forward in a stuffy hotel meeting room on the first night of the Lushan Summit, suggest a more deep-seated displeasure with the influence of a group of cultural brokers or entrepreneurs whose power over poetry scenes is not so much a result of literary talent or individual contributions to modern poetry development but due to their access to money and political savvy. Such suspicions of poetry scene corruption became even more apparent when modern poetry came into contact with the non-poetry-reading public on Internet forums and weibo, as we shall see in the instances in which verse went viral, explored in the final chapter.

CHAPTER 4

Poetry in the News

If
the return key on your keyboard
works particularly well
then
feel free to join us
if you
happen to also stutter
or suffer from chronic constipation
then
before long
you'll become
a poet above all others

—ANONYMOUS

If Hu Shi could see the current Chinese poetry arena with its "endless new ideas," "scattered pear blossom," and "streaking" would he sigh and consider himself unworthy? Then again, who cares about Hu Shi? Who cares about poetry? Who cares about Chnese poetry? Only when poetry becomes entertainment and gossip do the idle masses stop to say a quick "oh!" before remarking, "once there was Chinese soccer, now there is Chinese poetry."

—DING WEIFENG, "*Post-90 youth commemorates 90 years of New Poetry*" (90 hou shaonian jinian 90 nian xin shi)

In late 2010, a little-known poet and businessman by the name of Nie Shebo posted an article on his Sina blog titled "Dangdai shige 'shi' bing" (The "ten" diseases of contemporary poetry). In a disdainful tone and with copious use of quotation marks around words such as "poems" and "poets," Nie holds forth on the ailments plaguing Chinese poetry in the twenty-first century: flattery, lofty speech, high-speed composition, elitism, unproductive vagrancy (a result of staring at the wall and lacking inspiration), gossip-mongering, vulgarity, Occidentalism, the emperor's new clothes syndrome, and weakly resting upon one's laurels. "Good medicine that is bitter to the taste is beneficial for the sick, good words that are hard to hear are beneficial for conduct," he admonishes his readers. To win praise from the masses and produce works that will stand the test of time, all that China's sick poets need to do is "walk into life" and calmly and honestly produce poems.

Although such a text could easily be regarded as the embittered ramblings of a poet yet to make an impact on the national literary consciousness, Nie's essay can be classified within a burgeoning genre of poetry criticism in contemporary China: commentary on the failures of modern poetry, its textual and moral decrepitude, and its inevitable demise at some unspecified future date. These writings can be found in all the media spaces addressed in this book and come from all manner of sources, including poets, critics, scholars, government officials, educational institutions, cultural organizations, and members of the non-poetry-reading public. As a representative of the Hangzhou Youth Literature Center remarks in this chapter's second epigraph, modern poetry is all too often seen by the Chinese masses as yet another instance of national failure and a cause of humiliation on a par with the much-maligned national soccer team, only capable of drawing public attention when made the momentary target of scandal or gossip.

This final condition should, however, give us reason to pause. The fact that poetry is remotely capable of becoming a topic of national conversation is a sign that people are more emotionally invested in this literary genre in China than are people in many other countries: as I argued in the introduction, modern poetry is subject to the public's cultural memory as well to poets' conscious construction of literary history. In the United Kingdom, for example, a controversy over who is set to become the next poet laureate might make the culture section of one or two national papers but is much less likely to be known to people who do not actively seek out information about poetry.[1] Indeed, despite widespread discourse about its marginalization in the face of a dominant commercial culture, modern Chinese poetry is not just alive and kicking *within* poetry scenes (as the previous chapters have shown) but also sporadically finds itself the center of attention outside of them when published and discussed in the national media by people other than poets and critics.

In this final chapter I examine instances in which modern poetry has made the headlines and consider the implications of mass media representations of modern poetry for the construction of literary history and for the cultural memory of poetry. Poetry's continued vitality in the age of the Internet is, I suggest, related in unexpected ways to its potential for *viral*ity: the ability to be transmitted from person to person through multiple media spaces, to get people talking, and to arouse feverish debate about what constitutes a poem and who is worthy of the honorific "poet" in China today. It is in these debates around the genre of modern poetry that the outermost boundaries of poetry scenes can be found. Whether responding to a mass spoofing of a fellow poet, propagating a specific poetry "form" (*ti*), or asserting a set of universal poetic standards, the standpoints that poets and audiences adopt in media-led discussions and circulations of modern poetry are ultimately what indicate where they are positioned in relationship to poetry scenes.

The viral circulation of poetry differs in significant ways from the modes of publication and interaction explored in the previous three chapters, not least because it involves the mass participation of far more people than those active on poetry scenes. Texts do not go viral of their own accord or by entirely mechanical, nonhuman means; they circulate from screen to screen, server to server as a result of human intervention and the fact that they trigger some shared reaction within the psyches of its audience, whether it be humor, disdain, repulsion, pride, shock, or anger. One concept that is widely used in English-language discussions of viral culture on the Internet is "meme," which Richard Dawkins proposed—albeit in a speculative way[2]—might be considered a cultural equivalent to the gene, a unit of culture that propagates by making a jump from brain to brain in a process broadly comparable to imitation.[3] The sense of self-agency implied by the meme fails, however, to reflect the degree to which Internet users make conscious (or at least semiconscious) decisions to share a text, image, or attitude with others when they post a link on social media, copy it to forums, or send it by email. Rather than being inherent within the meme itself, meanings are constructed through the interactive process of consensus formation that accompanies widespread cultural circulation. As one meme-skeptic suggests, the story of the meme does not describe the spread of a social infection; the word "viral" is also misleading in this regard. Instead, it is a tale of "how an *understanding* is shared among *minds* that are forever situated in their own contexts, having their own interests, and working toward their own ends." To put it even more simply, it is brains that are active, not memes.[4]

In the instances in which modern Chinese poetry went viral, poems and poetry forms did not circulate as a result of the actions of poetry scene participants *or* as self-replicating agents but were instead passed around by netizens who found in them a source of amusement, contention, or emotional satisfaction. Non-poetry-reading publics have quite different expectations of poetry than do poets who consider themselves part of the poetry arena or participants in live scenes of poetry, in part because of the emphasis that the education system places on classical Chinese poetry and on lyrical and patriotic modern Chinese verse. As we have seen, a general tendency in poetry scenes over the past three decades has been to write colloquial poems about everyday topics. This tendency has been heightened by the development of the Internet into the primary space for the writing and circulation of modern poetry; as I suggested in Chapter 1, the Internet's mix of oral and textual modes of interaction has contributed to what Pettitt calls a "lettered quasi-orality," marked on the Chinese Internet by a chatty style of poetry that allows poets to respond to the contingencies of online interaction. Colloquial poetry has much in common with the general approach to writing across the Chinese Internet, which is notorious for propagating an ever-growing vocabulary of creative slang.[5] This has not, however, prevented many netizens from speaking up in criticism against the current state of modern Chinese poetry, which they expect to "rise above" the everyday language of ordinary people.

This theme of "rising above" is central for understanding the contrasting urges of opening up and gatekeeping that run throughout this book and are integrally related to the dynamics of the Internet, printed texts, and oral communication. The Internet, as indicated by the activities of the School of Rubbish, has opened up poetry scenes to less conventional groups and poetics, allowing those who would not usually have access to print publication to make use of the free-for-all environment of Internet forums and blogs to form their own poetry communities and, by challenging the authority of existing groups, create space for themselves within future literary histories. This also, however, involved establishing gatekeeping practices of their own, recognizing poets as members of the community only if they can demonstrate mastery of the group's interpretive strategies for (in this instance) "worshiping the low." Poets who experiment with second-channel print publishing have attempted to open modern poetry to the market by enhancing the commercial appeal of poetry anthologies as physical objects and by emphasizing the spectacular nature and contingencies of live scenes of poetry. Again, this also involved taking on a gatekeeping role within poetry scenes by deciding which poets and texts should be included in the anthologies and how their contents should be organized and presented. Organizers of face-to-face poetry events have also tried to open poetry to a wider audience by holding poetry recitals in public spaces like outdoor squares and city halls. Perhaps inevitably, these experiments ended up highlighting the differences in class, taste, and ideology between the people and institutions whose collaboration was required to stage the events. The Lushan Summit, for example, has been remembered not for the successful synergy among real estate, local government organizations, and modern poets but for the prolonged debate it sparked over the topic of petty literati poetry, a subject that divided poetry scenes into those who believe in the social responsibility of modern poets and those who resent the suggestion that they should focus on anything other than the quality of their poetic art.

Only in the case studies I explore in this chapter has modern poetry truly been opened up to people outside poetry scenes through mass participation in poetry writing, circulation, and critique. The latter of these activities suggests that non-poetry-reading audiences, like poets themselves, are keen to identify a set of standards for modern poetry in order for it to "rise above" other, less formal kinds of writing; in other words, they have a gatekeeping desire of their own, even if it is mostly expressed through skepticism and mockery. I look at three examples of verse going viral: the mass spoofing of the female poet Zhao Lihua in 2006, the propagation of "Baby Lamb form" poems that spoofed the official-cum-poet Che Yan'gao in 2010, and the Quake Poetry phenomenon of 2008. Each of these took place primarily on the Internet, which as Foley suggests is full of new species of cultural phenomena that cannot be explained by the technology of the tAgora and are characterized by high levels of contingency and rule-governed variability.[6] And like the Low Poetry that swept across poetry forums in the first half of the 2000s, all of the case studies explored below were tied to the public nature of online communication, in which anyone with an Internet connection can potentially get involved and be heard.

One major difference, however, and a key reason why the examples examined in this chapter went viral and the School of Rubbish did not, was that they took place in an era of more numerous "species" of Internet applications that facilitate far greater levels of interaction between people on the inside *and* the outside of cultural networks. While random netizens would have been unlikely to stumble upon

Internet forums like *Beijing Review* or *Poetry Rivers and Lakes* and decide to get involved in the conversation themselves, with the advent of blogging and weibo services in the latter half of the 2000s, each individual user exists as a single node within the same huge social network. Consequently users are likely to be exposed to content from complete strangers just by seeing the recommended blog posts of the day appear at the bottom of the page or by browsing posts forwarded by friends in their weibo feed. Blogging and weibo are also more commercial and entertainment-oriented than poetry forums, populated not just by "ordinary netizens" but also by Chinese (and non-Chinese) celebrities who use weibo to advance their careers, interact with fans, and spread news and messages.

Although there had been a number of Twitter-like Chinese microblogging services in existence in 2007 and 2008 (Fanfou, TaoTao, and others), it was not until the Sina Weibo service was launched in August 2009 that microblogging really began to break out in China. Its popularization was aided by the fact that ordinary citizens were increasingly taking to weibo to spread news and information among themselves, thereby outdoing the ability of the state-run news media to report in a timely and truthful manner on events of national significance.[7] By July 2013 there were more than 330 million weibo users in mainland China, accounting for 56 percent of China's overall Internet population.[8] The overwhelming majority uses domestic services, as Twitter cannot currently be used in China without a Virtual Private Network (VPN) or other censorship-circumventing software. Although weibo posts are limited to 140 characters, not only do 140 Chinese characters contain a lot more information than the same number of English words, users also make extensive use of websites that condense longer texts or collections of pictures into small images that can be attached to the weibo and then enlarged by readers, effectively allowing users to surpass the word limit. China's weibo platforms offer a variety of features designed to cater to local tastes, such as the ability to comment on the bottom of other people's weibo posts and the practice of message threading, whereby users can see all responses to a particular post listed in chronological order of appearance. As a result, Sina Weibo resembles a more sophisticated kind of Bulletin Board System and, like the BBS examined in Chapter 1, contains high levels of contention surrounding a wide range of issues.[9]

One phenomenon indelibly associated with the rise of weibo is the social behavior of "surrounding and observing" (*weiguan*), also translated as "the surrounding gaze." This concept can be traced back to Lu Xun's early twentieth-century depictions of the gawking crowds (*kanke*) who regard the suffering of their fellow Chinese people with a curious, even macabre indifference.[10] Hu Yong notes that a new politics of the surrounding gaze has emerged in the age of the Internet, in which *weiguan* takes on positive connotations as the most minimal form of public participation (*gonggong canyu*). Even when not actively creating their own content, Chinese Internet users become subjectively involved in the construction and deconstruction of texts and ideas simply by exercising their right to surround and observe. As Hu suggests, this can be considered a kind of "organized strength without organization" that rests on the "microforces" (*wei dongli*) that arise when the masses become voluntarily engaged in a particular discussion or incident.[11] Another phrase used in connection with Chinese social media is "homebody activism" (*zhai yundong*), which implies that people can come together to make a difference in society and culture simply by tapping away on keyboards at home. This was precisely what happened in the instances of verse going viral examined in this chapter.

The Zhao Lihua spoofing incident and the high levels of "surrounding and observing" it contained were experienced by many Chinese poets as an attack on the things that they hold dearest, not least the value of colloquial poetry and their right to decide as a community what constitutes "good" poetry. Similarly, the spoofing of Che Yan'gao inflicted additional damage upon the already declining reputation of the poetry arena, causing poets to shift their discursive allegiance further toward live scenes. Poets launched a number of activities in response to both incidents to show their support for fellow poets and, perhaps more important, to reassert their own gatekeeping authority over the genre of modern Chinese poetry. Quake Poetry, on the other hand, appeared to reflect a deep-rooted appreciation for poetry and a healing potential that traversed institutional and ideological lines. By demonstrating a capacity to unite the country during a time of exceptional national significance, Quake Poetry suggested not only that differences between who is or is not "on the scene" can be put aside in the interest of a greater cause but also that modern poetry is far from immune to the media's shaping influence on cultural memory and the political mobilization of grassroots culture.

POETRY SPOOFS

In September 2006, something rather strange and unexpected happened in the world of modern Chinese poetry. On September 11, someone using the web ID Redchuanbo left a post on the education-oriented forum *Liangquanqimei* (www.llqm.com) under the heading "The most sweat-inducing poems in history" (Shishang zui han de shi).[12] The poems contained in the post were all by the female poet Zhao Lihua, who, the poster revealed, had published poetry in official poetry journals such as *Poetry*, *People's Literature*, and *Poetry Selections* as well as in numerous poetry anthologies and individual collections, and had served as a judge for high-profile literary awards such as the Lu Xun Prize for Literature and the *Poetry Monthly* love poetry competition. The original poster concluded the short post with the exclamation, "It turns out / poetry / can also / be written / like this / !!!!!!!!" The post was forwarded to other Internet forums including www.MITBBS.com (Weiming kongjian), based in the United States, and the extremely popular Tsinghua University forum SMTH (Shuimu qinghua, www.newsmth.net). From that point on the post quickly went viral, with thousands of people reposting it to forums and blogs across the Chinese web, including hugely popular web portals like Sina, Sohu, Tianya, and QQ.

The first poem included in the original post by Redchuanbo, and one still widely cited as an example of contemporary poets plumbing the depths of poetic creation, was titled "Alone in Tennessee" (Yi ge ren lai dao Tiannaxi) and reads as follows: "Without a shadow of a doubt / my pancakes / are the best / in the entire world."[13] Forum participants responded with bemusement and outrage that this type of writing could be considered a "poem."[14] Netizens also started to compose their own spoof versions of Zhao's poems, all written using simple colloquial language, short lines, and mundane subject matter. A typical example read: "If / the return key on your keyboard / works particularly well / then / feel free to join us / if you / happen to also stutter / or suffer from chronic constipation / then / before long / you'll become / a poet above all others"—with the character wet (*shi*) standing in as a lewd homophone for the *shi* in poet (*shiren*).[15] Another, titled "Sorrow" (Youchou), lamented, "Professor Zhao Lihua / in America / is a famous poet / but me / I'm alone in sorrow." A website (now defunct), www.zhaolihua.com, was created on September 14 to act as a depository for Zhao's poetry, spoof poems, news articles, and netizens' comments and was advertised in news articles and blog posts across the Internet.[16] One enterprising netizen even set Zhao's poem "Alone in Tennessee" to music in the style of a revolutionary military song and shared it on video-streaming websites.[17]

Those who were not parodying Zhao's poetic style were busy critiquing it, as it seemed tens of thousands of otherwise poetically apathetic Chinese people had suddenly turned into armchair poetry critics. Zhao's literary credentials proved a prominent source of consternation, in particular her membership of the China Writers' Association and widely stated identity as a "top-ranked national author" (*guojia yiji zuojia*). Her impressive biography was reproduced alongside the most parodied of Zhao's poems, as if to demonstrate how very little talent can get you a long way. Hundreds of thousands of netizens expressed collective horror at what had happened to their country's poetic tradition, often in the form of poems composed using the same split-line style of poetry now being referred to, in a pun on Zhao Lihua's name, as "Pear Blossom form" (*lihua ti*—the *lihua* in Zhao's name actually translates as "beautiful China"). One poem acerbically described the collective realization that had resulted from reading Zhao's works: "poetry is not dead / Lihua taught me using her flowery [*huali*] verse / that I can write poetry too."[18] The criticisms soon extended to the state of the literary arena as a whole, with many assuming that Zhao must have used underhanded means to find her way into the Writers' Association, as she could not possibly have done so on the basis of her poetry.

The debate moved from the Internet to the print media, with almost every national newspaper in China reporting on what had by now turned into a large-scale "spoofing incident" and reproducing some of the most amusing Pear Blossom poems. Even party-run newspapers like the *People's Daily* carried write-ups of the affair. Celebrities and well-known bloggers including Han Han were quick to jump on the bandwagon, taking the opportunity to launch a full-blown condemnation of the state of modern Chinese poetry and the cliquishness and corruption of the poetry arena. Han's provocative essay "How come modern poetry and poets still exist?" and two accompanying pieces titled "Poets are anxious, have stopped writing poetry" (Shiren ji le, bu xie shi le) and "Firmly support poets turning hooliganism into a school" (Jianjue zhichi shiren ba liumang shuacheng yizhong liupai) were reproduced in print newspapers and across the Internet. As one of China's most famous bloggers with an active following of several million readers and thus an important opinion leader (*yijian lingxiu*) in China, Han played a powerful role in escalating the criticisms aimed at poets. His most famous comment was his sarcastic and often-repeated suggestion that "the only technique that modern poets need to master is how to hit the enter key." It was not long before friends and colleagues of Zhao Lihua began to fight back on her behalf as well as the behalf of contemporary Chinese poetry by attesting to the value of her writing, to her integrity, and to the numerous achievements of living poets. Among them was Shen Haobo. The fierce retorts to Han that Shen posted on his blog attracted tens of thousands of hits and thousands of comments and prompted the web portal Sina to invite him and Zhao Lihua (who had never met in person) to respond to the spoofing and the subsequent debate in a face-to-face studio chat that was streamed live over the Internet.[19]

Despite the fact that Zhao's credentials and publishing history had led netizens to associate her with government-sponsored literary activity and the elitist connotations of the poetry arena, the poets who sprang to her defense were mostly inhabitants of the live scenes that have been the focus of this book: writers for whom Internet forums, unofficial poetry journals and second-channel anthologies, and face-to-face poetry events constitute the primary spaces of poetic and social interaction. On the evening of September 30, the Third Generation poet Yang Li organized a poetry recital in Zhao's honor, held in Beijing's Disanji Bookstore under the slogan "Supporting Zhao Lihua and defending poetry" (*liting Zhao Lihua, baowei shige*). After a number of conventional readings, the poet and performance artist Su Feishu took to the stage and proceeded to strip completely naked in front of a gob-smacked audience before attempting to recite his poetry. The electricity in the bookstore was quickly cut, the audience hurried away, and the event's organizers were accosted by security guards; Su himself was later arrested and detained for ten days in police custody.[20]

This event, which was "incidentized" in the media as the Naked Recital Incident or Naked Poetry Incident—hence the reference to "streaking" (*luoben*) in the second epigraph to this chapter—further escalated media coverage of the Zhao Lihua spoofing. The recital even found itself featured on the evening news when Beijing TV aired a lengthy report that included several spoof poems, an overview of the current publishing situation for contemporary poetry, and carefully edited footage of Su's naked recital.[21] Another twist occurred with the release on the same day of a website, www.dopoem.com, which automatically produces "modern poems" according to preprogrammed sentence structures when a few key words are entered by the "poet." According to news reports, over one hundred fifty thousand spoof poems were created this way within just a few days.[22] Netizens and the media alike took this development as further proof, as if it were needed, that *anyone* can write poetry these days—even machines.

In October 2006, roughly a month after the incident began, an academic conference was convened in Beijing's National Museum of Modern Chinese Literature (Zhongguo Xiandai Wenxueguan) to analyze the Zhao Lihua affair, titled "Overthrow! A Forum on Chinese Poetic Construction in the Context of Globalization and the Poetry of Zhao Lihua" (Dianfu! Quanqiuhua yujing xia de hanyu shige de jiangou ji Zhao Lihua shige yantaohui). It was jointly organized by a number of Beijing-based poets, sponsored by the semi-official poetry journal *Poetry Monthly: Second Half of the Month* (Shige yuekan: Xia ban yue), the unofficial literary journal *Bole*, and the web portal *Leisure Park* (Lequyuan), and was attended by journalists from national newspapers and television channels including Beijing TV, CCTV, and Hong Kong's Phoenix TV, thus guaranteeing that it would be turned into a small-scale media event in its own right. Zhao Lihua herself was present, making her first public appearance since the incident began. The online spoofing and media coverage had turned Zhao into an overnight celebrity, adding her to the extremely short list of contemporary poets known to the average non-poetry-reading Chinese citizen and in many cases making her the only name that people could think of when the topic of poetry came up in conversation.

Zhao had done her best throughout the autumn of 2006 to defend herself to the public, posting lengthy articles and poetry selections on several newly opened blogs to explain that the parodied poems had been written during an earlier period of literary experimentation and were not at all representative of her overall style and that some of those most widely reproduced under her name (including a witty poem about flowery underpants) had not even been her own work. In a four-point essay titled "What I want to say" (Wo yao shuo de hua) that she posted on September 15, Zhao laid out her personal standards for good poetry and thoughts on the nature of spoofing and offered some names of contemporary poets she admired, adding that they are all "currently on contemporary live scenes of poetry." In an interview with Guangzhou's *Yangcheng Evening News*, she expressed hope that her writings would ultimately be judged by history, not by the spoofing activities of people today, and that poetic quality was far more important than "attending meetings, taking part in polemics, flirting online, holding forums, commissioning poetry reviews, doing interviews, raising flags, making demands, joining 'schools,' judging prizes, cajoling sinologists, and scrambling up to be a dignified monarch of the poetry arena."[23] Nonetheless, the unprecedented media attention showered upon contemporary poetry in 2006 seemed to have made the public aware for the first time that this was more or less what poets had been busying themselves with in recent years.

BABY LAMB FORM POEMS

The Zhao Lihua incident set the stage for several later public "discoveries" of contemporary poetry, all of which were accompanied by the dual realization that, first, poetry is nothing like as hard to write as most people had previously thought, and second, that there exists a whole world of poetry activities and writing styles to which most people had been completely oblivious. Most later incidents have taken place on weibo, which offers even more direct and rapid circulation of texts and opinions than the blogs and forums that were predominantly used in the spoofing of Zhao. One began at 7:00 pm on October 19, 2010, when the results of the Lu Xun Prize for Literature were announced online, which included the 2009 poetry collection *Yearning for Warmth* (Xiangwang wennuan) by the Wuhan poet Che Yan'gao. At 11:16 pm, a man named Chen Weijian, whose Sina blog states him to be a Zhejiang native and editor in chief of the magazine *Popular Song*, updated his Sina Weibo with a post that read: "After 'Pear Blossom form' 'Baby Lamb form'? Behold the winner of the poetry section of the fifth Lu Xun Prize for Literature, Wuhan City Party Secretary Che Yan'gao's poem 'Xu Fan': 'Xu Fan's beauty is a pure woman's beauty / I've always wanted to meet her but my wish has not yet come true / actually when I was young we lived very close / just a wall separated us / she lived on that side of the Western commercial district racetrack, and my house / was on this side of the Western commercial district racetrack / later she became famous / and happily married / making films which won her acclaim and filled many seats."[24] Several factors led to Chen's Weibo post attracting attention: the mention of an official literary prize named after

China's most canonical modern literary figure; the fact that the winner was also a high-level government official; and the poem itself, not only composed using the kind of casual, colloquial style that had brought notoriety to Zhao Lihua but also featuring a well-known actress from Wuhan. Most crucially, Chen had coined the perfect tagline with which to critique Che's poetry: "Baby Lamb form" (*yanggao ti*), a play on two characters of Che's name, *yan* and *gao*.

Chen's original weibo was forwarded several thousand times and attracted over two thousand comments; many more weibo users forwarded other people's forwards, and very quickly Che's "Baby Lamb form" had gone viral. Chen followed up eight minutes later with another post that predicted, "Che Yan'gao's 'Baby Lamb form' poetry will become popular. [Here is] 'Liu Yifei': 'I met Liu Yifei long ago, when she was very young / in the third grade at elementary school / one time she and my daughter took to the stage together / the camera in my hand recorded a little Indian girl / naturally beautiful, hands pressed together, rocking in a lotus pose / the wind followed her, taking with it a hall full of applause / at the time I said to the school principal: Poyang Street Elementary School will be proud / when this child grows up / she'll be an international star for sure."[25]

Like "Xu Fan," this celebrity-themed poem about the Hubei-born actress and singer Liu Yifei elicited netizens' dismay that such writing could be called "a poem" and that its author was deemed worthy of a national literary award, as well as discussion of Che's "dubious" identity as a government official. Many weibo comments dripped with sarcasm, using Internet slang like "magical horses are all floating clouds" (*shenma dou shi fuyun*), a pun-like expression meaning "it's all nonsense," or "judges, your moms are calling you home to study the *Book of Songs*," a play on the popular 2009 phrase "Jia Junpeng, your mom's calling you home for dinner" (*Jia Junpeng, ni ma han ni huijia chifan*).[26] More significant for the spread of Baby Lamb form poetry, many commentators offered spoof versions of Che's poems composed using almost identical sentence structures. One read: "Party Secretary Che's revoltingness is a fake man's revoltingness / I've always wanted to slap him but my great wish has not yet come true [. . .] now he has become popular / and the controversy has begun / he wrote many revolting crappy poems that somehow won prizes / I feel revolted by his poem 'Xu Fan' / in reality he is infatuated with Xu Fan / outside of his dreams he is infatuated with the Xu Fan within his poems." The impetus behind many of these spoof poems was an indignation that not only was *this* the current state of Chinese poetry but that the winner of an official literary prize was, himself, a government official. Cries of corruption rang out across the Internet, and Che was obliged to defend himself in the national media. He did so by making claims reminiscent of those of Zhao Lihua four years previously: the poems being circulated online were not representative of his work and had been part of a literary experiment with colloquial writing; his success in the competition had absolutely nothing to do with his being an official; and he is in fact extremely serious about literature, dedicating the hours between 5:00 and 7:40 each morning to his writing.[27]

Unlike the Zhao Lihua affair, the Baby Lamb form incident did not lead to a concerted effort by other poets to defend the target of the spoofing. This was in part because, unlike Zhao, Che is not a participant in the live scenes of poetry examined in this book, and thus has fewer well-known poet friends, and in part because the man who started the spoofing, Chen Weijian, is also a poet with a distrust of China's official literary institutions. Media reports did, however, manage to elicit a few responses from well-known contemporary writers. In a news article, Chun Sue admitted that she actually quite liked Che's poems and found them "very direct and very modern." After being bombarded with interview requests, Zhao Lihua offered an open response to the media on her blog, stating, "the Lu Xun Prize for Literature has dog fart all to do with Lu Xun" and accusing people who come up with phrases like "Pear Blossom form" and "Baby Lamb form" of being "stupid cunts" (*shabi*).[28] The Beijing writer Yan Yanwen argued that the incident was set to be the "death certificate" for the Lu Xun Prize for Literature and pointed to further evidence that China's official literary institutions are corrupt, including the fact that the Lu Xun judges had acknowledged Che's status as a government official in their statement explaining why they awarded him the poetry prize ("it is hard to come by a tough-minded City Party Secretary with such a soft poetic heart").[29] Where they did occur, interventions from poets and writers only reinforced the cultural significance of the "Baby Lamb form" spoofing incident, ensuring that it was imprinted more deeply in the minds of China's media consumers.

The viral circulation of Pear Blossom and Baby Lamb form poetry can be attributed to the popularity of interactive forms of online media such as forums, blogs, and weibo and to the social functions and behaviors these media and poetry forms allowed. Foremost among these social behaviors is the practice of spoofing. The subversive potential of spoofing as practiced on the Chinese Internet encompasses three aspects: problematizing individual authorship by "remixing" existing creative works, destabilizing the hierarchical status quo of Chinese media by relying upon grassroots cultural production, and an iconoclastic attitude toward mainstream and official grand narratives.[30] Each of these can be observed in the poetry form spoofings of Zhao Lihua and Che Yan'gao, although, as we have begun to see, media institutions as well as Chinese netizens also played a role in their propagation, suggesting that their significance transcended grassroots concerns.

An important issue to consider is precisely who or what was being spoofed in each instance and why. In the case of Zhao Lihua and Pear Blossom form poetry, the answer seems clear: it was the poet herself, her poetry credentials, and the literary organizations to which she belongs that were the primary objects of ridicule, as well as the Chinese "poetry arena" as an abstract whole whose many publications, prizes, and gatekeeping mechanisms were seen as offering far from sufficient confirmation of a poet's true literary abilities. Many of the critiques of Zhao and her colloquial style of poetry had the air of character assassination, labeling her the "Lotus of the Poetry Arena" (Shitan furong), which referred to the infamous Internet personality Shi Hengxia, more commonly known by her nickname Sister Lotus or Sister Hibiscus (Furong jiejie).[31] This analogy implied that Zhao was out of touch with the limits of her poetic abilities and in possession of an inflated ego like that of Sister Lotus. Moreover, because much of the fuss over Sister Lotus had centered on her less-than-perfect physical appearance, the comparison also took on chauvinistic overtones, as if implying that female poets are meant be judged on their looks as much as their poems.

The Baby Lamb form spoofs had similar implications insofar as it made the poet Che Yan'gao himself the target of the spoofing efforts, as well as his status as a government official and the assumed corruption within the literary arena that led to his being recognized by the Lu Xun Prize for Literature. Accusations that he lacked poetic talent were soon subsumed by widespread disgust over his day job. Che's inclusion in the list of winners apparently left some commentators livid with anger: one contributor to the popular Internet forum *Mop* (Maopu) posted a series of condemnations that each ended with a string of exclamation or question marks in a popular style of online writing known as "roaring form" (*paoxiao ti*). They included "Seize corrupt official poets!!!! Bring justice to those who give gifts of dirty money and accept bribes, restore purity to the Lu Xun prize, and restore truth to all under heaven!!!!!!"[32] Evidently the spoofing of Che and the Baby Lamb form poems had touched a deeper nerve among China's Internet population, who saw this as another instance of official abuses of power and privilege in contemporary society on par with the infamous "my dad is Li Gang" (*wo ba shi Li Gang*) incident that had gone viral on the Internet around the same time.[33]

A major factor in the circulation of the Pear Blossom and Baby Lamb forms was the delight with which netizens participated in the mass critiques of Zhao Lihua's and Che Yan'gao's poetry. As Zhao herself surmised in the Sina-hosted online chat on October 10, 2006, the underlying reason for the attacks on her poems was not that they were badly written or that people did not understand them but simply that most readers had not come into contact with contemporary poetry before—and if they had, had rarely been given the opportunity to criticize it and its authors with such abandon. From one perspective, then, netizens' glee in deriding Zhao's and Che's poetry could be seen as a grassroots seizure of discursive power from the country's literary elite, an assumption of gatekeeping authority to judge for themselves what makes "good" poetry rather than leaving the task of evaluation and canonization to critics, schools, universities, and official literary institutions. But from another angle, the spoofs were less an indication of serious literary engagement than of the public's communal knee-jerk reaction to discovering poems that looked and sounded completely unlike anything they had read or studied. One poet observed that most of those involved in the spoofing were students ranging from middle school to undergraduate age who had been exposed only to classical Chinese poetry and a very limited number of modern poems through their formal education.[34] Their strong and at times vicious reaction to Zhao's poetry was thus not born of a hatred of modern poetry per se but was, as Shen Haobo argued, a result of being confronted with writings that did not meet their more classically and lyrically oriented expectations of poetry. China is after all a "poetry nation" (*shiguo*), Shen remarked, and so it would stand to reason that the Chinese public should possess a "deep love" for this literary genre.

EARTHQUAKE POETRY

In May 2008, sandwiched between the Zhao Lihua incident and the spoofing of Che Yan'gao, China experienced yet another mass poetry movement that hit the news headlines, suggesting that Shen's comments about the Chinese people's "deep love" for poetry were not so misplaced. This time the impetus was not the discovery of a new "form" of poetry or the suspicion of corruption in the literary arena but a far more tangible event: the May 12, 2008, Sichuan Earthquake. Centered on the county of Wenchuan, the earthquake was felt as far away as Beijing and Shanghai and took the lives of around sixty-nine thousand people, leaving many millions more injured, bereaved, and homeless. Starting the day after the quake hit, people began to post original poems on Internet forums and blogs as a way of processing their shock and grief. Poems were composed in both modern and classical styles by well-known poets who had long been active in China's poetry scenes, as well as by "ordinary netizens" who were reported to have written not a single poem in their entire lives. Many of their poems went viral, forwarded and reposted hundreds and thousands of times across the Internet and sent from person to person using text messages and email.[35]

The poems that received the warmest reception online were reproduced in newspapers and magazines, published in print anthologies, recited on television and radio, and performed at poetry recitals and charity events. Some of those were then adapted into multimedia versions combining words, music, images, and video, which were also circulated widely through the Internet and on television. Several titles were assigned to this mass outpouring of poetry, including Wenchuan Poetry (Wenchuan shige), Quake-Resistance Poetry (Kang zhen shi), and simply Quake Poetry (Dizhen shi). It became one of China's most talked-about cultural phenomena of 2008, extensively reported on by the news media and analyzed at length by poets and critics. Like the Zhao Lihua incident, Quake Poetry can be considered one of the defining incidents in Chinese poetry in the first decade of the new millennium, whose implications for the effects of the media on modern Chinese poetry are profound.

News articles initially focused on the diversity and numbers of people writing poetry in response to the earthquake and the emotional effects of these poems, "consoling those who lost relatives in the disaster, inspiring those helping in rescue efforts, and eulogizing the fortitude shown by Chinese people in times of great calamity."[36]

Some exclaimed, "The entire population is writing poetry!" (*quanmin xieshi*), a phrase that had been used during the mass spoofing of Zhao Lihua; others used the more formal designation Earthquake Poetry Transcriptions (Dizhen shichao). Whereas Quake Resistance Poetry implies a unifying narrative of Chinese people coming together to resist the disaster as if fighting a common enemy, this latter designation resonates instead with mass literary movements like the Tiananmen Poetry (Tiananmen shichao) of 1976. The word "transcriptions" (*chao*) insinuates that the poems appearing in print were simply textual versions of works that had already been spreading from person to person through other media spaces. Several news articles directly compared Quake Poetry to Tiananmen Poetry, taking both as evidence of poetry's continued hold over the Chinese national consciousness and hinting at an analogy between the two events regarding the power of the public to forge their own emotional and cultural responses to national events.

While the netizen authors of Quake Poetry remained mostly anonymous throughout the publication and reception of their poems, poetry scene participants published earthquake-themed poems using their real names, thereby identifying themselves as poet-citizens of varying levels of renown. The following poem was posted on May 24, 2008, on *Poetry Rivers and Lakes*. It was written by Gu He and is titled "After the Earthquake Was Over, I Admit" (Dizhen guo hou, wo chengren). The final section reads as follows:

> I admit
> I didn't cry
> I didn't donate
> I didn't pray either
> all that time I was worrying about getting that job
> all that time thinking about how to chat up the girl who works in the
>   supermarket
> and how to earn enough cash to buy that new complete set of works by
>   Borges
> but I'm still a person too

The poem requires little by way of interpretation: the narrator admits having put quotidian concerns before grief or philanthropy yet refuses to believe this behavior makes him less of a human being. In general, online forums like *Poetry Rivers and Lakes* witnessed a wider range of emotional, intellectual, and verbal responses to the earthquake than those evident in netizen-penned poems, including anger, provocation, profanity, and black humor. Some poets objected outright to the existence of Quake Poetry, arguing that a more natural reaction to the tragedy would be creative silence. Zhou Zan, for example, pointed out that most Quake Poetry had unconsciously adopted a Scar Literature (*shanghen wenxue*) style, implying it had placed knee-jerk emotional catharsis before literary sophistication and disagreed with claims that the earthquake had instigated a "poetry fever."[37] Xie Youshun remarked that as time passes and the earthquake is forgotten, poetry, too, will probably "return to its original state," and thus Quake Poetry cannot be considered evidence of a widespread poetic renaissance.[38]

Despite such voices of caution, the overall response to the earthquake among Chinese poetry scenes was one of support, and poets expressed hope that their work could aid in fund-raising movements and console the people of China.[39] Many poetry critics wrote favorably of the phenomenon, equating it with grassroots poetry and seeing it as evidence of a newly liberal atmosphere in mainland China regarding poets' freedom to respond to events of national significance. Quake Poetry not only appeared to confirm the significance of poetry as an art form in modern China but also provided poets with unexpected print publishing opportunities and invigorated discussions about the relationship between poetry and "the era" along similar lines to the petty literati debate of 2006. Although there was a significant level of disagreement among poets and critics regarding the impact of Quake Poetry on the development of modern Chinese poetics, most observers were able to describe the phenomenon in a way that affirmed their preexisting beliefs about the status and ideal role of modern poetry in Chinese society and how poets must "face up to" contemporary events.

For the most part, however, it was poems produced by members of the non-poetry-reading public, not by recognized poets, that went viral in May 2008. One poem in particular stands out as having spread rapidly across the Internet as well as via television, radio, print publications, and face-to-face events. It is titled "Child, Quickly Grab Hold of Mama's Hand" (Haizi, kuai zhua jin mama de shou) and in most versions the heading is followed by the additional clause "composed for the children who died in the Wenchuan earthquake" and the date of composition: May 13, 2008. There are many variations of this poem in existence, but most linear text versions read more or less as follows:

Child, quickly
grab hold of Mama's hand
the path to heaven
is too dark
Mama's afraid
you'll bump your head
quickly
grab hold of Mama's hand
let Mama join you on your way
Mama
is afraid
the path to heaven
is too dark
I can't see your hand
since the fallen walls
stole away the sunlight
I'll never again see
your tender eyes
child
go now
the road ahead
has no more sadness
no more unfinished textbooks
or Papa's fists
you must remember
how Papa and I look
so in the next life we can be together again
Mama
don't worry
the path to heaven is a little crowded
there are lots of classmates and friends
we're saying
don't cry
every child's mama is our mama
every child is Mama's child
in these days without me
give your love to those living children
Mama
don't cry
your tears won't light up
our path
let us, alone,
slowly take our leave
Mama
I'll remember how you and Papa look
I'll remember our promise
in the next life we'll be together again

Even in its original form as a linear text poem written in short lines with a rhyme scheme based around the word "hand" (*shou*), it is easy to see why this poem was a hit. Its simple, rhythmic style makes it conducive to memorization and recitation, as does the use of two different voices to express the perspectives of mother and child. The tone is sad, a little sentimental, but ultimately reassuring, with the promise of reunification in the next life. The poem's virality could be gauged by its publication in nearly one hundred newspapers and magazines, its reproduction on thousands of blogs, forums, and other websites, its inclusion in most officially published anthologies of Quake Poetry, and its subsequent metamorphosis into multimedia poems. Certain lines of the poem sound familiar to the point of cliché. An online search revealed that the exact words of the final line, "in the next life we'll be together again," had featured in the lyrics to a 1993 pop song by the Taiwanese singer Su Rui titled "Holding Hands" (Qianshou).[40]

The viral circulation of "Child" spurred a communal effort among netizens to discover the author of the poem, a process known in Internet slang as a "human flesh search" (*renrou sousuo*). This quest suggested that although the multiple variations and viral circulation of the poem reflected a media dynamic that has more in common with the arena of oral tradition, many audiences approached Quake Poetry through the lens of the textual arena, assuming it to be subject to single authorship, fixity, and the propriety nature of texts. At least six people came forward to claim they had written the poem, but after further investigation most journalists and critics concluded that the true author was a twenty-four-year-old man from Shandong province named Su Shansheng, who was revealed to have not completed his high school education and who claimed to have written only three poems in his entire life.[41] Some netizens suspected that Su was lying about having written the poem and expressed disgust that anyone should use "fake sentiment" to exploit the tragedy and become a celebrity. Their resentment may have been fueled by Su's surprise revelation that "Child" was, itself, a variation on an earlier poem he had written for a girlfriend who had passed away titled "Darling, Quickly Grab Hold of My Hand" (Qin'ai de, kuai zhua jin wo de shou), which he posted on his Sina blog in December 2005.[42]

Within the first few days of being posted online on May 13, 2008, "Child, Quickly Grab Hold of Mama's Hand" had been adapted into multimedia versions that were uploaded to the Internet and broadcast on television. Most versions consisted of a combination of words, music, sound, and images in a powerful embodiment of what Foley calls "variation within limits" that is a defining characteristic of culture produced within the oAgora and eAgora.[43] In a three-day period of searching online I identified twenty distinct multimedia variations of the text, some referred to as poems, some as songs, some as videos, and some as music videos or MVs. Although it is not always clear where they were first posted or through which medium they first circulated, all were uploaded online in mp4 or flash video (.flv) format onto video-sharing websites including YouTube, 56.com, Youku, Sina, and Sohu.

The most common type of adaptation of "Child" is centered on a spoken recital of the poem and features some combination of journalistic photographs of the destruction caused by the earthquake, background music, and subtitles carrying the text of the poem. One version features the voice of a female narrator accompanied by somber orchestral music that eventually swells into the pop song "[We Don't] Only Love by Halves" (Cai ai dao yiban) by a Taiwanese girl group. The photographs are explicit, including close-up images of dead bodies and parental grief. Reproduced countless times in newspapers, on television, and online in the weeks after the earthquake hit, images such as these contributed to what some psychologists term "flashbulb memories": vivid, commonly shared memories created through the media that over time induce in their viewers a powerful sense of having been present for a historically significant event.[44] By appearing in almost all the multimedia adaptations of "Child, Quickly Grab Hold of Mama's Hand," the photos formed a recurring visual theme and ensured that the words of the poem would forever be associated with the physical spectacle of the earthquake and the ensuing public grief.

A second type of adaptation is one in which the poem is sung to a melody rather than recited. I identified two different pop song variations of the poem and the score for one other musical adaptation. Another type of adaptation can be found in videos recorded from television broadcasts of recited and musical versions of the poem, copied from television to computer (sometimes via a cell phone camera pointed at the screen) and then uploaded onto the Internet. One video is a clip of the poem being read aloud on a Dragon TV news program hosted by media celebrity Yu Dan and the presenter Luo Xin. The video begins with an emotional Yu discussing the aftermath of the earthquake and her personal reaction to the tragedy. A minute in, Luo mentions that he and Yu recently received a text message containing the poem "Child, Quickly Grab Hold of Mama's Hand." He proceeds to take out his cell phone, search for the poem, and recite it live on air. The camera zooms in for a close-up of Yu Dan's face, tears rolling down her cheeks. By the end both presenters are crying, and the remainder of the video shows them lamenting their inability to contribute toward earthquake relief efforts beyond the sum of money they had already donated.[45]

Yet another multimedia variation can be found in commercially produced music videos of the poem. One, produced in June 2008, features a group of fifty Hong Kong singers recording the more widespread song version composed by Wu Mengqi. It begins like many multimedia versions with a photograph of a clock with its hands permanently stuck at 2:28 pm, the precise time the earthquake hit. Smoke rises from the bottom of the screen as the image fades out and then in again to video footage of the singers in a recording studio, hands over headphones, singing into their microphones as the "lyrics" scroll across the bottom of the screen. A pared-down version of this arrangement was performed live at the eleventh anniversary celebrations of Hong Kong's handover to the PRC on June 30, 2008, broadcast on TVB Jade.[46] Its appearance on such a politically symbolic stage suggested that the poem had by this point been fully appropriated by Chinese government authorities, which were using it to propagate a key narrative about the unity of the Chinese people's response to a national catastrophe. While introducing the performance, the TVB Jade presenters emphasized the anonymity of the poem's author (even though Su Shansheng had long been identified as the author in the mainland Chinese media), in doing so sending an implicit message about the spontaneity of popular grief that, in China, finds expression through the genre of poetry. That the anniversary celebrations featured a musical adaptation of "Child" also seemed to reflect the Chinese government's desire to encourage the emerging concept of "cultural China," in which events that affect the well-being of Chinese people are felt as keenly in China's Special Administrative Regions, Taiwan, and overseas Chinese communities as they are within the PRC.

The circulation and appropriation of netizen-penned spoof poems and Quake Poetry by the media (and by extension the Chinese party-state whose ideological guidelines the media must follow) has its own historical precedent. From the "going to the people" (*dao minjian qu*) movement of the 1910s and 1920s, through Mao's demands that artists and writers adapt folk culture to serve the needs of the communist revolution, to the Multimillion Poem Movement of the Great Leap Forward, and even down to the inclusion of traditional folk songs on popular TV shows such as *Super Girl* (Chaoji nüsheng) in 2004–6, Chinese intellectuals, the media, and the state have time and again looked to ordinary people for creative inspiration and ideological support.[47] "Web friends" (*wangyou*) and "netizens" (*wangmin*) could be seen as the latest terms to join a lexicon that includes many other words and phrases such as "among the people," "popular" or "folk" (*minjian*, *pingmin*, or *minzhong*), "mass" or "the masses" (*qunzhong* or *dazhong*), and, of course, "the People" (*renmin*).

The frequent broadcasting of video and song versions of "Child, Quickly Grab Hold of Mama's Hand" on national television in May and June 2008 implied that the Chinese party-state was well aware of the gains to be had in encouraging this form of emotional catharsis. The repeated images of familial grief, of "Grandpa" Wen Jiabao visiting the affected earthquake zone, and of organized charity events that were heavily featured in Quake Poetry poem-videos bolstered an image of unity and national strength that the CCP has been intent on promoting since the 1980s. Cultural appropriation of this kind is a key part of the ruling elite's strategy to reclaim ideological legitimacy in the eyes of the Chinese public during the shift from a socialist to a capitalist political and economic system and reflects the party-state's reconfiguration of the media as a part of the overarching category of culture, used more for image management than for purely propagandistic purposes.[48] Although the authorities later cracked down on activists' attempts to investigate the number of deaths caused by the earthquake and the reasons for the collapse of so many schools, in the immediate aftermath of the earthquake, netizen-produced culture like the poem "Child" was adopted and circulated in such a way as to cast it in support of the government's nation-building goals.

On one level, then, Quake Poetry—unlike the spoofing of Zhao Lihua—was notable for demonstrating a high degree of creative consensus and emotional cohesion among its producers and consumers (or "prosumers"), suggesting not just a convergence of media channels but also a level of synergy between social groups and cultural and political institutions. Like all the instances of verse going viral that I have examined, it highlighted the speed with which the Internet, and interactive social media in particular, can enable poems to reach the screens and minds of people across the country and elsewhere in the world. Quake Poetry also acquired patriotic overtones, suggesting a "mutually reinforcing relationship" between modern Chinese poetry and China's official discourse of nationalism, which Yuezhi Zhao argues aims to reshape individuals in China's increasingly inequitable society into family members united by their shared pursuit of national dignity, wealth, and power.[49] What the earthquake seemed to have defined, according to media portrayals and the multimedia variations on netizen-penned Quake Poems, was the ability of the Chinese people to unite around something other than wealth and power: in this case, life itself and the health and happiness of those affected by the earthquake. Thus despite being widely depicted in the news media as a vernacular, populist phenomenon, Quake Poetry was far from immune from the ideological influence of the Chinese party-state, acting through the conjunction of a broad network of people, institutions, and media platforms.

HISTORY AND CULTURAL MEMORY

The phenomena I have described in this chapter were all products of collisions and collaborations between modern Chinese poetry and the (usually) non-poetry-reading public, which took place through and with the assistance of the mass media and, to varying degrees, the Chinese party-state. Sparks flew in each instance, whether owing to a public humiliation in the hands of the masses or the sheer enthusiasm with which members of the public approached the writing and deconstruction of modern poetry. That poetry was able to arouse such public interest despite ongoing discourse about its sociocultural marginalization suggests the need to look beyond the textual ambitions and community-related goals of contemporary poets to consider the historical contexts in which these incidents occurred, as well as the deeper cultural beliefs affecting the behaviors of those involved in consuming, critiquing, and producing poems. The case studies in this chapter also illuminate the tensions between the history of modern Chinese poetry as written and controlled by participants in China's poetry scenes and a sense of cultural memory that belongs equally to non-poetry-reading publics and is vital to China's identity as a "nation of poetry."

The historical contexts surrounding the viral spoofings of Pear Blossom and Baby Lamb form poetry were technological as well as social and political. The Zhao Lihua spoofing in 2006 came at a time when Internet forums were widely being used by online communities for sharing jokes and gossip and when growing numbers of cultural celebrities were taking to blogs to enhance their online presence and make their thoughts and writings more immediately available to the public. As Jing Wang has suggested, China's blogging revolution has "pushed viral communication to new heights," and blogs have proved ripe for the viral spread of content that often tests the boundaries of government censors and online enforcers of harmonious society.[50] Zhao herself, as well as a number of her high-profile supporters and detractors, used blogs to share their views on the spoofing incident with their legions of followers. Although Zhao had not been at all well-known before the spoofing began, it was partly her adept use of the one-to-many broadcast capacity of blogging and the function of web portals like Sina as an amplifier of celebrity voices that enabled her side of the story to be told, while also intensifying the atmosphere of contention that surrounded the affair.

The spread of Baby Lamb form poetry in 2010 was in large part a collective response to growing suspicions of corruption within the poetry arena, already raised during the spoofing of Zhao Lihua four years earlier and echoing widespread concern throughout China about political corruption during a period of uneven economic growth, land grabbing, and the various natural and man-made disasters of the early twenty-first century. It was no coincidence that Baby Lamb form poetry went viral in one of the fastest years of growth for weibo and just months after more than two hundred poetry forums had been deleted by NetEase, described by some as the end of the "poetry forum era." It also prolonged the national conversation about the legitimacy of colloquial poetry, as Che Yan'gao's prize-winning poems shared with those of Zhao Lihua a laid-back, conversational tone of voice and simple written form that many netizens believed unworthy of official literary accolades. It was interesting to observe how poets who value colloquial language as the most authentic life source of modern Chinese poetry responded to the widespread criticisms of what was now being derogatorily termed "saliva poetry" (*koushui shi*). Yi Sha, for example, saw netizens' disgust with Zhao's poems as evidence that colloquial poetry is "still avant-garde," despite having been in existence for over twenty years. His commentary appealed to live-scene discourse at the same time as it recalled the Panfeng Debate about the relative legitimacy of Intellectual and Popular writing styles: "If a person's writing ignores or avoids the live scenes of the original sounds of language [*yuyan de yuansheng xianchang*]," he argued, "then at the very least I can conclude that it is a kind of writing with low ambitions."[51]

Finally, Quake Poetry was clearly a direct result of the devastating earthquake of May 12, 2008, but also took place in the months leading up to the 2008 Beijing Olympic Games, widely seen as China's "coming-out party" to the world. The heightened sense of national consciousness that defined 2008 could also be observed in Quake poems, the majority of which were expressions of grief and national pride in the wake of such a huge loss of life.[52] As we have seen, many were circulated in the form of multimedia poems on video-sharing sites like Youku and Tudou, which were also undergoing a period of rapid growth and commercialization in 2008.[53] Like the synergies among big businesses, local government organizations, and poetry communities explored in Chapter 3, this outpouring of poems and their multimedia variations seemed to suggest that modern poetry could still perform a symbolically powerful, unifying function within contemporary Chinese society. A new narrative emerged in 2008 that poetry *was* of use to more than just poets after all, thus implicitly answering the question posed by Han Han in response to the Zhao Lihua affair of "How come modern poetry and poets still exist?" As one observer put it, "The Wenchuan earthquake shook souls like a typhoon. Poetry is the most direct means of releasing and expressing emotions that accumulate in the soul, and from this perspective poetry has not died, as its function cannot be replaced by any other medium. The crux of the matter is that poetry is able to pluck at the heartstrings."[54]

What role, then, do these media spectacles play in forging public impressions of modern poetry and creating cultural memory? The first three chapters of this book were concerned with the interactions between media dynamics and the desire of poets to belong to poetry scenes constituted of social activity that unfolds across multiple media spaces and publicizes and affirms poets' own understandings of modern poetry. At the same time as this reflects a live-scene style focus on the here and now of poetic interaction, it also reflects the importance attached to literary history, as poets are keenly aware of the need to leave behind a legacy and express the value of what they do in relation to what has come before. These activities could equally be understood as efforts to explore, circumscribe, and expand upon the generic parameters of modern poetry according to each poet's or poetry group's interpretive principles and literary ambitions. By forming and publicizing poetry communities, joining in debates, publishing their work through multiple media spaces, and aiding in the creation and propagation of poetry-related incidents and events, poets effectively lay claim to the genre of modern Chinese poetry, making clear through a variety of gatekeeping tactics who and what they believe worthy of the signifiers "poem" and "poet." The viral media spectacles that have been the subject of this chapter have the potential to render much of their efforts futile, as the formation of cultural memory is governed as much, if not more, by the mass media as it is by the efforts of cultural producers. If you were to ask a random member of the news-reading public about their impressions of contemporary Chinese poetry in the second half of the 2000s, you would be far more likely to hear something about Pear Blossom form, naked poets, or poetry machines than anything else.

Considering the ways in which communicative memories turn into cultural memory over time can help illuminate the reasons for this. As Astrid Eril and Ann Rigney explain, the concept of cultural memory—as opposed to other kinds of memory—is based on the assumption that memories become collective as a result of being continually shared among individuals by means of symbolic artefacts, a process that creates a sense of communal belonging that transcends space and time. Media are central to this. Rather than acting in a transparent manner as passive transmitters of information, as evoked by the image of an anthology quietly passing down poetry from generation to generation of readers, they mediate between current audiences and historical experiences, thus shaping collective understandings of the past and setting the stage for future ways of remembering in society.[55] Nor are mass media neutral channels of communication. They are continually absorbed in their own internal logics and dynamics, such as the need to win and maintain audiences and exhibit social responsibility without, in single-party political systems such as China's, being seen to diverge too far from the political status quo. While the Chinese media can at times help amplify the profile of poets by reporting on poetry scene activities, their strategy of sensationalizing the news to attract readers also functions to render more superficial the terms on which non-poetry-reading audiences understand poetry. In many instances, this involves reducing coverage to the misleadingly dichotomous question of "Is modern poetry dead?" and/or "Is poetry experiencing a crisis?" The spoofings of Zhao Lihua and Che Yan'gao were taken as rhetorical fuel for those in the "yes" camp, with Quake Poetry pointing in the direction of "no" by showing how, under certain conditions, a wider proportion of the population can find pleasure in reading and writing poetry.

The caveat "under certain conditions" is important. One of the narratives circulated in the media throughout the Quake Poetry movement came from a quotation by the Qing dynasty poet Zhao Yi (1727–1814): "the misery of the state leads to the emergence of great poets" (*guojia buxing shijia xing*).[56] By participating in this discourse, observers connected the "renaissance" of modern poetry that followed the Sichuan Earthquake to each incidence of great literature produced during times of national crisis, such as the periods of political upheaval and popular suffering that marked the gaps between stable dynastic rule in imperial China. This backward-looking, genealogical mode of thinking can be understood in light of the distinctions between history and cultural memory theorized by Pierre Nora and developed in scholarship on modern China by Ban Wang, Marc Andre Matten, and others.[57] Memory and history, as Nora argues, seem to exist in "fundamental opposition" to each other. While memory exists in a state of perpetual evolution and connects human experience to the present, history is the intellectual act of reconstructing that which no longer exists. At its heart is a critical discourse that is opposed to and suspicious of the existence of spontaneous memory and that sets out to suppress and destroy it.[58]

In the introduction I referred to Ban Wang's ideas about the interrelation between history and memory and the difficulties involved in distinguishing between the two. This is particularly true in an age in which memory and history alike are filtered and archived through the media. As Nora argues, "real memory," or memory that is kept alive through the social and unviolated behaviors of primitive or archaic societies, barely exists in today's modern era, having been supplanted by a constructed form of modern memory that depends on words and images for its survival. Rather than being spontaneous, natural, and perpetually linked to the present, what is called "memory" today is itself historically mediated, dilated, and multiplied by the countless acts of testifying and documenting that underpin modern sites of remembrance such as museums and television archives. As a result of such mediation, memory becomes increasingly inseparable from, or as Nora puts it, "ineluctably engulfed by," history.[59]

The mass poetry incidents described in this chapter suggest the continued pull of the cultural memory of poetry over Chinese society, with the media's attempts to connect Quake Poetry to every past instance of poetry benefiting from "the misery of the state" implying that there is value in the social form of poetry that is *not* controlled by the historicizing urges of China's living poets, even as these attempts inevitably contribute to the denaturalization of the public's "real memory" of poetry. This points to a contradiction at the heart of media representations of verse going viral. On the one hand, virality is taken as proof that poetry, and the cultural memory that surrounds it, is "not dead after all" and that China has reasserted its identity as a nation of poetry. On the other hand, modern poets are accused of not being up to the task of representing Chinese poetry in the modern world and their colloquial verse incapable of living up to collective memory of the greatness of China's poetic tradition. Poets, too, seem ambivalent toward the potential offered by the online public's mass involvement in poetry writing and critique. The fact that many celebrated both the viral spoofings of colloquial poets and Quake Poetry as proof of a nationwide "poetry fever" could also be understood in light of Nora's ideas about the relationship between history and cultural memory, in which each is reliant upon the other. *Lieux de mémoire*, or "sites of memory"—places and objects such as museums, archives, and calendars—are formed by the interactions between history and memory, a process that results in their "reciprocal overdetermination." Their fundamental purpose is to put a stop to the process of forgetting by halting time and materializing the immaterial. While there is a desire to remember inherent in these sites, they are made possible by the intervention of history and change and exist "because of their capacity for metamorphosis, an endless recycling of their meaning and an unpredictable proliferation of their ramifications."[60]

Such words could stand as a perfect description of poetry in China. What Ban Wang conceptualizes as a "critical historical consciousness" observable in the push and pull between memory and history in May Fourth–era China is also on display in the activities of China's contemporary poets, who benefit in terms of prestige and public attention from the cultural memory that continues to surround the genre of poetry at the same time as they cherish their creative independence from both poetic tradition and the political uses of literature, striving for authorial control over their own literary histories. The goal of writing history in May Fourth– and socialist-era China seemed to lie, Wang suggests, in constructing an imaginary continuity from past to present that ignored any gaps or breaks in an effort to legitimize the current political order. Since the 1980s, two contradictory tendencies have emerged. On the one hand, the championing of modernization carries with it a commitment to forget the struggles of the past and problems of history, replacing them with the "invisible hand of the market." Meanwhile, the new mythology of the market is called into question by a continued pull toward memory, a retrogressive gaze that encompasses both nostalgia for the past and skepticism toward the processes of globalization unfolding in the present.[61] According to Wang, it is the tensions between this "forward-looking acceleration" and "backward drag" that characterize modern Chinese cultural history.

This situation has only been compounded by the conjuncture in the early twenty-first century, a time in which China is moving further toward a fully capitalist and individualistic mode of economic and cultural production, marked by the emergence of a new, powerful class of entrepreneurs and overshadowed by the risks inherent in what many are arguing is an undeniably neoliberal mode of governance. While the transition toward a capitalist economic system and the cultural system reforms of recent decades are widely believed to have demystified high culture and stripped it of its public influence and aura for producers and consumers alike, the case studies examined in this chapter suggest that there remains a fundamental need for poetry in China, not just as an activity of cultural elites and niche literary communities but also as a source of self-identification for the otherwise non-poetry-reading public. Just as attracting negative reactions from rival poetry groups can be taken as acknowledgment of the existence of controversial poetry communities like the School of Rubbish, so too can the broader online public's occasional "surrounding and observing" of modern poets and poems be seen as tacit recognition of the continued centrality of poetry to China's national identity. The activities of poetry scene participants described throughout this book counteract both the dominant narrative that holds that high culture as a whole is struggling to maintain its relevance to everyday life *and* the Chinese party-state's attempts to promote individualization and self-interest as the preferred mode of living in capitalist society. The behaviors of netizens, too, indicate that collective activism surrounding forms of "high" culture is still a possibility, even if it takes place at home ("homebody activism") in the form of discursive rather than physical action, and the methods have become more deconstructive, satirical, and skeptical than ever before.

In conclusion, then, the impulses behind these instances of mass writing and critiques of modern Chinese poetry are far more complicated than terms such as "viral" and "meme" imply. The underlying motivations of netizens who contributed to the mass spoofings of poetry were, first, the suspicion that there was an unholy alliance at play between poetry and power, with "poets" receiving perks and accolades for what was surely terrible quality writing, and second, the expectation that poetry must be more than short colloquial commentaries on the trivialities of daily life or, as it came to be known, saliva poetry. Both of these are underpinned by the assumption that poetry should "rise above" as a form of culture untainted by money or political corruption and aesthetically more difficult and refined than everyday speech. Perhaps the most basic implication of all these examples of verse going viral is this: in an era when culture (including literature) is increasingly being used as a fast track to individual success, wealth, and fame, and when even the government encourages vulgarization as long as it brings in money and distracts from the deeper issues troubling the nation, surely *something* should remain sacred. And if that something is not poetry, one of the oldest, purest, and surest symbols of Chinese civilization, then what else could it possibly be?

Conclusion

I began this book by suggesting that modern poetry in China finds itself in a uniquely paradoxical situation. Written off by many journalists, netizens, and critics as hopelessly marginalized and out of touch with contemporary reality, it somehow manages to cling to some of its allure as the epitome of Chinese cultural achievement and the favored literary activity of many of the nation's elites. There are four possible solutions to this apparent paradox, which turns out to be not so paradoxical after all. In line with my cultural studies approach, these solutions are not intended as perfect or complete explanations, and neither are they mutually exclusive: each is tied to the other, and none could exist on its own. While they are derived from the situation of modern poetry in early twenty-first-century China, I would propose that they have implications for other areas of culture and countries, especially for cultural forms whose auras are thought to be weakened in an era of commercialization and mass media. I will also reconsider the question of agency or power, pay a return visit to the poem by Li Wei that opened the book, and end by contemplating the cultural implications of these new media scenes in an ever more technologically advanced future.

The first solution to the paradox of poetry's supposed marginalization lies in the concept of scenes. One reason many people are under the mistaken assumption that poetry no longer exists (or if it does, must be hobbling along on its last legs) is that they are not part of the scenes in which cultural activity takes place, which I have defined as historically conditioned and loosely affiliated networks of people involved in producing, circulating, and evaluating the contents of a cultural form. Cultural activity looks startlingly different depending on where the observer is positioned in relation to a scene. Being on the inside does not mean that you share with all other scene participants the same understanding of what your cultural form entails or how it should be produced and presented to others, but it does mean that you are more likely to be privy to the contentions and incidents that shape its calendar year and to the sense of liveliness and effervescence that emerges when people are connected to each other and when culture *happens*, in the present tense. Being on the outside does not preclude you from knowing that the scene exists, as you can always attend events as a member of the public or hear about it from time to time in the media. It does mean, however, that you are much less likely to understand the norms that shape this area of culture or be familiar with the hierarchies of people and discourses that give it shape. Scenes tend to be tight-knit, especially in the case of traditionally "high" forms of culture; while its members may talk about desiring a bigger audience or needing to "open up" to make a public impact, they on the whole prefer to be responsible for their own gatekeeping practices.

My second related argument is that the category of "poetry" is a social and not purely a textual form: it cannot be reduced to individual poems and any attempt to do so would be bound to fail, as it is usually the case that neither audiences nor authors can reach a consensus on what precisely "a poem" might be. Instead poetry encompasses both poems and all the activities that immediately surround them, including the literary, the economic, the political, and the mediatic. If modern poetry's health is judged solely by the percentage of print books and journals dedicated to it or the amount of media coverage given to the publication and discussion of modern poems, then yes, it is undeniably marginalized and cannot possibly hope to compete with the more entertainment-oriented genres and media of fiction, television, film, popular music, and computer games. But if you also take into account the space that face-to-face poetry activity takes up within Chinese cities and the volume of poetry-related activity and communication that occurs online, then the conclusion is quite the opposite: the category of poetry still occupies a vital position in contemporary Chinese culture. A related point concerns the question of where exactly the margins lie. Michelle Yeh once suggested that modern poetry has always existed in a state of marginality that, over time, has come to define its intellectual perspective and give rise to its power and creativity.[1] This is a wise observation, and for many poets the sense of being removed from the country's cultural or political center is far from a bad thing. However, it is worth bearing in mind that "the margins" and "the center" are relative terms that depend entirely on where you are standing. If you are able to position yourself anywhere within the scene, you are not in the margins at all but *are* the center.

To claim that poetry exists as a social form is not to say that poetry does not also deserve to be treated as literature and that meaning cannot be found in the aesthetic analysis of individual poems as written texts. But as Foley suggests, understanding culture as no more than a series of texts can only take us so far. Unless cultural reality is reimagined as a unique snapshot of a specific moment in space and time viewed from a single perspective, he argues, texts will never possess complete explanatory power as they can offer only fragmented analysis and not "holistic embodiment."[2] Understanding cultures as networks that are themselves ideally represented and supported by other networks (political, economic, and so on) is a way of acknowledging that cultures do not stand still: they are constantly emerging, morphing, and adapting to their environments, making it remarkably difficult to pin them down and subject them to analysis. This is why I have adopted the concept of the conjuncture, recognizing that the situation I describe in the first decade of the twenty-first century represents a unique set of circumstances conditioned by the complex interaction between multiple contexts that might never come together in quite the same way again.

My third suggestion relates to the significant amounts of economic capital that have been expended on modern Chinese poetry in the new millennium, which might also imply a contradiction: poetry is said to be economically dysfunctional yet it has brought in large donations of money and logistical support from cultural entrepreneurs, big businesses, and local government organizations. The most obvious explanation for this is philanthropic: poetry benefits from the kindness of others who channel their generosity toward this worthy and impoverished cause. This, however, does not quite account for the extent to which poetry has become embroiled in real estate promotion and local branding efforts in the last decade or so. Poetry is seen as a sensible financial investment by businesses and entrepreneurs in part because it has *not* been implicated in the market economy and has thus retained something of its former allure as a nationally important and spiritually "pure" activity that can help businesses appear more civilized and refined. This is the logic of the cultural economy, being promoted by the Chinese party-state under the umbrella of cultural system reforms: culture is used to promote business, and cultural and economic capital turn out to be almost synonymous terms of value.[3]

The involvement of individual cultural brokers like Tan Kexiu can also be seen as an extension of the "DIY way of life" that is promoted by the Chinese government as the ideal way of living under neoliberal conditions in which individuals take responsibility for their own life choices and deal with the possibilities—and the risks—inherent in "this brave new way of living."[4] While the government sees the DIY way of life as a way of encouraging individualization and the growth of the middle class, for Chinese poets it has conversely allowed a greater degree of collectivism, as inflows of cash secured by individual entrepreneurs with a love of poetry help stage lavish events at regular intervals throughout the country. Attending poetry events is a must for many poets who wish to be present in live scenes of poetry and a way of asserting their poetry citizenship by participating in the here and now of collective poetry activity.

My fourth solution to the marginalization paradox is that poetry is at once subject to the historical consciousness of modern poets *and* the non-poetry-reading public's cultural memory of poetry. While poets attempt to exert their influence over the discursive formation of history by creating "incidents," naming, writing essays and publishing books, forming communities and groups, and performing gatekeeping functions within their communities, the non-poetry-reading public remembers that China is supposed to be a "nation of poetry" and stubbornly holds onto the conviction that the best poetry ever written (and, most likely, ever to be written) was the classical verse of the Tang and Song dynasties, penned by poets who are long dead. This is a belief that is perpetuated at home, where many children are encouraged by parents to memorize classical poems from the age of three, by the country's formal education system, which teaches far more classical than modern Chinese poems, and by the mainstream media, which in the early twenty-first century functions as both a sounding board for popular opinion and a tool for ideological governance in the hands of the Chinese party-state.

One might be tempted to conclude that the category of "poetry" as a whole has been dispatched to memory and deleted from the present as it no longer seems relevant or necessary to China's nation-building goals. According to this line of thinking, modern poetry is a failure because it does not make money (even as it benefits from it), does not enhance China's global reputation (especially when the poems are as "bad" as Zhao Lihua's "Alone in Tennessee"), and does not even entertain, unless subjected to mass spoofing and parody. As one observer noted, modern poetry is often seen as little more than a cause for embarrassment, comparable to China's much-berated national soccer team. From one angle, the efforts of poetry scene participants are designed to counteract this narrative: rather than simply being an "illumination from the past,"[5] poetry is shown to be relevant to—if not lighting up—the present, demonstrated particularly vividly in the emergence over the past two decades of a new poetics of presence, defined by Yu Jian in 1993 as "accepting responsibility and existing as a poet of the 'live scene.'"[6]

Another goal of this book has been to take up the challenge of understanding culture as subject to complex distributions of power that are not simply defined by the opposition between domination and resistance, or by the opposition between the Chinese party-state and citizens who may not approve of everything (or, in some cases, anything) their government does. This has involved taking a performative approach to issues of culture and power, conceptualizing the negotiations that take place among poetry scene participants as performative interactions between various participants in modern Chinese society.[7] Just as China's official ideology of "socialism with Chinese characteristics" and the academic discourse of "postsocialism" make room for the coexistence of residual socialist ideology with capitalist economic policies and, similarly, the government's current emphasis on the culture industry implies both a drive toward privatization and a continued belief in the importance of culture to the party-state, so too have cultural communities like the poetry scenes studied in this book succeeded in productively negotiating between political, economic, and literary demands that can often appear to be at odds with each other.

That is not to say, of course, that these conflicting demands coexist in perfect harmony or that poetry can only benefit from the unexpected collaborations between political and business representatives that support much contemporary poetry activity. As we have seen, contention exists in every media space of poetry publication and reception and can often be traced to the suspicion that poets have either sold out to money and power or have taken on too authoritarian a role in their gatekeeping of poetry scenes. It is possible, too, that poetry's reputation as a pure or aesthetically elevated cultural form has taken a permanent hit as a result of the current trend of free-flowing colloquial poetry and the spoofing incidents discussed in the last chapter and that the "poetry arena" will forever be associated with compromise with, if not capitulation to, political and economic forces. Nonetheless, contention is part and parcel of cultural scenes, which will always be enlivened by ideological and interpersonal tensions owing to the passion with which scene participants approach their chosen area of culture.

To a certain extent language itself, in the form of discourse, can be used to buffer against the more contentious and damaging accusations leveled against poetry scenes, evidenced by the way in which many poets have turned away from the elitist connotations of the term "poetry arena" to embrace a more democratic, participatory discourse of "live scenes." The fact that even live scenes have become a source of debate, with some poets accusing others of promoting a "fake live scene discourse" (*wei xianchang shuo*), suggests, however, that infighting is inevitable.[8] Not only is language itself highly political, subject to both poetry politics and the party-state's sensitivity toward potentially subversive speech, but contention is also seen as advantageous to many poetry scene participants. While some more academically minded poets fear that the "circus-style" cultural performances that characterize the "catwalk" of poetry distract from the more important task of writing good-quality poems that bear witness to history and stand the test of time (a very textualist approach to poetry),[9] for many other poets these performances are, in fact, a central part of poetry as a social form. By actively involving themselves in the contingencies of poetry activity and the debates and incidents it invariably contains, poets are not being swept along in a kind of permanent present tense as live-scene discourse might seem to imply but are engaging with and ultimately helping produce the history of poetry, which remains a cultural form of great symbolic power in early twenty-first-century capitalist China.

To offer one final example of how poems come into all of this and to steer the discussion back to the subject of media, another central concern of this book, I would like to return to Li Wei's poem "Is Zhang Ziyi Beautiful or Not?" The path that this poem has taken since its initial publication in 2006 illustrates the fact that rather than being passively subjected to the government's control over the media, poetry scene participants are adept at appropriating and manipulating different media platforms in ways that allow them to assert their gatekeeping agency over the value and standards of modern Chinese poetry and thus express their own subjectivities as individual poet-citizens. Li Wei's poem also serves as an illustration of the varying media dynamics that poetry encounters on its journeys through space and time, which include the contingencies and multiple pathways of face-to-face and online communication as well as the relatively controlled and fixed dynamics of print-based publication.

The public reception of "Is Zhang Ziyi Beautiful or Not?" began, unusually, with its publication in print in the June 2006 edition of the official poetry journal *Poetry Monthly*. Even this tells us how much has changed within poetry publication since the turn of the millennium: in previous decades, the idea that such a vulgar, celebrity-obsessed poem might find its way into a state-run literary journal would be unimaginable. Shortly after publication, it reappeared on the online poetry forum *Poetry Rivers and Lakes* after it was posted there by Xu Jiang, who had offered to help out his technologically challenged friend by sharing some of his writings on the Internet. It was not until it was featured in January 2007 in the inaugural Chinese Poetry Charts (Zhongguo Shige Paihangbang), however, that the poem began to attract more widespread attention.

These charts were conceived of by a group of Nanjing-based academics and poetry critics calling themselves the Modern Han Poetry Research Project, who stated that their goal was one of "responsibly overcoming the failures of journals, organizations, and small cliques, and providing a fair assessment of the writings, people, and publications of each year."[10] Instead of being featured as one of the top ten "good" poems of 2006, Li Wei's poem found itself listed at number two in the Mediocre Poetry Chart (Yongshibang), one place below a poem by the well-known male poet and representative of Intellectual Writing, Sun Wenbo. Media outlets across China reported on the charts, running such gleeful headlines as "Ten poets climb the 'mediocre poetry chart,' Sun Wenbo makes no. 1, Zhao Lihua nowhere to be seen."[11] Most reports seemed to find Li Wei's poem about Zhang Ziyi more titillating than anything else. Many took the poem's contents at face value, using it as an opportunity to stir misogynistic debate about whether Zhang Ziyi really *is* as beautiful as she is made out to be. A few poets responded to the media storm that surrounded the Chinese Poetry Charts by defending Li's poem on instant messaging services and accusing the men who launched the charts of being "mediocre scholars" themselves.

Five months later in June 2007, I attended a poetry event in a performance hall of the Tianjin College of Arts, organized by Xu Jiang and titled "The Blooming of *Sunflower*" (*Sunflower* is the name of Xu Jiang's long-running unofficial poetry journal). In attendance were many poets from Beijing, Tianjin, and the surrounding area, including the usual suspects who had been associated with *Poetry Rivers and Lakes* since the turn of the millennium: Shen Haobo, Yi Sha, Xu Jiang, Hou Ma, Zhong Dao, Yang Li, Ma Fei, and others. As is typical at these events, male poets massively outnumbered their female counterparts, although there were a few women invited, including the young poet and novelist Chun Sue. Midway through the poetry recitation portion of the event, Li Wei took to the stage and announced, with a wicked grin, that the poem he had chosen to recite was called "Is Zhang Ziyi Beautiful or Not?" The audience erupted into enthusiastic applause before he had even started. Li's performance, delivered with gusto in his Tianjin dialect, was welcomed with guffaws and whoops of encouragement.

In 2012, I did an online search of the title of Li Wei's poem and found that its voyage had continued in the years since I had heard it recited in Tianjin. In June 2011 it was awarded a prize at a poetry recitation event held to mark the twentieth anniversary of the influential unofficial poetry journal *Poetry Reference*. The announcement of the poetry prize explained that although the poem had stirred up much discussion in 2007 as an example of poetic mediocrity, it was in fact one of the "best" works of recent years. Li Wei, the judges claimed, had pulled off an "ingenious comparison between the beauty of the popular movie star Zhang Ziyi and that of a female colleague from his office, thus demonstrating the huge gulf that separates the life values of the poet and those of the market." That same month, Li Wei's poem was featured as the recommended poem on a weibo column written by Yi Sha, titled the New Century Poetry Classics (Xin shiji shidian). Each day between April 2011 and April 2012, Yi selected a poem he liked that had been written since 2000 and shared his evaluation of the poem with his weibo followers and anyone else who sees the posts his followers share. Yi's commentary posed the question, "Is 'Is Zhang Ziyi Beautiful or Not?' mediocre or not?" and concluded that the judges of the Mediocre Poetry Chart got their assessment completely wrong in assuming that any poem that deals with popular culture must, by definition, be tasteless and crass. Li Wei did not give a hoot about Zhang Ziyi, Yi Sha noted, but cared only about his colleague Liu Ping.

In each of the live scenes that this poem encountered in the first five years of its existence—print publications, news websites, online poetry forums, concert hall stages, and weibo—it seemed to have acquired different meanings and performed different functions. Selected for publication in an official poetry journal, it served as an example of recent poetic writing that seemed to have its finger on the pulse of popular opinion. Featured in the Mediocre Poetry Chart, it was evidence of the deterioration of modern poetry in a consumer age and subject to the gatekeeping authority of the Modern Han Poetry Research Project. Recited in person by the poet himself, it functioned as a statement of authorial authenticity and an in-joke shared among a community of poets who possessed similar attitudes toward the value of colloquial poetry in China today. When it received accolades from unofficial literary institutions and was recirculated through weibo as part of Yi Sha's New Century Poetry Classics, it helped communicate to a broader audience of Internet users that poetry is alive and kicking in the twenty-first century and that it is ultimately poets, not "mediocre scholars" or journalists, who should be able to decide what makes good poetry.

All of this can tell us several things about the ways that meanings are produced through interactions among cultural producers, audiences, and media. Poetry as a literary genre has been experiencing a struggle over ownership in the past decade or so. On the one hand, poets have successfully used the communicative possibilities afforded to them by new media technologies and dynamics, experimenting with virtual identity, forming new poetry groups, engaging in intergroup debates, and using the Internet to organize and select the contents of print publications and face-to-face events. In the case of "Is Zhang Ziyi Beautiful or Not?" it was weibo that was most productive in wrestling back the symbolic value of Li Wei's poem from academics, who had cynically included it in their Mediocre Poetry Chart as a way of exploiting media narratives of modern poetry's terminal decline. In both instances, poetry scene participants employed the Internet as an interactive medium for determining what makes good-quality poetry and for sharing those standards with a wider audience.

These same Internet technologies have, on the other hand, opened up poets' writings and activities to a population of netizens whose education in modern poetry ended in the 1980s with selected works of Misty Poetry and Haizi but who still believe in the symbolic importance of poetry to China as a nation. Given half the opportunity, many of them are more than willing to "surround and observe" in order to poke fun at their country's cultural elites for both their social privileges and creative failings. China's news media seem to have played a large part in encouraging mass spoofings of poetry and in propagating narratives of modern poetry's demise. This could reflect one of two conflicting goals: either journalists have been complying with the government's understanding of news media as belonging within the broader category of culture and using news reports to communicate the continued importance of culture to the party-state's ideological and economic goals or they, too, have grown suspicious of the complicity between the poetry arena and power and publicized the spoofings as a subtle means of expressing dissatisfaction with a nation in which a government official who writes trite poems about local celebrities can, somehow, be awarded state-sponsored literary prizes. It is also possible that both objectives have been achieved at once.

Oral performance has always opened poetry up to different ways of reading and listening, and sounds and subjective interactions between performer and audience can produce meanings that are entirely absent on the printed page, as demonstrated by the audible delight generated by Li Wei's recitation of his poem in Tianjin in 2007 and the unscripted events precipitated by the Big Square Poetry Festival in Beijing in 2006, described in Chapter 3.[12] Some observers have begun to suggest that a similar dynamic is at play when poetry moves onto the Internet, a process that is often imagined in terms of evolution. Li Xia, for example, outlines the progress of human civilization from a hunter-gatherer society through agrarian, industrial, postindustrial, and finally Internet civilization.[13] His suggestion that the Internet is ushering in a return to the kind of oral literature (*koutou wenxue*) of the people (*minjian*) that prospered before the invention of print echoes what scholars working within the Western tradition have termed the "Gutenberg parenthesis," the idea that print publication constitutes but a single, relatively short chapter in the history of human communication and that once it is over (an end date that is drawing ever closer), something newer and more convenient will take its place.[14]

However, the "new" media dynamics that have come to the fore in the age of the Internet are not so new: qualities such as openness, contingency, mass participation, immediacy, and informality existed for many millennia before the age of print in the arena of oral tradition. Foley calls the assumption that oral communication evolved into written communication and is now evolving into electronic communication an "evolutionary fallacy," attributable to the ideology of the text in that it assumes that the superior kind of communication is that which can be confined to a singular textual creation by a singular author and consumed by a singular audience.[15] Like the Gutenberg parenthesis, it also assumes, incorrectly, that the history of each technology can be "bracketed off" and that once the Internet has established itself as the world's primary medium for cultural exchange, the history of print will effectively be over.[16]

This leads me to my final question: Might the social phenomena and viral patterns of China's "new media scenes" be symptomatic of a broader epochal shift in Chinese media and culture, and perhaps even in the ways that cultures are produced, circulated, and made meaningful across the technologically developed world? I stand by my basic assertion that the stories I have told relate first and foremost to the contemporary Chinese conjuncture and the tensions that exist between different understandings and uses of media and culture, as well as between modern poetry history and the cultural memory that surrounds poetry in China. At the same time, it seems pertinent to ask whether these tensions indicate a turning point in culture more generally, at least in countries where the Internet has already become an integral part of everyday life. This is not intended as an evocation of the Gutenberg parenthesis or a claim that the age of print will soon be over once and for all: as we have seen, "old" media dynamics continue to make their influence felt in a variety of ways, and the gatekeeping authority of print publication is not likely to end any time soon. To pose a slightly different question: Is it possible that the aura of culture is, and perhaps always has been, best understood as residing not so much within "texts themselves" (and is thus *not* undermined by mass reproduction through media technologies, as Walter Benjamin famously suggested, or threatened by the much-bemoaned marginalization of high cultural forms) but in the social interactions and contentions that ensue when people participate in the creation and circulation of culture—in short, in the human networks through which cultural meaning is made?

If communication technologies continue to develop in the direction they have been so far in the new millennium, world cultures from here on out are destined to be permanently online and accessible (to those who have access to these technologies, an important caveat given economic and social inequalities) by gestures or voice command, not hidden within physical media such as books, CDs, and film. Boundaries between texts and media are already less clear-cut than ever before, a tendency that we might expect to continue by losing, for example, the artificial distinction between poems and song lyrics or the lines between films and computer games that partake of the same imaginary world. Nor will it be necessary to seek out other human bodies to enjoy the sense of community that culture provides: more and more of us are in perpetual contact through social media and communication technologies, which are being integrated into our bodies and living environments in increasingly pervasive ways. Thus while the specific modes of poetry activity that have been the focus of this book are a product of the conjuncture in China's early twenty-first century, cultures—and the memories that surround them—are becoming ever more participatory, contingent, diverse, and technologically mass-mediated, not just by the traditional custodians of cultural taste but by anyone who has the resources and impetus to get involved. It will be fascinating to observe how the social form of Chinese poetry responds.

APPENDIX: POETRY SURVEY QUESTIONS

Real name and pen name:

Poetry-related identity (poet, critic, researcher, editor, etc.):

Year of birth (optional):

Place of residence:

Other profession(s):

Poetry group membership(s):

Published poetry collections, if any:

1. How do you understand the notion of "live scenes" of poetry? In what ways do you think this concept differs, if at all, from the "poetry arena"?

2. Have you attended poetry recitation events before? If so, how many do you usually attend a year?

3. What do you think are the benefits and disadvantages of poetry recitation?

4. How do you think your poetry differs when it is recited aloud as opposed to written on the page?

5. What meaning does print publication hold for you?

6. What is your opinion of poetry polemics? How willing are you to join in debates between poets and between poetry groups?

7. What role do you think the media should play in poetry scenes?

8. What are your thoughts on poetry criticism? Do other people's critiques affect the way you write?

9. Do you see any conflict between "individual writing" and membership in poetry schools or communities?

10. Are you at all worried about the future of New Poetry?

GLOSSARY OF CHINESE TERMS

A Fei 阿斐
A Xiang 阿翔
Ai Qing 艾青
An Qi 安琪
baguanren 把关人 gatekeeper
baihuawen 白话文 vernacular Chinese
Bai Xiaosheng 百晓生
banzhu 版主 [Internet] forum moderator
Bei Dao 北岛
Beihui guixian 北回归线 *Tropic of Cancer*
Beijing daxue Weiming shigejie 北京大学未名诗歌节 Peking University Weiming Poetry Festival
Beijing pinglun 北京评论 *Beijing Review*
Beijing wenxue 北京文学 Beijing Literature
Beijing Zhongkun Touzi Jituan 北京中坤投资集团 Beijing Zhongkun Investment Group
Bei Ta 北塔
boke 博客 blog
Boke wang 博客网 Bokee
bu zaichang zhe 不在场者 people who are not present [on the scene]
Cai ai dao yiban 才爱到一半 [We Don't] Only Love by Halves
cai shi 采诗 to select poems
canque de bianxuan 残缺的编选 crippled anthologizing
caogen 草根 grassroots
cao ni ma 草泥马 grass mud horse
Cao Pi 曹丕
Changsha Gaoxin Bocai Shiyan Xuexiao 长沙高新博才实验学校 Changsha High-Tech Bocai Experimental School
Changsha Houtian Cehua Guwen Youxian Gongsi 长沙后天策划顾问有限公司 Changsha Houtian Planning Consultancy Company Limited
Chang Shan 长山
chao 潮 tide, wave
Chaoji nüsheng 超级女声 Super Girl
chaozuo 炒作 to [self-]publicize, hype
chema fei 车马费 travel expenses

Che Yan'gao车延高
Chen Dongdong 陈东东
Chen Chongyi 陈仲义
Chen Jiagang 陈家刚
Chen Kaige 陈凯歌
Chen Pingyuan 陈平原
Chen Weijian 陈维建
chengdan 承担 to bear [responsibility]
Cheng Guangwei 程光炜
chongdi 崇低 worship the low
chonggao 崇高 worship the high, lofty, sublime
Chuanyue hanyu de shige zhi guang 穿越汉语的诗歌之光 The light of poetry, cutting through the Chinese language
Chuntian de rufang jie 春天的乳房劫 Spring's Breast Plunder
ci shi ci di 此时此地 here and now
cucao 粗糙 crude
Dachang shige jie 大场诗歌节 Big Square Poetry Festival
Dagong shige 打工诗歌 Migrant Worker Poetry
Datou Yaya 大头鸭鸭 Big Headed Ducky
dai 代 generation
Dai Jinhua 戴锦华
Dai Wangshu 戴望舒
danwei 单位 work unit
dangdai 当代 contemporary
dangxiaxing 当下性 contemporary spirit
dao minjian qu 到民间去 going to the people
Deng Hong邓鸿
Deng Xiaoping 邓小平
diceng 底层 the lower rungs
di er qudao 第二渠道 second channel [publishing]
dimian shiren 地面诗人 ground surface poets
Di san dai 第三代 Third Generation
Di san dai hou shige zhuanti taolunhui 第三代后诗歌专题讨论会 Post–Third Generation Poetry Forum
Di san ji 第三极 Third Pole
Di san tiao daolu 第三条道路 Third Way
Di shichao 低诗潮 Low Poetry Movement
Di shige yundong 低诗歌运动 Low Poetry Movement
Dizhen guo hou, wo chengren 地震过后，我承认 After the Earthquake Was Over, I Admit
Dizhen shi 地震诗 Quake Poetry
Dizhen shichao 地震诗抄 Earthquake Poetry Transcriptions
Dianfu! Quanqiuhua yujing xia de hanyu shige de jiangou ji Zhao Lihua shige yantaohui 颠覆！全球化语境下的汉语诗歌的建构暨赵丽华诗歌研讨会 Overthrow! A Forum on Chinese Poetic Construction in the Context of Globalization and the Poetry of Zhao Lihua
Dianyingjia Xiehui 电影家协会 Film Artists' Association
Ding Weifeng丁伟锋
Douban 豆瓣
Du Fu 杜甫

Duoduo 多多
Duoyu 朵渔
egao 恶搞 spoof
Fa Qing 法清
fayan 发言 to speak out, speech
fanchang 反常 contrary and common
Fanfou 饭否
Fan Si 凡斯
fanglang 放浪 unrestrained
fang si fang sheng 方死方生 both dead and alive
fei chonggao 非崇高 not-lofty
Feifei 非非 Not-Not
fei guanfang 非官方 unofficial
fei ling 非灵 not-soul
fei lixing 非理性 not-rational
fei rou 非肉 not-flesh
fei shi shidai 非诗时代 not a time for poetry
fenqing 愤青 angry youth
fenghui 峰会 summit
Feng Ru Song 风入松 Forest Song
Feng Xiaogang 冯小刚
Fu Mahuo 符马活
Furong jiejie 芙蓉姐姐 Sister Lotus
ge 歌 song
Ge Mai 戈麦
gerenhua xiezuo 个人化写作 individualized writing
gonggong canyu 公共参与 public participation
gonggong lingyu 公共领域 public sphere
Gu Cheng 顾城
Gu He 古河
guanfang 官方 state-sponsored, official
guanfang shuofa 官方说法 official talk
guangchang 广场 square
guguai 古怪 weird
Guo Lusheng 郭路生
guilaizhe 归来者 returnee
guojia buxing shijia xing 国家不幸诗家幸 the misery of the state leads to the emergence of great poets
guojia yiji zuojia 国家一级作家 top-ranked national author
Guo Moruo 郭沫若
Haiyan zhi ge 海燕之歌 Song of the Storm-Petrel
Haizi 海子
Haizi, kuai zhua jin mama de shou 孩子，快抓紧妈妈的手 Child, Guickly Grab Hold of Mama's Hand
Han Bo 韩博
Han Dong 韩东
Han Han 韩寒
Han Zuorong 韩作荣
He Xiaozhu 何小竹
hexie 河蟹 river crab
hexie shehui 和谐社会 harmonious society
heise de yanjing 黑色的眼睛 black eyes
Hong Zhu 洪烛
Hong Zicheng 洪子诚
hou kouyu 后口语 post-colloquial
Hou Ma 侯马
hou menglong 后朦胧 post-Misty
hou xin shiqi 后新时期 post–New Era
hou zhengzhi xiezuo 后政治写作 Post-Political Writing
Hu Jiujiu 胡赳赳

Hunan Kaida Caixin Touzi Youxian Zeren Gongsi 湖南凯达财信投资有限责任公司 Hunan Kaida Financial Investment Corporation Limited
Hu Shi 胡适
Hu Xudong 胡续冬
Hu Yong 胡泳
Huacheng Chubanshe 花城出版社 Flower City Publishing House
huali 华丽 flowery
huayu kongjian 话语空间 discourse space
huayuquan 话语权 discursive power
huanyuan 还原 return to the original
Huang Lihai 黄礼孩
Huang Nubo 黄怒波
Huang Xiang 黄翔
Huang Zhenlin 黄振林
Huida 回答 The Answer
huise 晦涩 opaque
huiyi 会议 meeting
huodong 活动 event, activity
Huozhe 或者 *Or*
jishi zhuyi 纪实主义 on-the-spot realism
*Jia Junpeng, ni ma han ni huijia chifan*贾君鹏，你妈喊你回家吃饭 Jia Junpeng, your mom's calling you home for dinner
Jiashen fengbao ershiyi shiji Zhongguo shige dazhan 甲申风暴二十一世纪中国诗歌大展 Jia Shen Storm Twenty-First Century Chinese Poetry Grand Exhibition
Jia Zhangke 贾樟柯
jian 鉴 mirror
jiancha 检查 to audit
jianrui 尖锐 edgy
Jiang Hao 蒋浩
Jiangnan Buyi 江南布衣 Southern China Cloth
Jiang Tao 姜涛
jiaoliu 交流 exchange
jie 界 realm, world
jie 节 festival
jiegui 接轨 integration
Jieke 解渴 Thirst-Quenching
Jintian 今天 *Today*
jingdianzuo 经典作 canonical texts
juhui 聚会 gathering
juyou keligan 具有颗粒感 gritty
jueqi 崛起 rise
Kan hai 看海 Watching the Ocean
kanhao 刊号 International Standard Serial Number (ISSN)
kanke 看客 gawking crowds
Kang zhen shi 抗震诗 Quake-Resistance Poetry
Kongkongdangdang 空空荡荡 Empty
kouhao 口号 slogan
koushui shi 口水诗 saliva poetry
koutou wenxue 口头文学 oral literature
kuajie 跨界 boundary crossing
Kui 葵 *Sunflower*
Laji pai 垃圾派 School of Rubbish
Laji yixiang 垃圾意象 Rubbish Imagery
Laji yundong 垃圾运动 Rubbish Movement

La Jiadu 拉家渡
Lanhudie Zidingxiang 蓝蝴蝶紫丁香 Blue Butterfly Lilac
langsong 朗诵 recitation
langsonghui 朗诵会 [poetry] recital
Lao De 老德
lao qianbei 老前辈 old-timers
Lao Tian 老天
Lao Touzi 老头子 Old Man
Lei Feng 雷锋
Leng Shuang 冷霜
Li Bai 李白
Li Da 李达
lihe 离合 separate and unified
lihua ti 梨花体 Pear Blossom form
Li Hongqi 李红旗
Li Ji 李季
Li Mingpeng 黎明鹏
Li Qingguo 李青果
Li Qingzhao 李清照
Li Shaojun 李少君
liting Zhao Lihua, baowei shige 力挺赵丽华，保卫诗歌 Supporting Zhao Lihua and defending poetry
Li Wei 李伟
Li Xia 李霞
Liangquanqimei 两全其美 LQQM
Liang Xiaobin梁晓斌
liangxin 良心 conscience
Lin Mang 林莽
Liu Chun 刘春
Liu Dehua 刘德华 Andy Lau
liupai 流派 school
Liu Yifei 刘亦菲
Longmai shihui 龙脉诗会 Longmai Poetry Meeting
Lushan bieshu 麓山别墅 Lushan Villas
Lu Weiping卢卫平
Lu Xun 鲁迅
Luan Xiaojie 栾小杰
lunjian 论剑 polemic
luntan 论坛 forum
Lun wei minjian 论伪民间 On the fake popular
Lun wen 论文 Discourse on literature
luoben 裸奔 streaking
luohouyu 落后于 far behind
Luo Xin 骆新
Luo Ying 骆英
Luo Zhenya罗振亚
Ma Bin 马斌
Ma Fei 马非
Ma Hua 马骅
Manghan 莽汉 Macho Men
Mang Ke 芒克
Maopu 猫扑 Mop
Mao Zedong 毛泽东
Mei Lanfang 梅兰芳
meinü zuojia 美女作家 Beauty Writers
meisu 媚俗 kowtowing to the vulgar
menkan 门槛 gate, threshold
menglong 朦胧 misty, obscure
Mian Mian 棉棉
min'ganci 敏感词 sensitive words
minjian 民间 nongovernmental, popular, of the people
Minjian lichang 民间立场 the Popular Standpoint
minjian qiye 民间企业 privately owned enterprises
minjian shige kanwu 民间诗歌刊物 unofficial, independently

financed poetry journals, often abbreviated as *minkan* 民刊
minjian zhishifenzi 民间知识分子 popular intellectual
mingming 命名 naming
Mingtian 明天 *Tomorrow*
Mingtian E'erguna Zhongguo shige shuangnian zhan 明天额尔古纳中国诗歌双年展 Tomorrow E'erguna Chinese Poetry Biennial Exhibition
Mo Mo 默默
nandong 难懂 incomprehensible
Nanren 南人
niandu zhixing zhubian 年度执行主编 executive editor [of that year]
nianjian 年鉴 almanac, yearbook
Nie Shebo聂社波
Ning Ying 宁瀛
nüxing shige 女性诗歌 women's poetry
Ouyang Jianghe 欧阳江河
Panfeng shihui 盘峰诗会 Panfeng Meeting
Pan Shiyi 潘石屹
Pan Wei 潘维
Pang Qingming庞清明
pangran dawu 庞然大物 big beasts
paoxiao ti 咆哮体 roaring form
Peng Yanjiao彭燕郊
Pidan 皮旦
pidan 皮蛋 thousand-year-old egg
pingtai 平台 platform
putong 普通 ordinary, standard
qiling hou 70后 post-1970
Qiwulun 齐物论 On leveling things
Qiyue pai 七月派 July Group
Qianshou 牵手 Holding Hands
Qin'ai de, kuai zhua jin wo de shou 亲爱的，快抓紧我的手 Darling, Quickly Grab Hold of My Hand
qingchang 清场 cleansing the scene
Qiu Zhijie 邱志杰
Qu Yuan 屈原
quanmin xieshi 全民写诗 the entire population is writing poetry
quanzi 圈子 circles
qunti 群体 group
Renmin chouhonghong 人民臭烘烘 The People Stink
renmin daibiao shiren 人民代表诗人 People's Representative Poet
Renmin wenxuejiang 人民文学奖 People's Literature Award
renqi 人气 popularity [especially on the Internet]
renrou sousuo 人肉搜索 human flesh search
Rong Guangqi 荣光奇
routi 肉体 flesh
Ruan Qingquan 阮庆全
Sajiao pai 撒娇派 School of Coquetry
Sanchongzou 三重奏 *Trio*
Sang Ke 桑克
shabi 傻逼 stupid cunt
shalong 沙龙 salon
shan shi 删诗 to delete poems
shanghen wenxue 伤痕文学 Scar Literature
she 社 society
shencha 审查 to audit, censorship

Shen Deqian 沈德潜
Shen Haobo 沈浩波
shenma dou shi fuyun 神马都是浮云 magical horses are all floating clouds, i.e., "it's all nonsense"
Shen Qi 沈奇
shenti xiezuo 身体写作 body writing
Shen Wu 神五
Sheng Xing 盛兴
shi 湿 wet
Shi cankao 诗参考 *Poetry Reference*
shi ci'er 诗词儿 the words [to a poem]
shidai 时代 era
shi de guodu 诗的国度 nation of poetry
shige chongbai 诗歌崇拜 cult of poetry
shige huodongjia 诗歌活动家 poetry activist
shige jie 诗歌界 poetry world
Shige yuekan 诗歌月刊 *Poetry Monthly*
Shige yuekan: Xia ban yue 诗歌月刊：下半月 Poetry Monthly: Second Half of the Month
shiguo 诗国 nation of poetry
Shiji 史记 Record of History
Shiji zhi jiao: Zhongguo shige chuangzuo zitai yu lilun jianshe yantaohui世纪之交：中国诗歌创作姿态与理论建设探讨会 Turn of the Century: A Forum on Creative Trends and Theoretical Construction in Chinese Poetry
shijian 事件 incident
shijianhua 事件化 incidentization [turning into an incident]
shi jianghu 诗江湖 poetry rivers and lakes
Shi jianghu: wangluo shige dang'an 诗江湖：网络诗歌档案 Poetry Rivers and Lakes: Avant-Garde Poetry Files
shijie geming 诗界革命 poetry world revolution
Shijing *Book of Songs*
Shikan 诗刊 *Poetry*
shiminggan 使命感 sense of historical mission
shiniao xiezuo 屎尿写作 shit and piss writing
Shiren he wei 诗人何为 What are poets for?
Shishang zui han de shi 史上最汗的诗 The most sweat-inducing poems in history
shisheng 失声 to lose one's voice, cry out
Shi shenghuo 诗生活 *Poemlife*
Shishishang de Ma Heling 事实上的马鹤铃 The Actual Fact of Ma Heling
shitan 诗坛 poetry arena
shitan 屎坛 arena of shit
shitan ditu 诗坛地图 poetry arena map
Shitan furong 诗坛芙蓉 Lotus of the Poetry Arena
shitan hexie 诗坛和谐 poetry arena harmony
Shi tansuo 诗探索 Poetry Exploration
Shi xilie 屎系列 Shit Series
shi yan zhi 诗言志 poetry

expresses what is intently on the mind

shiyi jusuo xianchang caifeng 诗意居所现场采风 live-scene folk-song collecting at the poetic residence

Shi zha 诗札 Poetry epistles

Shi Zhi 食指

shoubian 手边 present at hand

Shoujie Lushan xin shiji shige mingjia fenghui 首届麓山新世纪诗歌名家峰会 First Lushan New Century Famous Poets Summit

shoutu youze 守土有责 to bear the responsibility of defending [one's] own territory

Shucai 树才

shuhao 书号 International Standard Book Number (ISBN)

shushang 书商 book agent, book dealer

Shu Ting 舒婷

Shuihuzhuan 水浒传 *Water Margin*

Shuimu qinghua 水木清华 SMTH

Sima Qian 司马迁

sitan 死坛 arena of the dead

Song Xiaoxian宋晓贤

Song Zuifa 宋醉发

Souhu 搜狐 Sohu

Su Feishu 苏非舒

Su Rui苏芮

Su Shansheng 苏善生

Suiyue de yizhao: Jiushi niandai wenxue shuxi shige juan 岁月的遗照：九十年代文学书系诗歌卷 *A Portrait of Years Gone By: Literature of the Nineties, Poetry Volume*

Sun Wenbo 孙文波

Tamen 他们 Them

Tamen shinian shixuan 他们十年诗选 Them Ten-Year Poetry Selection

tan 坛 altar, arena

Tan Kexiu 谭克修

Tan Zhongchi谭仲池

Tang Xiaodu 唐晓渡

TaoTao 滔滔

titan 体坛 sporting arena

tizhi 体制 the system

Tiananmen shichao 天安门诗抄 Tiananmen Poetry

Tian Xiaoqing 田晓青

Tianya 天涯 *Horizons*

Tianya shihui 天涯诗会 *Tianya Poetry Society*

Tudou 土豆

tuzhu shiren 土著诗人 aborigine poets

tuanti 团体 group

Wansheng Shuyuan 万圣书园 All Sages Bookstore

Wang Ao 王傲

Wang Gui 王贵

Wang Jiaxin 王家新

wangkan 网刊 webzine, e-zine

wangluo shige 网络诗歌 Internet poetry

wangluo shiren 网络诗人 Internet poets

wangluoti shige 网络体诗歌 Internet-form poetry

wangmin 网民 netizen

wangming 网名 web-name

Wang Mingyun 王明韵

Wangyi 网易 NetEase

Wang Yin 王寅
wangyou 网友 web friends
weibo 微博 microblogs
wei dongli 微动力 microforces
Weige zhun ru Zhongguo shichang 伟哥准入中国市场 Viagra Gains Entry to the Chinese Market
weiguan 围观 to surround and observe, the surrounding gaze
Wei Hui 卫慧
Wei le laji wo laji 为了垃圾我垃圾 For the Sake of Rubbish I Am Rubbish
Weiming kongjian 未名空间 No Name Space, MITBBS
wei minzu shige fuxing er nuli 为民族诗歌复兴而努力 working hard for the renaissance of the people's poetry
wei shenghuo de shige 为生活的诗歌 poetry for life's sake
wei shenme bu rang Shen Haobo zai shufu yixie ne 为什么不让沈浩波再舒服一些呢 Why not make Shen Haobo feel even better?
Wei shenme bu zai shufu yixie ne 为什么不再舒服一些呢？Why Not Make It Feel Even Better?
wei shige de shige 为诗歌的诗歌 poetry for poetry's sake
wei xianchang shuo 伪现场说 fake live-scene discourse
Wenchuan shige 汶川诗歌 Wenchuan Poetry
wenhua chanye 文化产业 culture industry
wenhua jingyi 文化经济 cultural economy
wenhuare 文化热 high-culture fever
wenhua tizhi gaige 文化体制改革 cultural system reforms
Wen Jiabao 温家宝
Wenlian 文联 abbreviated version of Zhongguo Wenxue Yishujie Lianhehui
Wenloucun jishi 文楼村记事 Records of Wenlou Village
wentan 文坛 literary arena
wenyi 文艺 literature and art
wenyi qingnian 文艺青年 artistic youth
Wo ai zhe tudi 我爱这土地 I Love This Land
wo ba shi Li Gang 我爸是李刚 my dad is Li Gang
women zai yiqi 我们在一起 we are together
Wu Ang 巫昂
Wu Mengqi吴梦奇
wutai 舞台 stage
wu ti 无体 no essence
Wu Wenguang 吴文光
wu yong 无用 no application
Xi Chuan 西川
Xi Du 西渡
Xiabanshen 下半身 Lower Body
xiake 侠客 knight-errant
xianchang 现场 live scene
xianchang biaoyan 现场表演 live performance
xianchang zhibo 现场直播 live broadcasting
xianchanggan 现场感 feeling of live scenes
xianchangxing 现场性 liveness
xiandai 现代 modern
Xiandai shige luntan 现代诗歌论坛 *Modern Poetry Forum*

xianfeng 先锋 avant-garde
xianshi 现实 revealing the real [as in *xianshizhuyi* 现实主义 realism]
xianzaishi 现在时 present tense
Xiangchou 乡愁 Nostalgia
Xiangwang wennuan 向往温暖 *Yearning for Warmth*
xiang xia 向下 aim down
Xiangxin weilai 相信未来 Believe in the Future
Xiao Hai 小海
xiao wenren shige 小文人诗歌 petty literati poetry
Xiao wu 小武 *Xiao Wu* or *The Pickpocket*
Xiaoxiang chenbao 潇湘晨报 Xiaoxiang Morning News
Xiao Yin 小引
Xiao Ying 萧映
Xiao Yu'er 小鱼儿
Xie Youshun 谢有顺
xiezuo chuban 协作出版 cooperative publishing arrangements
Xinlang 新浪 Sina
Xinnian xin shi hui 新年新诗会 New Year New Poetry Show
Xin Pipan Xianshi Zhuyi Shige 新批判现实主义诗歌 New Critical Realist Poetry
Xinrui shiren menglie pengji "xiao wenren shige' 新锐诗人猛烈抨击'小文人诗歌' Sharp poets harshly criticize "petty literati poetry"
Xin Shi 新诗 New Poetry
Xin shiji shidian 新世纪诗典 New Century Poetry Classics
Xin shi Yanjiusuo 新诗研究所 New Poetry Research Institute
Xin Zuopai 新左派 New Leftism
Xin Ziyouzhuyi 新自由主义 Neoliberalism
Xingxing 星星 *Stars*
xiuxian 休闲leisure
Xu Fan徐帆
Xu Jiang 徐江
Xu Jingya 徐敬亚
xushi 叙事 narrative
Xu Xiangchou 徐乡愁
Xu Zhimo 徐志摩
xueshuhui 学术会 [academic] conference
xuerou 血肉 flesh and blood
xueyuan pai 学院派 academic group
Xunlian xiaozhu tianshang fei 训练小猪天上飞 Training Piglets to Fly in the Sky
Yan Jun 颜峻
yantaohui 研讨会 [academic] conference
Yan Wo 燕窝
Yan Yanwen阎延文
Yang Chunguang 杨春光
yanggao ti 羊羔体 Baby Lamb form
Yang Ke 杨克
Yang Li 杨黎
Yang Lian 杨炼
Yang Xiaomin 杨晓民
Yeshou 野兽 Beast
Yeya Shalong 野鸭沙龙 Wild Duck Salon
Yi 翼 *Wings*
yiban duzhe 一般读者 ordinary reader
Yi dai ren 一代人 This Generation
Yi ge ren lai dao Tiannaxi 一

个人来到田纳西 Alone in Tennessee
yijian lingxiu 意见领袖 opinion leader
Yi Sha 伊沙
yishi 仪式 ceremony
yishu shang women bingcheng: zhenzheng de, yongheng de minjian lichang 艺术上我们秉承：真正的永恒的民间立场 In art we adhere to the true, eternal, Popular Standpoint
Yi Tou Xueqi Fanggang de Zhu 一头血气方刚的猪 A Feisty Pig
yiwen cuxiao 以文促销 using culture to promote business
Yin Lichuan 尹丽川
yinyong 吟咏 to chant
yingtan 影坛 cinematic arena
Yongshibang 庸诗榜 Mediocre Poetry Charts
yongsu 庸俗 tacky
Youchou 忧愁 Sorrow
Youguan dayantan 有关大雁塔 Of Wild Goose Pagoda
youguo youmin 忧国忧民 to worry about the nation and the people
Youku 优酷
Yu Dan 于丹
Yudu 余毒 Residual Poison
Yu Guangzhong 余光中
Yu Jian 于坚
yule 娱乐 entertainment
Yuxiang 雨巷 Rainy Alley
yuyan de yuansheng xianchang 语言的原声现场 the live scenes of the original sounds of language
Yuan Mei 袁枚
Yue Gencheng乐根成
yundong 运动 movement, campaign
Zaibie kangqiao 再别康桥 A Second Farewell to Cambridge
zaichang 在场 [on the scene] presence
zaichangzhe 在场者 people present [on the scene]
zanzhu 赞助 to sponsor
Zang Di 臧棣
zaoxue 造血 hematopoietic
zeren bianji 责任编辑 responsible editor
zhai yundong 宅运动 homebody activism
Zhang Baoquan 张宝全
Zhang Guangtian 张广天
Zhang Jiayan 张嘉谚
Zhang Ning 张宁
Zhang Qinghua 张清华
Zhang Shuguang 张曙光
Zhang Taozhou 张桃洲
Zhang Xin 张欣 (CEO of SOHO China)
Zhang Xin 张新 (literary historian)
Zhang Xinyu 张新煜
Zhang Yimou 张艺谋
Zhang Ziyi piaoliang bu piaoliang? 章子怡漂亮不漂亮？ Is Zhang Ziyi Beautiful or Not?
Zhao Lihua 赵丽华
Zhao Yi 赵翼
zhenggui 正规 proper
zhenghe 整合 consolidation
zhengque daoxiang 正确导向 correct guidance of public opinion

Zheng Xiaoqiong 郑晓琼
Zhi Feng 支峰
zhimian xianchang de piping 直面现场的批评 criticism that confronts live scenes
zhishi 知识 knowledge
Zhishifenzi xiezuo 知识分子写作 Intellectual Writing
Zhi xiangshu 致橡树 To the Oak Tree
zhongchan jieceng 中产阶层 the middle class
Zhong Dao 中岛
Zhongguo Shige Hui 中国诗歌会 China Poetry Society
Zhongguo Shige Paihangbang 中国诗歌排行榜 Chinese Poetry Charts
Zhongguo shige de lian 中国诗歌的脸 Faces of Chinese Poetry
Zhongguo shitan 1986 xiandaishi qunti dazhan 中国诗坛1986现代诗群体大展 Grand Exhibition of Modernist Poetry Groups on China's Poetry Arena in 1986
Zhongguo Wenxue Yishujie Lianhehui 中国文学艺术界联合会 Chinese National Federation of Writers and Artists
Zhongguo Xiandai Wenxueguan 中国现代文学馆 National Museum of Modern Chinese Literature
Zhongguo xin shi nianjian 中国新诗年鉴 *Chinese New Poetry Almanac*
Zhongjian dai 中间代 the Middle Generation
Zhou Enlai 周恩来
Zhou Jun 周军
Zhou Yunpeng 周云蓬
Zhou Zan 周瓒
zhuyi 主义 ism
Zhu Ziqing 朱子庆
Zhuangzi 庄子
Zi yue 子曰 Confucius Sez
Zuguo a, wo qin'ai de zuguo 祖国啊，我亲爱的祖国 Motherland, Ah, My Dear Motherland
Zuguo, huo yi meng wei ma 祖国，或以梦为马 Motherland, Or a Dream as a Horse
Zuojia Xiehui 作家协会 Writers' Association
Zuopin 作品 *Literary Works*
Zuoyi Zuojia Lianmeng 左翼作家联盟 League of Left-Wing Writers

NOTES

INTRODUCTION

1. I use here Meow Hui Goh's translation of this phrase, which she adapts from Stephen Owen's translation of *zhi* as "what is intently on the mind." Goh, *Sound and Sight*, 122.

2. Xinhua, "Shei hai zai xie shi, Zhongguo hai you shiren ma?" (Who still writes poetry and does China still have poets?); Xinhua, "Dangdai shige weihe 'jimo'?" (Why is contemporary poetry so lonely?).

3. These activities are not limited to modern-style poetry; as Tian Xiaofei shows, writing old-style poetry is also still a popular activity in China today, although it does not have the same institutional support as modern poetry and is mostly written as a "private and personal undertaking." Tian, "Muffled Dialect Spoken by Green Fruit."

4. Hartley, Burgess, and Bruns, "Introducing Dynamics."

5. Cao Pi, "Lun wen" (Discourse on literature), translated in Owen, *Readings in Chinese Literary Thought*, 58. The applicability of this famous line to modern Chinese literary practices is discussed, among other places, in Denton, "General Introduction," 18–19; Hockx, *Questions of Style*, chap. 6; Van Crevel, *Chinese Poetry in Times of Mind, Mayhem and Money*, 448.

6. See, e.g., Zhou, *Historicizing Online Politics*; Zheng, *Technological Empowerment*; Zhao, *Communication in China*; Yang, *The Power of the Internet in China*; Sun, *Internet Policy in China*; Lagerkvist, *After the Internet, Before Democracy.*

7. This pertains more to the reception of cultural studies in the Western world. For an overview of its scholarly reception in China, see Wang, "Cultural Studies in China."

8. Grossberg, *Cultural Studies in the Future Tense*, 54, 9.

9. Damon and Livingston, *Poetry and Cultural Studies*, 2. The authors suggest that a cultural studies understanding of poetry should begin with a rough social definition that encompasses anything that is claimed to be poetry at any time (3).

10. Harrington, *Poetry and the Public*, 5, 20.

11. For more on the involvement of poetry in the Great Leap Forward, see Chen, "Multiplicity in Uniformity."

12. Grossberg, *Cultural Studies in the Future Tense*, 25, 40, 41.

13. Wang, "What Is Political Theater?" 86.

14. Scott, *Conscripts of Modernity*, 4.

15. Hartley, *Communication, Cultural and Media Studies*, 241.

16. Grossberg, *Cultural Studies in the Future Tense*, 50.

17. Shoemaker and Vos, *Gatekeeping Theory*, 1.

18. For more on cultural citizenship, see Andrew et al., *Accounting for Culture*; Stevenson, *Cultural Citizenship*.

19. Fong and Murphy, "Introduction: Chinese Experiences of Citizenship at the Margins," 2.

20. Zhang, *Postsocialism and Cultural Politics*, 3, 11, 4, 55.

21. Berry, *Postsocialist Cinema in Post-Mao China*; Gong, *Uneven Modernity*; Hockx, *Internet Literature in China*; McGrath, *Postsocialist Modernity*; Lu, *Chinese Modernity and Global Biopolitics*; Visser, *Cities Surround the Countryside*.

22. Lu, *Chinese Modernity and Global Biopolitics*, 209–10.

23. Gong, *Uneven Modernity*, 7.

24. Harvey, *A Brief History of Neoliberalism*, 120.

25. Robison, introduction, vii; Robison, "Neoliberalism and the Market State," 4.

26. Zhao, *Communication in China*, 6–7.

27. Ren, *The Middle Class in Neoliberal China*, 14.

28. Ibid., 146–47.

29. Wang and Lu, "Introduction: China and New Left Critique," x–xii.

30. For more on migrant worker poetry, see Gong, "Toward a New Leftist Ecocriticism in Postsocialist China"; Inwood, "Between License and Responsibility."

31. Straw, "Scenes and Sensibilities," 248.

32. In other words, I follow Foucault's later understanding of discourses as "tactical elements or blocks operating in the field of force relations." Foucault, *The History of Sexuality*, 101–2.

33. Examples include Zhang Xiuzhong, ed., *Zhongguo shitan de zuori jinri he mingri* (The yesterday, today, and tomorrow of China's poetry arena), published by Shanghai shudian in 1928; Pu Feng, *Xiandai Zhongguo shitan* (China's modern poetry arena), published by Shige chubanshe in 1938; and *Zhongguo shitan* (China's poetry arena), published by Zhongguo shitanshe in 1948.

34. Zhang, "Bearing Witness," 18; Zhang, "Transfiguring the Postsocialist City," 96; Berghuis, *Performance Art in China*, 135; Berry, "Jia Zhangke and the Temporality of Postsocialist Chinese Cinema," 119; Braester, "Excuse Me, Your Camera Is in My Face," 201.

35. For an ethnographic study of the *genba* of Japanese hip-hop, see Condry, *Hip-Hop Japan*.

36. Wang, *Yuyan dadian* (A great Chinese dictionary).

37. Yeh, "Frontier Taiwan," 3–4.

38. For more on Republican-era literary societies, see Hockx, *Questions of Style*; Denton and Hockx, *Literary Societies of Republican China*.

39. For more on the socialist cultural bureaucracy, see Link, *The Uses of Literature.*

40. See, especially, McDougall and Louie, *The Literature of China in the Twentieth Century*; Yeh, "Contemporary Chinese Poetry Scenes"; Yeh, "The 'Cult of Poetry' in Contemporary China"; Van Crevel, *Language Shattered*; Van Crevel, "The Horror of Being Ignored and the Pleasure of Being Left Alone"; Van Crevel, "Unofficial Poetry Journals from the People's Republic of China"; Van Crevel, *Chinese Poetry in Times of Mind, Mayhem and Money.*

41. Dai, *Yinxing shuxie* (Invisible writing), 219.

42. Ibid., 224–26.

43. Qiu, *Zhongyao de shi xianchang* (The important thing is the live scene), 2.

44. Zhang, "Zhongguo dangdai xingwei yishu de meixue zhi si" (Thoughts on the aesthetics of Chinese contemporary performance art).

45. Berghuis, *Performance Art in China*, 135.

46. Huang, "Dangqian xiju yishu moshi jian de ronghe yu paichi" (Fusions and repulsions between current forms of theatrical art), in *Dangdai xiju* 6 (2002).

47. Wu, *Xianchang* (Document), 274–75.

48. Quoted in Dai, *Yinxing shuxie* (Invisible writing), 225.

49. Zhang, "Bearing Witness"; Robinson, "From 'Public' to 'Private.'"

50. Zhang, "Bearing Witness," 19.

51. Ibid., 20.

52. Berry, "Getting Real," 123.

53. Dai, *Yinxing shuxie* (Invisible writing), 226.

54. See the Appendix for the complete set of questions included in this questionnaire.

55. Wang, *High Culture Fever*, 160.

56. Hartley, Burgess, and Bruns, "Introducing Dynamics," 2.

57. Foley, "The tAgora: Exchanging Tangible Goods."

58. Foley, "Contingency."

59. Foley, "The oAgora: Oral Networks to Surf."

60. Foley, "Systems Versus Things."

61. Foley, *Oral Tradition and Internet Technology*, 8.

62. Yi, "Zuo da de 'Shi jianghu'" ("Poetry rivers and lakes" made big).

63. Miller and Shepherd, "Questions for Genre Theory from the Blogosphere," 285.

64. For discussion of the hive mind and the power of collective organization, see Shirky, *Here Comes Everybody.*

65. A similar point is made by Jing Wang: "Precisely because it is hard to monitor the spread of viral content online, Chinese digital networks are a breeding ground for creative expression that tests the boundaries of the norm." Wang, *Brand New China*, 302.

66. Gong and Yang, "Digitized Parody," 3.

67. Zhao, *Communication in China*, 36.

68. Ibid., 84.

69. Ibid., 7, 14.

70. Ibid., 32–33.

71. Ibid., 35–36. Rebecca MacKinnon makes a similar point in her discussion of dissent on the Chinese Internet, suggesting that while public debate and certain forms of online activism are growing, the state's methods of control and manipulation have ultimately been successful in preventing democracy movements from taking off in China. MacKinnon, *Consent of the Networked*, 42.

72. Barmé, *In the Red*, chap. 11.

73. For more on the history and functions of CCTV, see Zhu, *Two Billion Eyes*.

74. Zhao, *Communication in China*, 86.

75. Wang, "Culture as Leisure and Culture as Capital," 70–71.

76. Zhao, *Communication in China*, 108–9, 120.

77. Wang, "Culture as Leisure and Culture as Capital," 86.

78. Ren, *The Middle Class in Neoliberal China*, 69–76.

79. Ibid., 16.

80. Ibid., 18–19.

81. Ibid., 147.

82. Zhao, *Communication in China*, 121.

83. Ren, *The Middle Class in Neoliberal China*, 99.

84. As discussed in Crespi, *Voices in Revolution*, chap. 7.

85. Scholarly contributions include Cheng, *Zhongguo dangdai shige shi* (A history of Chinese contemporary poetry); Hong and Liu, *Zhongguo xin shi shi* (A history of Chinese contemporary new poetry); Luo, *Ershi shiji Zhongguo xianfeng shichao* (Twentieth-century Chinese avant-garde poetry); Zhang, *Ershi shiji Zhongguo xin shi shi* (A history of twentieth-century Chinese new poetry); and Zhou, *Touguo shige xiezuo de qianwangjing* (Through the periscope of poetic writing).

86. Van Crevel, *Chinese Poetry in Times of Mind, Mayhem and Money*, 9.

87. Braester, *Witness Against History*.

88. Wang, *Illuminations from the Past*, 103.

89. Assmann, "Collective Memory and Cultural Identity," 126.

90. For detailed discussion of China's revolutionary poetry recitation aesthetics, see Crespi, *Voices in Revolution*, chap. 6. For analysis of Mao's poetry, see Zhang and Vaughan, *Mao Zedong as Poet and Revolutionary Leader*.

91. Hong and Liu, *Zhongguo dangdai xin shi shi* (A history of Chinese contemporary new poetry), 111.

92. Tan, "Dangdai xin shi jingduanhua wenti ji xin shi jiaoyu wenti piantan" (A brief discussion of the canonization of contemporary new poetry and the problem of new poetry education).

93. Liu, "Jianguo yilai zhongxue jiaocai xin shi jiaoyu de fazhan" (The development of new poetry education through middle school textbooks since the establishment of the PRC).

94. Wang, *Illuminations from the Past*, 3.

95. Ibid., 5.

96. As was the case with CCTV's *New Year New Poetry Show* (Xinnian xin shi hui), a television show consisting of staged recitations by famous TV presenters and actors of well-known modern poems broadcast each Chinese New Year during 2005–10. The videos and list of poems from each show can be found here: http://www.360doc.com/content/12/0226/21/8088618_189858819.shtml. From 2011 on, the show was renamed *New Year Poetry Show* and reconfigured to include more classical than modern poems.

97. Haft, *Selective Guide to Chinese Literature, 1900–1949*; Hockx, *A Snowy Morning*; Hockx, *Questions of Style*; Hong and Liu, *Zhongguo xin shi shi* (A history of new poetry in China); Lin, *Modern Chinese Poetry*; McDougall and Louie, *The Literature of China in the Twentieth Century*; Van Crevel, *Language Shattered*; Yeh, *Modern Chinese Poetry*.

98. Van Crevel, *Language Shattered*.

99. As translated in Yeh, "Chinese Literature from 1937 to the Present," 611.

100. Xu, "Jueqi de shiqun" (Poetry groups on the rise).

101. Tian, "Shisan lu yanxian" (Route no. 13), 33. According to Tian, local students were invited onto a makeshift stage to recite poetry; he recalls one young girl reciting Fang Han's poem "On the Road" (Zai lushang) with particular zeal. The film director Chen Kaige, then a student at the Beijing Film Academy, also participated by reciting Shi Zhi's "Believe in the Future" and Bei Dao's "The Answer" in a typically revolutionary style. See Chapter 3 for more on the history of poetry recitation in China.

102. Jing Wang argues that writers in the first half of the 1980s maintained their belief in literature's sensational impact on society and in their "sacred mission" as the most avant-garde of China's cultural and political critics. This belief helped characterize literature as an institution that possessed the ability to bring about an ethical rebirth of the nation. Wang, *High Culture Fever*, 160.

103. Day, "Grand Poetry Exhibition of 1986."

104. Van Crevel, *Chinese Poetry in Times of Mind, Mayhem and Money*, 16.

105. Yeh, "The 'Cult of Poetry' in Contemporary China," 64–68. For more on the canonization of Haizi, see Kunze, *Struggle and Symbiosis*; Van Crevel, *Chinese Poetry in Times of Mind, Mayhem and Money*, chap. 3.

106. Hong and Liu, *Zhongguo dangdai xin shi shi* (A history of Chinese contemporary new poetry), 248–49.

107. Wang Guangming, cited in Luo, *Ershi shiji Zhongguo xianfeng shichao* (Twentieth-century Chinese avant-garde poetry), 237.

108. Shen, "Shei zai na 'jiushi niandai' kai shuan?" (Who's fooling "the nineties"?).

109. Quoted in Van Crevel, *Chinese Poetry in Times of Mind, Mayhem and Money*, 428, 438. Van Crevel suggests that an uppercase "P" be used in the word "Popular" to indicate its poetry-political connotations, even though "popular" is far from being an exact translation of the complex Chinese word *minjian* (408–9).

110. Li, "Naming and Antinaming," 200, 199.

111. Van Crevel, *Chinese Poetry in Times of Mind, Mayhem and Money*, 10, 25.

112. Ibid., 30–45.

113. Liu, "Gender Politics in Jin Yong's Martial Arts Novels," 182.

114. Song, "Space, Swordsmen, and Utopia," 155–57.

115. Yang, *The Power of the Internet in China*, 173–75.

116. Van Crevel translates "poetry rivers and lakes" as "poetry vagabonds." Van Crevel, *Chinese Poetry in Times of Mind, Mayhem and Money*, 330.

117. Bai, "Shitan yingxiong zuoci paihangbang" (Poetry arena heroes ranked by order of seating); Zhang, "The Return of the Pioneer," 8.

118. Day, *China's Second World of Poetry*, 426.

119. Zhou, *Touguo shige xiezuo de qianwangjing* (Through the periscope of poetic writing), 10. For more on the commercialization of fiction, see Kong, *Consuming Literature*.

120. For more on the formation of the Middle Generation, see An, "Guanyu zhongjiandai" (About the middle generation).

121. Much has been written in Chinese on female-authored poetry and poetry communities, including a substantial section in Zhou, *Touguo shige xiezuo de qianwangjing* (Through the periscope of poetic writing). At present, the only English-language monograph dedicated to women's poetry is Zhang, *The Invention of a Discourse*.

122. Naming has a long history in modern Chinese literature; in 1928, Lu Xun satirized this tendency among his colleagues: "The fearful thing about the Chinese literary [arena] is that everyone keeps introducing new terms without defining them." Cited in Anderson, *The Limits of Realism*, 1. I have replaced Anderson's translation of *tan* as "scene" with "arena" to be consistent with the language of this book.

123. Wang, *Illuminations from the Past*, 25.

124. Liu, *Menglongshi yihou* (After misty poetry).

125. Chen, *Touches of History*; Jiang, *"Xin shi ji" yu Zhongguo xin shi de fasheng* ("New Poems" and the emergence of China's New Poetry).

126. Foley, "Arena of Oral Tradition."

127. Straw, "Scenes and Sensibilities," 254.

128. Foley, "Culture as Network."

129. Crespi, *Voices in Revolution*, 171–73.

130. Yeh, "'There Are No Camels in the Koran,'" 11–12.

131. Xu, "Where Has the Aura Gone?" 33–35.

CHAPTER 1

1. Li, "Ershiyi shiji" (Twenty-first century).

2. Chen, "Jin wu nian wangluo shitan shi xiang guancha" (Observations on poetry phenomena in the online poetry arena in the last five years).

3. Hockx, "Virtual Chinese Literature," 673.

4. Foley, *Oral Tradition and Internet Technology*, 83.

5. Zhao, *Communication in China*, 305.

6. Liu, *Urban Youth in China*; Herold and Marolt, *Online Society in China*; Sun, *Internet Policy in China*; Voci, *China on Video.*

7. Yang, *The Power of the Internet in China*, 3, 209, 1.

8. Ibid., 55, 159.

9. Yang, "Social Dynamics in the Evolution of China's Internet Content Control Regime," 288–89.

10. MacKinnon, "Flatter World and Thicker Walls?" 33.

11. For more analysis of online opinion shaping practices, see Marolt, "Grassroots Agency in a Civil Sphere?"

12. Yang, *The Power of the Internet in China*, 209, 211.

13. Ibid., 214–16. For more on Internet use among socially disenfranchised groups, see Qiu, *Working-Class Network Society.*

14. Yang, *The Power of the Internet in China*, 73.

15. Wang, "Dui 'wangluo shige' de chubu kaocha he yanjiu" (Preliminary investigations and research into Internet poetry). For a detailed investigation into the functioning of Chinese poetry forums, see Hockx, "Virtual Chinese Literature."

16. Disanji shikan, "Zhongguo shige de minjian jiyi" (The unofficial memory of Chinese poetry). Further evidence of the impact of this mass forum closure is evidenced by the fact that of the fifty-one websites featured in Michael Day's 2005 list of influential avant-garde poetry forums (http://leiden.dachs-archive.org/poetry/list.html), only two were still operational by 2013.

17. This was not the first time that poetry forums had been subject to unexpected mass closures; a similar thing happened in 2003, when many forums hosted by NetEase were shut down, leading to a "consolidation" (*zhenghe*) of online poetry forums. Chen, "Jin wu nian wangluo shitan shi xiang guancha" (Observations on poetry phenomena in the online poetry arena in the last five years).

18. Ibid.

19. Yang, "The Internet as Cultural Form," 111.

20. See, e.g., Disanji xinwen fayanren, "Xin shiji shi nian Zhongguo shige de xianzhuang he weilai yantaohui jiyao" (Summary of the forum on the current state and future of Chinese poetry in the first decade of the new millennium).

21. Yu, "Blogging Everyday Life in Chinese Internet Culture," 424.

22. Ibid., 425.

23. China Internet Network Information Center (CNNIC), "The 32nd Statistical Report on Internet Development in China."

24. Han, "The Influence of Microblogging on Personal Public Participation."

25. He, "'Shige zai wang shang'—wangluo shige" (Poetry on the Internet—Internet poetry). He writes, "if you don't read blogs then you have no way of knowing how deep poetry's waters have become."

26. Disanji xinwen fayanren, "Xin shiji shi nian Zhongguo shige de xianzhuang he weilai yantaohui jiyao" (Summary of the forum on the current state and future of Chinese poetry in the first decade of the new millennium).

27. Yang, "Wangluo huanjing xia de shige xiezuo" (Poetry writing in an online environment).

28. Sang, "Hulianwang shidai de zhongwen shige" (Chinese poetry in the age of the Internet), 259.

29. Pettitt, "Media Dynamics and the Lessons of History," 63.

30. Hjarvard, "The Mediatization of Society," 121–22. Italics in the original.

31. Hansen, *Bodies in Code*, 144.

32. Farrall and Herold, "Identity vs. Anonymity," 167.

33. Giese, "Speaker's Corner or Virtual Panopticon," 22.

34. Irwin, *Scenes*, 206.

35. See, e.g., Turkle, *Life on the Screen*; Landow, *Hypertext 2.0*; and Matusitz, "Deception in the Virtual World." For a Chinese example, see Ouyang, *Wangluo wenxue lungang* (A thesis on Internet literature).

36. Turkle, *Life on the Screen*, 10.

37. Wang, "Dui 'wangluo shige' de chubu kaocha he yanjiu" (Preliminary investigations and research into Internet poetry).

38. Lao Xiang, "Lao Taozi zenme le?" (What's up with Old Man?).

39. Pidan, "Lun zuowei yundong de lajipai" (On the School of Rubbish as a movement); Pidan, "Lajipai jiyao" (School of Rubbish synopsis).

40. Pidan, "2005 nian beiwanglu" (2005 memorandum).

41. For more on the topic of Internet celebrity, see Roberts, "China's Internet Celebrity."

42. Authors of vernacular fiction in imperial China often published under pseudonyms, in part to avoid the negative associations of this relatively "lowly" literary genre, and many of China's most influential early modern writers published under pen names, including Lu Xun (Zhou Shuren) and Lao She (Shu Qingchun).

43. Bolter, *Writing Space*, 206.

44. Lao Touzi, "Shi zha" (Poetry epistles).

45. Ibid.

46. As in the phrase *zhongti, xiyong* (Chinese essence, Western application).

47. Møllgaard, *An Introduction to Daoist Thought*, 92.

48. Bei, *August Sleepwalker*, 33. Han Dong's poem "Of the Wild Goose Pagoda" (Youguan dayanta) is often cited as a powerful example of antiloftiness and antiheroics in Third Generation poetry writing.

49. Day, *China's Second World of Poetry*, 305–6.

50. Lao Touzi, "Zhongguo laji pai shige daibiaozuo shi shou zuopin yu dianping" (Ten representative works and commentary on China's School of Rubbish poetry).

51. This refers to the poem "This Generation" (Yi dai ren), which includes the words *heise de yanjing* (black eyes). Michelle Yeh's translation is as follows: "Dark night has given me dark eyes / With which I search for light." Yeh, *Modern Chinese Poetry*, 82.

52. McDougall and Louie point out that this not in fact a poem at all but a single stanza in Bei Dao's longer poem "Notes from the City of the Sun."

They explain that the common reading of the character "net" as "a condemnation of the lack of freedom in Chinese life and the despair of those caught in its toils" is in fact a "creative misunderstanding" but do not suggest an alternative interpretation. McDougall and Louie, *The Literature of China in the Twentieth Century*, 433–34.

53. Cited in Huber, Middeke, and Zapf, *Self-Reflexivity in Literature*, 7.

54. Glazier, *Digital Poetics*.

55. Bachleitner, "The Virtual Muse," 338.

56. Hayles, "The Time of Digital Poetry," 206.

57. Internet searches of the last few lines reveal mention of similar song lyrics elsewhere and perhaps a Hungarian poem.

58. http://hk.netsh.com/eden/bbs/6411/html/tree_7544870.html.

59. Xu, "Xu Xiangchou wenxuan" (Collected writings of Xu Xiangchou).

60. Fish suggests that interpretive communities are constituted of people who share similar interpretive strategies for writing rather than reading texts, or for "constituting their properties." These strategies exist before the act of reading begins and affect what the reader sees in any given text. Fish, *Is There a Text in This Class?* 13.

61. Van Crevel, *Chinese Poetry in Times of Mind, Mayhem and Money*, chap. 9. For more on Yi Sha's life and poetics see Inwood, "Yi Sha"; Van Crevel, "Rejective Poetry."

62. Day, *China's Second World of Poetry*.

63. Translated in Van Crevel, *Chinese Poetry in Times of Mind, Mayhem and Money*, 317.

64. Ibid., 310.

65. Yu, "Shiren he wei?" (What are poets for?), 236.

66. Shen, "Huida jingbao jizhe de 11 ge wenti" (Replying to 11 questions from a Jingbao reporter).

67. Pidan, "Lajipai jiyao" (School of Rubbish synopsis).

68. Lao Touzi, "Shi zha" (Poetry epistles).

69. This poem can be found in *Laji pai wangkan [di wu qi] (shi shi zhuanhao)* (School of Rubbish Webzine Issue no. 5: Shit Poetry Special), http://www.yanruyu.com/jhy/author/39729.shtml.

70. Zhang, "Di shige yundong" (The Low Poetry Movement).

71. Xiao, "Laji xiezuo qiangdang chulong, gongcheng maotou zhizhi xiabanshen" (Rubbish writing appears with a bang, its spears pointed straight at the Lower Body).

72. Xu, "Zhongguo lajipai" (China's School of Rubbish).

73. Laiji shidai, "Di yi huihe" (The first exchange).

74. Lanhudie zidingxiang, "Zhongguo lajipai zhuming shiren, guanshui dashi Lanhudie zidingxiang da wangyou wen" (Famous poet from China's School of Rubbish and master of the School of Spam Blue Butterfly Lilac answers Internet friends' questions).

75. These include a book launch party held on July 10, 2004, in Guangzhou to mark the release of the first edition of the journal *Rubbish Movement* (Laji yundong), an event that was attended by more than thirty poets and artists, as well as journalists from several online and print media organizations.

Han, "Xin shiji shi nian Zhongguo xin shi dashiji" (Memorandum of events in the first decade of Chinese new poetry in the new century).

76. Lao Touzi, "Lajipai xuanyan" (School of Rubbish manifesto).

77. The distinction between social learning and the traditional Cartesian understanding of knowledge and learning is discussed in Grinnell, "From Consumer to Prosumer to Produser," 596.

78. Gong, "Toward a New Leftist Ecocriticism in Postsocialist China," 151–52.

79. This conversation has been archived by Jiang Pinchao and can be accessed here: http://blog.boxun.com/hero/2006/jiangpinchao/306_1.shtml.

80. For example, Barmé and Davies argue that although debates that took place on the Chinese Internet in 2000–2001 suggested that most writers could enjoy a few minutes of online fame, more permanent reputations were still being established in traditional print media. Barmé and Davies, "Have We Been Noticed Yet?" 103.

81. Chang, "2003 nian zhongguo shige zhuanhao" (Chinese poetry 2003 special).

82. Xiao, "2003 nian huayu wangluo shige bu wanquan shuli" (An incomplete assessment of Chinese language Internet poetry in 2003).

CHAPTER 2

1. Van Crevel, *Chinese Poetry in Times of Mind, Mayhem and Money*, 8.

2. Lazer, *Opposing Poetries*, 128.

3. From a methodological point of view, it is worth bearing in mind that the willingness of these editors and publishers to submit themselves to my detailed questioning was likely motivated in part by the desire to see their publications featured in English-language scholarship. I have endeavored to maintain a level of skepticism, especially regarding their more obviously self-promoting pieces of information, but for the most part take their accounts of the more mundane details of the editing and publication process to be true. Where possible, I have compared oral accounts to written recollections in prefaces, postscripts, and blogs, although much of the information provided to me in interviews is not available elsewhere.

4. Popular writing, according to Van Crevel, draws on Chinese experience and pride in national traditions such as Tang and Song dynasty classical poetry. Van Crevel, *Chinese Poetry in Times of Mind, Mayhem and Money*, 410.

5. Kong, *Consuming Literature*, 40.

6. Ibid., 65; Xin, *Publishing in China*, sec. 5.1.2.

7. For a comprehensive overview of the meanings and categories of unofficial publication within Chinese poetry production, see Van Crevel, "Unofficial Poetry Journals from the People's Republic of China."

8. See the Appendix.

9. Zhang, "From Counter-canon to Hypercanon in a Postcanonical Age," 614.

10. Yu, "Poems in Their Place."

11. Ibid., 169.

12. Sima Qian, *Shiji* (Record of history) (Shanghai: Zhonghua shuju, 1959), 47.1936, quoted in ibid., 172.

13. For a detailed case study of how successive generations of editorial and ideological efforts can shape the reputation of individual authors and thus produce literary history, see Tian, *Tao Yuanming and Manuscript Culture.*

14. Tompkins, *Sensational Designs*, 187.

15. Unless otherwise stated, the publishing details provided in this chapter are taken from interviews I conducted with Yang Ke and other members of the *Almanac*'s editorial committee in 2007 and 2009.

16. Yang, "98 gongzuo shouji" (98 work notes)," 517–18; Yang, "'Zhongguo xin shi nianjian' de jiazhi duo nian hou hui gengjia mingxi" (The value of the *Chinese New Poetry Almanac* will be clearer in years to come).

17. All the figures cited in this section of the chapter are taken from interviews with Yang Ke and other members of the editorial committee (Li Qingguo, Fu Mahuo, and Song Xiaoxian), Guangzhou, May 29, 2007.

18. Interview with Yang Ke, part of *Nanfang zhoumo*, "'Zhongguo xin shi nianjian' shige chonghui minjian de keneng" ("Chinese New Poetry Almanac": The possibility of poetry returning to the people).

19. According to Yang Ke, Yang Maodong had originally planned to send employees to individual bookshops across the country that had failed to pay suppliers for the *Almanac* but soon abandoned this practice after making an expensive train journey from Guangzhou to a bookshop in Shenyang, only to discover a mere seventy copies of the *Almanac* had been sold.

20. Yang, "Zhongguo shige xianchang" (Live scenes of Chinese poetry).

21. Garnham, *Capitalism and Communication*, 161–62.

22. Dai, *Yinxing shuxie* (Invisible writing), 25.

23. Zhou Yongming, writing about *minjian* political writers on the Internet, argues their identities are characterized by "flux, contradictions, and ambiguity" and that they are identified by their "conscious pursuit of a new citizenship centered around independence from state strictures in terms of both material well-being and freedom of thought." Zhou, "Living on the Cyber Border," 780–82.

24. Dai, *Shuxie wenhua yingxiong* (Writing cultural heroes), 11.

25. China Book Publishing Web, "Xinwen chuban zongshu yanli chachu 'xin cang da e' yi shu ji qi chubanzhe" (The General Administration of Press and Publication enforces strict punishments upon *A Great Evil Hidden in the Heart* and its publishers).

26. Zhao, *Communication in China*, 36.

27. See, e.g., McDougall, *Fictional Authors, Imaginary Audiences*, chap. 9.

28. Brokaw and Reed, *From Woodblocks to the Internet*, 33.

29. Zhang, quoted in Liu, "Jin 20 nian xin shi xuanben chuban de huimou yu pingshuo" (A look back at and reflection on the publication of poetry anthologies in the past twenty years), 20.

30. Tang Xiaodu believes this was the case with his *1998 Modern Chinese Poetry Almanac*, which was banned and withdrawn from bookshops shortly after publication: Tang suspects he was reported on by a jealous participant

in the poetry scene who used his labeling of some poetry as being from "Taiwan" (not "China's Taiwan") to get him into trouble with the censors. Tang Xiaodu, interview by the author, Beijing, July 8, 2007.

31. For a full list of critical writings that contributed toward and reflected upon the Panfeng Debate, see the appendix to Van Crevel, *Chinese Poetry in Times of Mind, Mayhem and Money*, chap. 12.

32. Yang, "98 work notes," 518–19.

33. Van Crevel, *Chinese Poetry in Times of Mind, Mayhem and Money*, 407.

34. Ibid., 10.

35. Yu, "Chuanyue hanyu de shige zhi guang" (The light of poetry, cutting through the Chinese language), 7.

36. Ibid., 8.

37. Ibid., 9. My translation of *pangran dawu* as "big beasts" follows Van Crevel, *Chinese Poetry in Times of Mind, Mayhem and Money*, 382. Han Dong uses the same phrase in his essay "Lun minjian" (On the Popular) to refer to the System, the Market, and the West.

38. For a discussion of this anthology and other key texts involved in the Intellectual-Popular polemic, see Van Crevel, *Chinese Poetry in Times of Mind, Mayhem and Money*, chap. 12.

39. An essay by Shen Haobo first explicitly pointed to these apparent miscarriages of publishing justice. Shen, "Shei zai na 'jiushi niandai' kai shuan" (Who's fooling "the nineties"?).

40. Yang Ke believes most of Xie Youshun's ideas expressed in this essay were gleaned directly from extended private communication with Yu Jian. Yang Ke, interview by the author, Guangzhou, May 29, 2007.

41. Xie, "Neizai de shige zhenxiang" (The inner true face of poetry), in *Nanfang zhoumo* (Southern Weekend), April 2, 1999, reprinted in *1999 Chinese New Poetry Almanac*, 526–29.

42. Ibid.

43. *Nandu zhoukan* (Southern Metropolis Weekly), "Yang Ke fangtan" (An interview with Yang Ke).

44. Yang, "Live scenes of Chinese poetry." All quotation marks are in the original.

45. Any details in this section not cited otherwise are based upon interviews I conducted with Yang Ke, Li Qingguo, Song Xiaoxian, and Fu Mahuo, Guangzhou, May 29, 2007.

46. This anthology takes its design cues from poetry websites and features photos of the poets and a window-like design.

47. Hartley, *The Politics of Pictures*, 3.

48. Renov, "Introduction," 8.

49. Yeh, "The 'Cult of Poetry' in Contemporary China"; Van Crevel, *Chinese Poetry in Times of Mind, Mayhem and Money*, 18.

50. Hockx, "Poets in Poems" (abstract); Van Crevel, "Not Quite Karaoke," 657.

51. Van Crevel, "Not Quite Karaoke," 657.

52. This exhibition, involving websites, newspapers, and literary journals, was partly modeled on Xu Jingya's "Grand Exhibition of Modernist Poetry Groups on China's Poetry Arena 1986." For a brief description of both, see Day, *China's Second World of Poetry*.

53. Yang, "2004–2005 'Zhongguo xin shi nianjian' gongzuo shouji" (2004–2005 "Chinese New Poetry almanac" work notes).

54. See Xi, "Shushang lichang yu yishu yuanze" (A book agent's standpoint and artistic principles).

55. Yang, "Nanfang ribao fangtan" (Interview with *Southern Daily*).

56. Xie, "Minjian yijing chengzhang wei zhuliu" (The popular has already grown into the mainstream).

57. Wu, "Xianchang" (Document), 274–75.

58. Ren defines life spectacles as mediated cultural processes that shape the ways that individuals function in and perceive everyday life, arguing that their proliferation parallels the growing importance of communication in contemporary capitalist societies. Ren, *The Middle Class in Neoliberal China*, 70.

59. Yang, "'2000 Zhongguo xin shi nianjian' gongzuo shouji" (2000 Chinese New Poetry Almanac work notes), 635.

60. Yang, "'2002–2003 Zhongguo xin shi nianjian' gongzuo shouji" (2002–2003 Chinese New Poetry Almanac work notes).

61. The table of contents can be accessed here: http://q.sohu.com/forum/14/topic/380709.

62. Lu, "Zhongguo shitan you Yang Ke!" (The Chinese poetry arena has Yang Ke!). A Google search of "2006 Chinese New Poetry Almanac list of contents" returned, in March 2008, no fewer than 152 pages of results.

63. Few people noticed that Shucai had not even selected his own poems, presumably part of his quest for objectivity.

64. Xu, "Lun wei minjian" (On the fake popular).

65. The *Spring and Autumn Annals* is the official history of the State of Lu and covers the period from 722 to 481 BCE. It is commonly thought to have been written by Confucius, although his authorship is contested by scholars. De Bary and Lufrano describe it as "a kind of old-fashioned gazette copied from ancient documents relative to public events and ceremonies." Bary and Lufrano, *Sources of Chinese Tradition*, 267.

66. Shen, "Dui Yang Ke shuo" (To Yang Ke).

67. As a result of the controversies that surrounded the editing of the 2006 edition of the *Almanac*, Yang Ke decided once again to make adjustments to the editorial procedures. From the 2007 edition onward he decided to select a different member of the editorial committee to be responsible for the majority of editorial responsibilities each year, without listing his or her name as acting editor. Yang hoped that this would avoid the poetry politics, jealousies, and factionalism that dogged the 2006 edition.

68. Guillory, *Cultural Capital*, viii, x.

69. Ibid., 28.

70. Anderson, *Imagined Communities*, 6.

71. In January 2008 Zheng Xiaoqiong's career took one step further up the ladder when she was made a deputy to the 11th Guangdong Province

People's Congress and assigned the task of representing the eight million rural migrant workers in Dongguan: a good indication of where writing poetry can still get you in China today.

CHAPTER 3

1. For more on the roles of repetition and memorization in oral practices of Chinese poetry, see Sun, *The Poetics of Repetition in English and Chinese Lyric Poetry.*

2. Foley, "Arena of Oral Tradition."

3. Foley, "Contingency."

4. Van Crevel, "The Horror of Being Ignored and the Pleasure of Being Left Alone"; Crespi, "The Poetry of Slogans and Native Sons"; Crespi, *Voices in Revolution*, chap. 7.

5. Crespi, *Voices in Revolution*, 24, 27, 58.

6. Ibid., 84.

7. Ibid., 142.

8. Ibid., 164–66.

9. Tang, *Chinese Modern*, 127.

10. This has actually happened; see Chapter 4.

11. Li Da (1890–1966) was one of the founding members of the Chinese Communist Party (CCP) and a well-known Chinese Marxist philosopher who worked for a year as propaganda chief of the CCP; Mei Lanfang was a male Chinese opera performer famed for playing *dan* (female) roles; like the comparison between Andy Lau, a popular Hong Kong star, and the former Nationalist Party leader Chiang Kai-shek, this analogy indicates an insurmountable chasm between role and actor, or between the poem and its reciter.

12. Shen, "Xiao bo Yu Jian de langsong guan" (A brief refutation of Yu Jian's views on recitation).

13. Pang, "Bo Yu Jian 'langsong shi shige de duantoutai' zhi waili xieshuo" (In refutation of Yu Jian's fallacies in "Recitation is poetry's guillotine"), http://blog.sina.com.cn/s/blog_4a5198df010005mo.htmltype=v5_one&label=rela_prevarticle.

14. See *Nanfang zhoumo* (Southern weekend), "Langsong: Hui shi zhi zui?" (Is recitation to blame for destroying poetry?). Zhang told me in an interview that he originally had no intention of writing this essay but was persuaded by the editor of the newspaper to come up with a conflicting argument.

15. Xinjingbao, "Xiju, yinyueren dazao 'kuajie' shige langsonghui" (Theatre people and musicians create a "boundary crossing" poetry recital).

16. Braester, "Chinese Cinema in the Age of Advertisement," 552–54.

17. Ren, "Redistribution of the Sensible in Neoliberal China," 241.

18. For more on corruption in Chinese real estate, see Sun, *Corruption and Market in Contemporary China*; Zhu, "The Shadow of the Skyscrapers."

19. Hu, "Dachang" (Big Square).

20. Middleton, *Distant Reading*, 92–93.

21. UNESCO, "Draft Programme and Budget, 2004–2005."

22. Ren, *The Middle Class in Neoliberal China*, 126.

23. Full details of the organizing committee of the Lushan Famous Poets Summit were included in the official announcement, posted on various news and poetry websites. See, e.g., Tan Kexiu's blog entry: http://blog.tianya.cn/blogger/post_show.asp?BlogID=341456&PostID=5579250&idWriter=0&Key=0.

24. Yue, "Zai shou jie lushan xin shiji shige mingjia fenghui xinwen fabuhui zhici" (An address at the press conference for the First Lushan New Century Famous Poets Summit).

25. Shen, "Ruhe lijie xianfeng" (How should we understand the avant-garde?).

26. Xiaowen, "Xinrui shiren menglie pengji 'xiao wenren shige'" (Sharp poets harshly criticize "petty literati poetry").

27. Van Crevel, "The Horror of Being Ignored and the Pleasure of Being Left Alone."

28. Braester, "Chinese Cinema in the Age of Advertisement," 551.

29. Ren, *The Middle Class in Neoliberal China*, 19.

30. Ren, "Redistribution of the Sensible in Neoliberal China," 241.

31. Braester, "Chinese Cinema in the Age of Advertisement," 564.

32. Feiniu7, "Wo weishenme yao ma Tan Kexiu" (Why I want to curse Tan Kexiu); Jiaoshou, "Tan Kexiu li fengrenyuan hai you duo yuan?" (How long until Tan Kexiu ends up in the lunatic asylum?).

33. Zhao, *Communication in China*, 86.

34. Crespi, *Voices in Revolution*, 181.

35. Higgins, "Iceland Baffled by Chinese Plan for Golf Resort."

36. Hawes, "Corporate CEOs as Cultural Producers," 95–96.

37. Most of the organizers of face-to-face poetry events I interviewed in 2006 and 2007 confirmed that large amounts of free publicity provided by the media was the primary motivation behind the sponsorship of otherwise commercially nonviable poetry events.

38. Zhao, *Communication in China*, 39; Ren, *The Middle Class in Neoliberal China*, 16.

39. Journalists invited to attend the Misty Poetry Forum, part of the 2005 Peking University Weiming Poetry Festival (Beijing daxue Weiming shigejie), were presented with a sum of ¥200 (US$33) each, financed by Huang Nubo. Several told me in private that they were only there for the money and would otherwise have no interest in reporting on the event. For more on the phenomenon of paid journalism in contemporary China, see Latham, "Nothing but the Truth."

40. *Hunan ribao*, "Zhimian shidai vs. geren jiushu" (Facing the era vs. personal redemption).

41. Crespi, *Voices in Revolution*, 176.

42. Duoyu's phrase "lose their voices" (*shisheng*) can also be translated as "cry out"; it is not entirely clear to me which meaning of the term he is invoking here, and it is possible the ambiguity is intentional.

43. Quoted in Chou, "Creative Space, Cultural Industry Clusters, and Participation of the State in Beijing," 200.

44. Ren, *The Middle Class in Neoliberal China*, 16.

45. Inwood, "Between License and Responsibility." Marston Anderson writes that realism has carried "the profoundest burden of hope for cultural transformation" in China since the earliest years of the Republic of China. Anderson, *The Limits of Realism*, 3.

46. Mao, "Talks at the Yan'an Forum on Art and Literature," 438.

47. Wang and Lu, "Introduction: China and New Left Critique," xii.

48. Anderson, *The Limits of Realism*, 7.

49. Denton, "General Introduction," 37.

CHAPTER 4

1. See, e.g., Moss, "My Run for Oxford Professor of Poetry Was Crushed by Viral Campaign—and a Distinguished Rival."

2. Burman, "The Misunderstanding of Memes."

3. Dawkins, *The Selfish Gene*, 192.

4. Burman, "The Misunderstanding of Memes," 78, 98.

5. See, e.g., China Digital Times, "Grass-Mud Horse Lexicon."

6. Foley, "The eAgora: Electronic Networks to Surf."

7. Sullivan, "A Tale of Two Microblogs in China," 775.

8. China Internet Network Information Center (CNNIC), "The 32nd Statistical Report on Internet Development in China."

9. Sullivan, "A Tale of Two Microblogs in China."

10. China Media Project, "The Surrounding Gaze."

11. Hu, quoted in ibid.

12. This Tianya post contains the original post on *Liangquanqimei* left on September 11 and shows how it was forwarded to the U.S.-based Chinese-language BBS *No Name Space* later that day and to the Tsinghua University BBS *Shuimu Qinghua* on September 12: http://www.tianya.cn/publicforum/content/culture/1/215671.shtml. The history of the initial spoofing of Zhao Lihua is elucidated on a Baidu forum in a post titled "A search for the developmental origins of Pear Blossom Form," which was taken from a comment left on Zhao Lihua's personal blog: http://tieba.baidu.com/p/140757527.

13. This poem and several others can be found in a news feature titled "Are netizens spoofing a female poet, or is a female poet spoofing poetry?" http://news.sohu.com/s2006/06nvshiren/.

14. They included a famous post left by the web ID Pear Blossom Cult (*lihua jiao*) on the Tianya BBS on September 13, which is widely cited as the originating site for the thread; see, e.g., http://baike.baidu.com/view/1404696.htm.

15. http://bbs.dahe.cn/read-htm-tid-702529–page-3.htm.

16. This website has been archived by Wayback Machine and its contents are available here: http://www.tianya.cn/publicforum/content/culture/1/215671.shtml.

17. See, e.g., http://www.tudou.com/programs/view/9Pznrzp3EmQ/.

18. http://news.163.com/06/0919/20/2RDLD1M4000121EP.html.

19. A transcript of their conversation can be read here: http://blog.sina.com.cn/lm/8/2006/1010/9183.html.

20. See, e.g., the Xinhua news article "Liting Zhao Lihua, nan shiren Su Feishu luoti langsong bei juliu" (Supporting Zhao Lihua, male poet Su Feishu's naked recital gets him arrested).

21. http://news.xinhuanet.com/video/2006–10/17/content_5212804.htm.

22. http://news.tom.com/2006–10–11/0027/08624238.html.

23. Zhao, "Zhao Lihua huida Yangcheng wanbao caifang" (Zhao Lihua replies to an interview with the *Yangcheng Evening News*).

24. http://www.weibo.com/1433655842/zFoqwijdV1.

25. http://www.weibo.com/1433655842/wroqwisJed.

26. This phrase was originally posted on a forum for the popular MMORPG *World of Warcraft* and went viral in part because of the apparently absurd idea that someone's mother would resort to using video game forums to make sure her son gets home in time for dinner.

27. Tengxun xinwen, "Jiwei shuji huo Lu Xun wenxuejiang 'yanggao ti' shi baohong wangluo" (Party secretary wins Lu Xun prize for literature, "Baby Lamb form" poems light up the web).

28. Zhao, "Lu Xun jiang he Lu Xun goupi guanxi dou meiyou" (The Lu Xun prize has dog fart all to do with Lu Xun). As Zhao notes in a later addition to this blog entry, the original title itself also turned into a "form" (*ti*) that went viral, inspiring hundreds of inventive questions from netizens such as "Does the Golden Rooster prize have anything to do with golden roosters?" "Does the Hundred Flowers prize have anything to do with flowers?" and "Does ants climbing up the tree [a spicy noodle dish with minced meat] have anything to do with trees?"

29. Tengxun xinwen, "Yan Yanwen: 'Yanggao ti' shi Lu Xun wenxuejiang de siwang zhengshu" (Yan Yanwen: "Baby Lamb form" is the death certificate for the Lu Xun prize for literature).

30. Meng, "Regulating Egao," 52–53.

31. Shi had taken the Chinese media by storm in 2005 with her blog-based narratives and "narcissistic commentary" of her attempts to gain entrance into China's top graduate programs by relying upon her dubious self-taught dancing skills and signature "S-shaped curves" and to find herself a rich and handsome boyfriend despite her (according to netizens) "fat" and "revolting" appearance. For more on Sister Lotus, see Roberts, "China's Internet Celebrity."

32. http://dzh.mop.com/whbm/20101027/0/OSgl5lI1da13df3l.shtml.

33. This incident occurred when Li Qiming, the perpetrator of a fatal car accident in Hebei, tried to use his father Li Gang's position as deputy director of the local Public Security Bureau to extricate himself from responsibility for his crime.

34. Shanshangshi, "Liting Zhao Lihua" (In support of Zhao Lihua).

35. According to several articles, the chat room of one Chinese website experienced an influx of over fifteen thousand poems on May 19 alone. See,

e.g., Wang, "Zai feixu shang chuli de shige jinianbei" (A poetry memorial standing tall above the ruins).

36. Jiang, "Dizhen shichao rang shige chonghui minjian" (Earthquake poetry transcriptions, returning poetry to the folk).

37. Zhou, "Da dizhen yu wenxue biaoda" (The big earthquake and literary expression).

39. Pu, "Xie Youshun: Shige yinggai yu shidai gandan xiangzhao" (Xie Youshun: Poetry should be in tune with the times).

39. See, e.g., "A proposal to all of China's poets from the website Poemlife and the journal Poetry and People," http://www.poemlife.com/PoemNews/news.asp?vNewsId=4008, in which the editors describe plans to hold fundraising poetry recitals in cities throughout Guangzhou province and request that poets write earthquake-themed poems to be recited at these events. Similar recitals were held across China, and most regions published their own volume of Quake Poetry.

40. My thanks go to Zang Di for pointing out this similarity.

41. Feng, "Su Shansheng: Wo gang hao shi luguo de daibizhe" (Su Shansheng: I was just a passing ghost-writer).

42. Ibid.

43. Foley, "Variation Within Limits."

44. Kirshenblatt-Gimblett, "Kodak Moments, Flashbulb Memories."

45. Some viewers remarked that the real reason Yu Dan was crying is because she donated so little (¥100,000) compared to her huge annual earnings as a best-selling author and media celebrity. Others cited such video clips as their first exposure to the poem and claimed that the sight of Yu and Luo's tears was immensely moving. See the comments section, http://blog.sina.com.cn/s/blog_51abadbe01009e5h.html.

46. http://www.youtube.com/watch?v=ZiJSPsjAyPg.

47. For an overview of uses of folk culture by Chinese intellectuals in the Republican era, see Hung, *Going to the People.*

48. Yu, *Media and Cultural Transformation in China*, 152; Ren, *The Middle Class in Neoliberal China*, 16.

49. Zhao, *Communication in China*, 86.

50. Wang, *Brand New China*, 164.

51. Yi, "Wo zuo gu wo shou" (I do therefore I speak).

52. For more on the events that took place in 2008, see Merkel-Hess, Pomeranz, and Wasserstrom, *China in 2008.*

53. Eldon, "As Leading Chinese Video Sites Tudou and Youku Battle on, More Reasons Emerge for 56.com's Downtime."

54. Wang, "Zai feixu shang chuli de shige jinianbei" (A poetry memorial standing tall above the ruins).

55. Erll and Rigney, *Mediation, Remediation, and the Dynamics of Cultural Memory*, 1, 3. For more discussion on media's effect on the formation of collective and cultural memory, see Meyers et al., *On Media Memory.*

56. Chen, "Lun: 'Guojia buxing shijia xing'" (On: "The misery of the state leads to the emergence of great poets").

57. Wang, *Illuminations from the Past*; Matten. *Places of Memory in Modern China*.

58. Nora, "Between Memory and History," 7–9.

59. Ibid., 18.

60. Ibid., 19.

61. Wang, *Illuminations from the Past*, 8.

CONCLUSION

1. Yeh, "Introduction: From the Margin," xxiii.

2. Foley, "Culture as Network."

3. Wang, "Culture as Leisure and Culture as Capital," 70–71.

4. Ren, *The Middle Class in Neoliberal China*, 19.

5. Wang, *Illuminations from the Past*.

6. Yu, "Shiren he wei?" (What are poets for?).

7. Wang, "What Is Political Theater?" 86.

8. Baiya, "Lun Hanyu shige xushu celue de zhuanxing (si)" (On the changes in narrative strategies in Chinese poetry [four]).

9. See, e.g., Jiang, "Xianchang yu yuanjing" (Live scenes and future prospects).

10. "'2006 nian shige paihangbang' zai Nanjing fabu" ("2006 poetry charts" are released in Nanjing).

11. Xinlang, "10 wei shiren dengshang 'yongshibang' Sun Wenbo lie bangshou Zhao Lihua mei shang bang" (Ten poets climb the "mediocre poetry charts," Sun Wenbo makes no. 1, Zhao Lihua nowhere to be seen).

12. For more on the meanings of oral poetry, see Bender, *Plum and Bamboo*; Bernstein, *Close Listening*; Crespi, *Voices in Revolution*; Foley, *How to Read an Oral Poem*; Middleton, *Distant Reading*.

13. Li, "Ershiyi shiji" (Twenty-first century).

14. Pettitt, "Media Dynamics and the Lessons of History."

15. Foley, "The eAgora: Electronic Networks to Surf."

16. Pettitt, "Media Dynamics and the Lessons of History."

BIBLIOGRAPHY

"'2006 nian shige paihangbang' zai Nanjing fabu" '2006年诗歌排行榜'在南京发布 ("2006 poetry charts" are released in Nanjing). http://woaxiang.blogcn.com/articles/%E2%80%9C2006%E5%B9%B4%E8%AF%97%E6%AD%8C%E6%8E%92%E8%A1%8C%E6%A6%9C%E2%80%9D%E5%9C%A8%E5%8D%97%E4%BA%AC%E5%8F%91%E5%B8%83.html.

An Qi 安琪. "Guanyu zhongjiandai: Wo canyu le yi ge shidai de shige jianshe" 关于中间代:我参与了一个时代的诗歌建设 (About the middle generation: I participated in the poetic construction of an era). http://www.zgyspp.com/Article/ShowArticle.asp?ArticleID=7497.

Anderson, Benedict Richard O'Gorman. *Imagined Communities: Reflections on the Origin and Spread of Nationalism*. New York: Verso, 2006.

Anderson, Marston. *The Limits of Realism: Chinese Fiction in the Revolutionary Period*. Berkeley: University of California Press, 1990.

Andrew, Caroline, Monica Gattinger, M. Sharon Jeannotte, and Will Straw, eds. *Accounting for Culture: Thinking Through Cultural Citizenship*. Ottawa: University of Ottawa Press, 2005.

Assmann, Jan. "Collective Memory and Cultural Identity." Trans. John Czaplicka. *New German Critique* no. 65 (1996): 125–33.

Bachleitner, Norbert. "The Virtual Muse: Forms and Theory of Digital Poetry." In *Theory into Poetry: New Approaches to the Lyric*, ed. Eva Müller-Zettelmann and Margarete Rubik, 303–46. New York: Rodopi, 2005.

Bai Xiaosheng 百晓生. "Shitan yingxiong zuoci paihangbang" 诗坛英雄座次排行榜 (Poetry arena heroes ranked by order of seating). http://www.chinapoesy.com/ShiCiZhiShie81733da-3664-4da8-af12-344eca8501d2.html.

Baiya 白鸦. "Lun hanyu shige xushu celue de zhuanxing (si)—dangxiaxing yuanze: Panqing Yu, Yi, Shen de wei xianchang shuo" 论汉语诗歌叙述策

略的转型 (四) : 当下性原则 : 辨清于、伊、沈的伪现场说 (On the changes in narrative strategies in Chinese poetry [four]: Clarifying Yu, Yi and Shen's fake live-scene discourse). http://blog.sina.com.cn/u/49c185d0010008l0.

Barmé, Geremie R., and Gloria Davies. "Have We Been Noticed Yet? Intellectual Contestation and the Chinese Web." In *Chinese Intellectuals Between State and Market*, 75–108. New York: Routledge, 2004.

Barmé, Geremie R. *In the Red: On Contemporary Chinese Culture.* New York: Columbia University Press, 2000.

Bary, William Theodore De, and Richard John Lufrano. *Sources of Chinese Tradition: From 1600 Through the Twentieth Century.* New York: Columbia University Press, 2001.

Bei, Dao. *August Sleepwalker.* Trans. Bonnie McDougall. New York: New Directions, 1988.

Bender, Mark. *Plum and Bamboo: China's Suzhou Chantefable Tradition.* Champaign: University of Illinois Press, 2003.

Benjamin, Walter. "The Work of Art in the Age of Mechanical Reproduction." *Illuminations*, 217–51. Trans. Harry Zohn. Ed. and intro. Hannah Arendt. New York: Shocken Books, 1969.

Berghuis, Thomas J. *Performance Art in China.* Beijing: Timezone 8 Limited, 2006.

Bernstein, Charles. *Close Listening: Poetry and the Performed Word.* New York: Oxford University Press, 1998.

Berry, Chris. "Getting Real: Chinese Documentary, Chinese Postsocialism." In *The Urban Generation: Chinese Cinema and Society at the Turn of the Twenty-First Century*, ed. Zhen Zhang, 115–36. Durham, NC: Duke University Press, 2007.

———. "Jia Zhangke and the Temporality of Postsocialist Chinese Cinema: In the Now (and Then)." In *Futures of Chinese Cinema: Technologies and Temporalities in Chinese Screen*, ed. Olivia Khoo and Sean Metzger, 111–28. Chicago: Intellect Ltd., 2009.

———. *Postsocialist Cinema in Post-Mao China: The Cultural Revolution After the Cultural Revolution.* Reprint. New York: Routledge, 2008.

Berry, Chris, Lu Xinyu, and Lisa Rofel. *The New Chinese Documentary Film Movement: For the Public Record.* Hong Kong: Hong Kong University Press, 2010.

Bolter, J. David. *Writing Space: Computers, Hypertext, and the Remediation of Print.* 2nd ed. Mahwah, NJ: Lawrence Erlbaum Associates, 2001.

Braester, Yomi. "Chinese Cinema in the Age of Advertisement: The Filmmaker as a Cultural Broker." *China Quarterly* 183 (2005): 549–64.

———. "Excuse Me, Your Camera Is in My Face: Auteurial Intervention in PRC New Documentary." In *The New Chinese Documentary Film Movement: For the Public Record*, ed. Chris Berry, 195–216. Hong Kong: Hong Kong University Press, 2010.

———. *Witness Against History: Literature, Film, and Public Discourse in Twentieth-Century China.* 1st ed. Stanford, CA: Stanford University Press, 2003.

Brodsgaard, Kjeld Erik. "The Democracy Movement in China, 1978–1979: Opposition Movements, Wall Poster Campaigns, and Underground Journals." *Asian Survey* 21, no. 7 (July 1, 1981): 747–74.

Brokaw, Cynthia Joanne, and Kai-wing Chow. *Printing and Book Culture in Late Imperial China.* Berkeley: University of California Press, 2005.

Brokaw, Cynthia, and Christopher A. Reed. *From Woodblocks to the Internet: Chinese Publishing and Print Culture in Transition, Circa 1800 to 2008.* Leiden: Brill, 2010.

Burman, Jeremy Trevelyan. "The Misunderstanding of Memes: Biography of an Unscientific Object, 1976–1999." *Perspectives on Science* 20, no. 1 (2012): 74–104.

Carey, James W. *Communication as Culture: Essays on Media and Society.* Rev. ed. London: Routledge, 2009.

Chang Shan 长山. "2003 nian zhongguo shige zhuanhao: Laji Laji geming" 2003年中国诗歌专号：垃圾革命 (Chinese Poetry 2003 Special: Rubbish Revolution). http://cyber.swnu.edu.cn/xinshi/bbs/showtopic.asp?TOPIC_ID=358&Forum_ID=27.

Chen, Pingyuan. *Touches of History: An Entry into "May Fourth" China.* Trans. Michel Hockx, Uga Sze Pui Kwan, Christopher Neil Payne, and Christopher Rosenmeier. Leiden: Brill, 2011.

Chen, S. H. "Multiplicity in Uniformity: Poetry and the Great Leap Forward." *China Quarterly*, no. 3 (July 1, 1960): 1–15.

Chen Sihe 陈思和. *Zhongguo dangdai wenxueshi jiaocheng* 中国当代文学史教程 (A course book of the history of contemporary Chinese literature). Shanghai: Fudan Daxue Chubanshe, 1999.

Chen Youkang 陈友康. "Lun: Guojia buxing shijia xing" 论"国家不幸诗家幸" (On: "The misery of the state leads to the emergence of great poets"). *Yunnan minzu daxue xuebao* 21, no. 3 (2004).

Chen Zhongyi 陈仲义. "Jin wu nian wangluo shitan shi xiang guancha" 近五年网络诗坛诗象观察 (Observations on poetry phenomena in the online poetry arena in the last five years). http://www.yanruyu.com/jhy/author/69892.shtml.

Cheng Guangwei 程光炜. *Zhongguo dangdai shige shi* 中国当代诗歌史 (A history of Chinese contemporary poetry). Beijing: Zhongguo Renmin Daxue Chubanshe, 2003.

China Book Publishing Web. "Xinwen chuban zongshu yanli chachu 'xin cang da e' yi shu ji qi chubanzhe" 新闻出版总署严厉查处'心藏大恶'一书及其出版者 (The General Administration of Press and Publication enforces strict punishments upon *A Great Evil Hidden in the Heart* and its publishers). http://www.shdf.gov.cn/newshtmt.html?id=8484&newsType=84.

China Digital Times. "Grass-Mud Horse Lexicon." http://chinadigitaltimes.net/space/Grass-Mud_Horse_Lexicon.

China Internet Network Information Center (CNNIC). "The 32nd Statistical Report on Internet Development in China." 2013. http://www1.cnnic.cn/IDR/ReportDownloads/201310/P020131029430558704972.pdf.

China Media Project. "The Surrounding Gaze 围观." *China Media Project*. http://cmp.hku.hk/2011/01/04/9399/.

Chou, Tsu-Lung. "Creative Space, Cultural Industry Clusters, and Participation of the State in Beijing." *Eurasian Geography and Economics* 53, no. 2 (March 1, 2012): 197–215.

Chow, Kai-wing, Tze-ki Hon, Hung-yok Ip, and Don C. Price, eds. *Beyond the May Fourth Paradigm: In Search of Chinese Modernity*. Lanham, MD: Lexington Books, 2008.

Chow, Kai-wing. *Publishing, Culture, and Power in Early Modern China*. Stanford, CA: Stanford University Press, 2004.

Condry, Ian. *Hip-Hop Japan: Rap and the Paths of Cultural Globalization*. Durham, NC: Duke University Press, 2006.

Crespi, John. "The Poetry of Slogans and Native Sons: Observations on the First China Poetry Festival." *MCLC Resource Center* (November 2005). http://mclc.osu.edu/rc/pubs/crespi.htm.

———. *Voices in Revolution: Poetry and the Auditory Imagination in Modern China*. Honolulu: University of Hawaii Press, 2009.

Van Crevel, Maghiel. *Chinese Poetry in Times of Mind, Mayhem and Money*. Leiden: Brill, 2008.

———. "The Horror of Being Ignored and the Pleasure of Being Left Alone: Notes on the Chinese Poetry Scene." *MCLC Resource Center* (2003). http://mclc.osu.edu/rc/pubs/vancrevel.html.

———. *Language Shattered: Contemporary Chinese Poetry and Duoduo*. Leiden: Research School CNWS, 1996.

———. "Not Quite Karaoke: Poetry in Contemporary China." *China Quarterly* no. 183 (2005): 644–69.

———. "Rejective Poetry: Sound and Sense in Yi Sha." In *Text, Performance, and Gender in Chinese Literature and Music: Essays in Honor of Wilt Idema*, ed. Maghiel van Crevel, Tian Yuan Tan, and Michel Hockx, 389–412. Leiden: Brill, 2010.

———. "Unofficial Poetry Journals from the People's Republic of China: A Research Note and an Annotated Bibliography." 2007. http://mclc.osu.edu/rc/pubs/vancrevel2.html.

Dai Jinhua 戴锦华. *Shuxie wenhua yingxiong* 书写文化英雄 (Writing cultural heroes). Nanjing: Jiangsu renmin chubanshe, 2000.

———. *Yinxing shuxie: 90 niandai Zhongguo wenhua yanjiu* 隐形书写:90年代中国文化研究 (Invisible writing: Research into 1990s Chinese culture). Nanjing: Jiangsu renmin chubanshe, 1999.

Damon, Maria, and Ira Livingston, eds. *Poetry and Cultural Studies: A Reader.* 1st ed. Champaign: University of Illinois Press, 2009.

Dawkins, Richard. *The Selfish Gene.* 30th Anniversary. New York: Oxford University Press, 2006.

Day, Michael. *China's Second World of Poetry: The Sichuan Avant-Garde, 1982–1992.* Leiden: Digital Archive for Chinese Studies, 2005.

———. "Grand Poetry Exhibition of 1986." *Digital Archive for Chinese Studies*, 2005. http://leiden.dachs-archive.org/poetry/exhibition.html. ———. "Online Avant-Garde Poetry in China Today." In *New Perspectives on Contemporary Chinese Poetry*, ed. Christopher Lupke, 201–18. New York: Palgrave Macmillan, 2008.

Denton, Kirk. "General Introduction." In *Modern Chinese Literary Thought: Writings on Literature, 1893–1945*, ed. Kirk Denton, 1–61. Stanford, CA: Stanford University Press, 1996.

———, ed. *Modern Chinese Literary Thought: Writings on Literature, 1893–1945.* Stanford, CA: Stanford University Press, 1996.

Denton, Kirk A., and Michel Hockx, eds. *Literary Societies of Republican China.* Lanham, MD: Lexington Books, 2008.

De Weerdt, Hilde. "Grief for Departed Women in Shi from Jin to Sui: Pan Yue's 'Daowang Shi.'" *Papers on Chinese Literature* 1 (1993): 21–39.

Ding Weifeng 丁伟锋. "90 hou shaonian jinian 90 nian xin shi: Hangzhou shaonian wenxueyuan jinian xin shi danchen 90 zhounian zushi" "90后"少年纪念90年新诗—杭州少年文学院纪念新诗诞辰90周年组诗 (Post-90 youth commemorates 90 years of new poetry: Poems from the Hangzhou Youth Literature Center to mark the 90th birthday of new poetry). http://www.hzqsn.com/wszt_wxy/104845.htm.

Disanji shikan 第三级诗刊. "Zhongguo shige de minjian jiyi: Boqu chouwen shi liangguang—2010 niandu Zhongguo shige shi da shijian" 中国诗歌的民间记忆:剥去丑闻是亮光—2010年度中国诗歌十大事件 (The unofficial memory of Chinese poetry: Underneath the scandals is a shining light, or ten big incidents in Chinese poetry in 2010). http://blog.sina.com.cn/s/blog_489db26e0100nwng.html.

Disanji xinwen fayanren 第三极新闻发言人. "Xin shiji shi nian Zhongguo shige de xianzhuang he weilai yantaohui jiyao" 新世纪十年中国诗歌的现状和未来研讨会纪要 (Summary of the forum on the current state and future of Chinese poetry in the first decade of the new millennium). http://www.yanruyu.com/jhy/author/105636.shtml.

Donald, Stephanie, Michael Keane, and Yin Hong. *Media in China: Consumption, Content and Crisis*. London; New York: RoutledgeCurzon, 2002.

Duoyu 朵渔. "Shiren nengfou miandui ziji?" 诗人能否面对自己？(Can poets face up to themselves?). http://hk.netsh.com/eden/oldbbs/741/html/tree_11243283.html.

———. "Zai lun shige piping jibenshang shi yi zhong zishuo zihua" 再论诗歌批评基本上是一种自说自话 (I'll say it again that poetry criticism is essentially talking to itself). http://www.zgyspp.com/Article/ShowArticle.asp?ArticleID=3484.

Edmond, Jacob. "Dissidence and Accommodation: The Publishing History of Yang Lian from *Today* to Today." *China Quarterly* 185 (2006): 111–27.

Edwards, Louise, and Elaine Jeffreys. *Celebrity in China*. Hong Kong: Hong Kong University Press, 2010.

Eldon, Eric. "As Leading Chinese Video Sites Tudou and Youku Battle on, More Reasons Emerge for 56.com's Downtime." *VentureBeat*. http://venturebeat.com/2008/06/24/as-leading-chinese-video-sites-tudou-and-youku-battle-on-more-reasons-emerge-for-56coms-downtime/.

Erll, Astrid, and Ann Rigney. *Mediation, Remediation, and the Dynamics of Cultural Memory*. Berlin: Walter de Gruyter, 2009.

Farrall, Kenneth, and David Kurt Herold. "Identity vs. Anonymity: Chinese Netizens and Questions of Identifiability." In *Online Society in China: Creating, Celebrating, and Instrumentalising the Online Carnival*, ed. David Kurt Herold and Peter Marolt, 165–83. New York: Routledge, 2011.

Feiniu7 非牛7. "Wo weishenme yao ma Tan Kexiu" 我为什么要骂谭克修 (Why I want to curse Tan Kexiu). http://harveywang.tianyablog.com/blogger/post_read.asp?BlogID=7994&PostID=6000087.

Fish, Stanley Eugene. *Is There a Text in This Class? The Authority of Interpretive Communities*. Cambridge, MA: Harvard University Press, 1980.

Foley, John Miles. "Arena of Oral Tradition." *Oral Tradition and Internet Technology*, 2011. http://www.pathwaysproject.org/pathways/show/Arena_of_Oral_Tradition.

———. "Contingency." *Oral Tradition and Internet Technology*. 2011. http://www.pathwaysproject.org/pathways/show/Contingency.

———. "Culture as Network." 2011. http://www.pathwaysproject.org/pathways/show/Culture_as_Network.

———. "The eAgora: Electronic Networks to Surf." *Oral Tradition and Internet Technology*. 2011. http://pathwaysproject.org/pathways/show/eAgora.

———. *How to Read an Oral Poem*. Champaign: University of Illinois Press, 2002.

———. "The oAgora: Oral Networks to Surf." *Oral Tradition and Internet Technology*. 2011. http://www.pathwaysproject.org/pathways/show/oAgora.

———. "Systems Versus Things." *Oral Tradition and Internet Technology*. 2011. http://pathwaysproject.org/pathways/show/Systems_versus_Things.

———. "The tAgora: Exchanging Tangible Goods." *Oral Tradition and Internet Technology*. 2011. http://www.pathwaysproject.org/pathways/show/tAgora.

———. "Variation Within Limits." 2011. http://www.pathwaysproject.org/pathways/show/Variation_Within_Limits.

Fong, Vanessa L., and Rachel Murphy. "Introduction: Chinese Experiences of Citizenship at the Margins." In *Chinese Citizenship: Views from the Margins*, ed. Vanessa L. Fong and Rachel Murphy, 1–8. New York: Routledge, 2006.

———, eds. *Chinese Citizenship: Views from the Margins*. New York: Routledge, 2006.

Foucault, Michel. *The History of Sexuality, Vol. 1: An Introduction*. Trans. Robert Hurley. New York: Vintage, 1990.

Fu Mahuo 符马活. *Shi jianghu: 2001 wangluo shige nianxuan* 诗江湖 : 2001 网络诗歌年选 (Poetry rivers and lakes: 2001 yearbook of Internet poetry). Xining: Qinghai Renmin Chubanshe, 2002.

Feng Chunjie 逢春阶. "Su Shansheng: Wo ganghao shi luguo de daibizhe" 苏善生 : 我刚好是路过的代笔者 (Su Shansheng: I was just a passing ghost-writer). http://dzrb.dzwww.com/dazk/dzzm/200805/t20080530_3651395.htm.

Garnham, Nicholas. *Capitalism and Communication: Global Culture and the Economics of Information*. London: Sage, 1990.

Giese, Karsten. "Speaker's Corner or Virtual Panopticon: Discursive Construction of Chinese Identities Online." In *Cyber China: Reshaping National Identities in the Age of Information*, ed. Françoise Mengin, 19–36. New York: Palgrave Macmillan, 2004.

Glazier, Loss. *Digital Poetics: The Making of E-Poetries*. 1st ed. Tuscaloosa: University of Alabama Press, 2008.

Goh, Meow Hui. *Sound and Sight: Poetry and Courtier Culture in the Yongming Era (483–493)*. Stanford, CA: Stanford University Press, 2010.

Gong, Haomin. "Toward a New Leftist Ecocriticism in Postsocialist China:

Reading the 'Poetry of Migrant Workers' as Ecopoetry." In *China and New Left Visions: Political and Cultural Interventions*, ed. Ban Wang and Jie Lu, 139–57. Lanham, MD: Lexington Books, 2012.

———. *Uneven Modernity: Literature, Film, and Intellectual Discourse in Postsocialist China*. Honolulu: University of Hawaii Press, 2012.

Gong, Haomin, and Xin Yang. "Digitized Parody: The Politics of Egao in Contemporary China." *China Information* 24, no. 1 (March 1, 2010): 3–26.

Grinnell, Claudia K. "From Consumer to Prosumer to Produser: Who Keeps Shifting My Paradigm? (We Do!)." *Public Culture* 21, no. 3 (2009): 577–98.

Grossberg, Lawrence. *Cultural Studies in the Future Tense*. Durham, NC: Duke University Press, 2010.

Gu, Edward X., and Merle Goldman. *Chinese Intellectuals Between State and Market*. London: Routledge, 2004.

Guillory, John. *Cultural Capital: The Problem of Literary Canon Formation*. Chicago: University of Chicago Press, 1993.

Haft, Lloyd, ed. *Selective Guide to Chinese Literature, 1900–1949: The Poem*. Leiden: Brill, 1990.

Han Dong 韩东. "Lun minjian" 论民间 (On the Popular). In *1999 Zhongguo xin shi xuan* 1999中国新诗选 (1999 Chinese New Poetry yearbook), ed. He Xiaozhu, 1-18. Xi'an: Shaanxi shifan daxue, 1999.

Han Han 韩寒. "Jianjue zhichi shiren ba liumang shuacheng yizhong liupai" 坚决支持诗人把流氓耍成一种流派 (Firmly support poets turning hooliganism into a school). http://www.bullogger.com/blogs/twocold/archives/17971.aspx.

———. "Shiren ji le, bu xie shi le" 诗人急了, 不写诗了 (Poets are anxious, have stopped writing poetry). http://www.bullogger.com/blogs/twocold/archives/17861.aspx.

———. "Xiandai shi he shiren zenme hai cunzai?" 现代诗和诗人怎么还存在？(How come modern poetry and poets still exist?). http://culture.163.com/06/0930/16/2S9HN8DH00281MU3.html.

Han Shanshi 寒山石. "Dui dangxia shitan de jiti shenpan: Cong Zhao Lihua xianxiang shuo xiaqu" 对当下诗坛的集体审判：从赵丽华现象说下去 (A collective judgment on the contemporary poetry arena: Discussing the Zhao Lihua phenomenon). http://www.shigebao.com/html/articles/12/2047.html.

Han Zongbao 韩宗宝. "Xin shiji shi nian Zhongguo xin shi dashiji" 新世纪十年中国新诗大事记 (Memorandum of events in the first decade of Chinese new poetry in the new century). http://blog.sina.com.cn/s/blog_3d81a08401017jlr.html.

Hansen, Mark B. N. *Bodies in Code: Interfaces with Digital Media*. New York: Routledge, 2006.

Harrington, Joseph. *Poetry and the Public: The Social Form of Modern U.S. Poetics*. 1st ed. Middletown, CT: Wesleyan University Press, 2002.

Hartley, John. *Communication, Cultural and Media Studies: The Key Concepts*. London: Routledge, 2011.

———. *The Politics of Pictures: The Creation of the Public in the Age of Popular Media*. New York: Routledge, 1992.

Hartley, John, Jean Burgess, and Axel Bruns, eds. *A Companion to New Media Dynamics*. New York: Wiley-Blackwell, 2013.

———. "Introducing Dynamics." In *A Companion to New Media Dynamics*, ed. John Hartley, Jean Burgess, and Axel Bruns, 1–11. New York: Wiley-Blackwell, 2013.

Harvey, David. *A Brief History of Neoliberalism*. 1st ed. New York: Oxford University Press, 2007.

Hawes, Colin. "Corporate CEOs as Cultural Producers." In *The New Rich in China: Future Rulers, Present Lives*, ed. David S. G. Goodman, 85–98. New York: Routledge, 2008.

Hayles, N. Katherine. "The Time of Digital Poetry: From Object to Event." In *New Media Poetics: Contexts, Technotexts, and Theories*, ed. Adalaide Morris and Thomas Swiss, 181–210. Cambridge, MA: MIT Press, 2006.

He, Baogang. "Chinese Intellectuals Facing the Challenges of the New Century." In *Chinese Intellectuals Between State and Market*, ed. Merle Goodman and Edward Gu, 263–79. New York: RoutledgeCurzon, 2004.

He Ping 何平. "'Shige zai wang shang'—wangluo shige" '诗歌在网上'—网络诗歌 (Poetry on the –Internet—Internet poetry). *Dangdai zuojia pinglun* 5 (2008).

Herold, David Kurt, and Peter Marolt. *Online Society in China: Creating, Celebrating, and Instrumentalising the Online Carnival*. 1st ed. New York: Routledge, 2011.

Higgins, Andrew. "Iceland Baffled by Chinese Plan for Golf Resort." *New York Times*, March 22, 2013, sec. World/Europe. http://www.nytimes.com/2013/03/23/world/europe/iceland-baffled-by-chinese-plan-for-golf-resort.html.

Hjarvard, Stig. "The Mediatization of Society: A Theory of the Media as Agents of Social and Cultural Change." *Nordicom Review* 29, no. 2 (2008): 105–34.

Hockx, Michel. *Internet Literature in China*. New York: Columbia University Press, 2014.

———. "Links with the Past: Mainland China's Online Literary Communities and Their Antecedents." *Journal of Contemporary China* 13 (February 2004): 105–27.

———. "Poets in Poems: The Author as a Character in Modern Chinese Poetry" (abstract). http://www.international.ucla.edu/china/events/print-event.asp?eventid=4570.

———. *Questions of Style: Literary Societies and Literary Journals in Modern China, 1911–1937*. Leiden: Brill, 2003.

———. *A Snowy Morning: Eight Chinese Poets on the Road to Modernity*. Leiden: CNWS Publications, 1994.

———. "Virtual Chinese Literature: A Comparative Case Study of Online Poetry Communities." *China Quarterly* 183 (2005): 670–91.

Hong Zhu 洪烛. "Weihe shuo wangluo gaibian le Zhongguo shige?" 为何说网络改变了中国诗歌 (Why do we say the Internet has changed Chinese poetry?). http://wenxinshe.zhongwenlink.com/home/blog_read.asp?id=4053&blogid=50369.

Hong Zicheng 洪子诚, ed. *Zai Beida ketang du shi* 在北大课堂读诗 (Reading poetry in the Beijing University classroom). Wuhan: Changjiang Wenyi Chubanshe, 2002.

———. *Zhongguo dangdai wenxueshi* 中国当代文学史 (A history of contemporary Chinese literature). Beijing: Beijing Daxue Chubanshe, 1999.

Hong Zicheng 洪子诚 and Liu Denghan 刘登翰. *Zhongguo dangdai xin shi shi* 中国当代新诗史 (A history of Chinese contemporary new poetry). Beijing: Beijing Daxue Chubanshe, 2005.

Hu Jiujiu 胡赳赳. "Dachang: Zuowei meijie de shige shi women zai yiqi" 大场：作为媒介的诗歌使我们在一起 (Big Square: Poetry is a medium for bringing us together). http://blog.sina.com.cn/s/blog_49c75f8b01000424.html.

Huang Zhenlin 黄振林. "Dangqian xiju yishu moshi jian de ronghe yu paichi" 当前戏剧艺术模式间的融合与排斥 (Fusions and repulsions between current forms of theatrical art). *Dangdai xiju* 当代戏剧 (Contemporary theater) 6 (2002). http://paper.buduo.cn/05/19278648.asp.

Huber, Werner, Martin Middeke, and Hubert Zapf. *Self-Reflexivity in Literature*. Würzberg: Königshausen and Neumann, 2005.

Hunan ribao 湖南日报 (Hunan Daily). "Zhimian shidai vs. Geren jiushu: 'Xiao wenren shige' yinbao shitan lun" 直面时代vs.个人救赎：'小文人诗歌'引爆诗坛论 (Facing the era vs. personal redemption: "Petty literati poetry" causes a storm in the poetry arena) (August 23, 2006). http://blog.tianya.cn/blogger/post_show.asp?idWriter=0&Key=0&BlogID=341456&PostID=6527036.

Hung, Chang-tai. *Going to the People: Chinese Intellectuals and Folk Literature, 1918–1937*. Cambridge, MA: Harvard University Asia Center, 1985.

Inwood, Heather. "Between License and Responsibility: Reexamining the

Role of the Poet in Twenty-First Century Chinese Society." *Chinese Literature Today* 2, no. 1 (2011): 49–55.

———. "Yi Sha: Running His Race in the Ninth Lane." *Chinese Literature Today* 2, no. 2 (2012): 7–10.

Irwin, John. *Scenes: New Social Worlds in Urban Settings*. Beverly Hills, CA: Sage Publications, 1977.

Jenkins, Henry. *Convergence Culture: Where Old and New Media Collide*. New York: New York University Press, 2006.

Jiang Tao 姜涛. "Xianchang yu yuanjing" 现场与远景 (Live scenes and future prospects). In *Zhongguo xin shi baipishu*, ed. Tan Wuchang, 556–58. Beijing: Kunlun chubanshe, 2004.

———. *"Xin shi ji" yu Zhongguo xin shi de fasheng* "新诗集"与中国新诗的发生 ("New Poems" and the emergence of China's New Poetry). Beijing: Beijing Daxue Chubanshe, 2005.

Jiang Xiaoling姜小玲. "Dizhen shichao rang shige chonghui minjian" 地震诗抄让诗歌重回民间 (Earthquake Poetry Transcriptions, returning poetry to the folk). http://news.xinhuanet.com/book/2008–06/04/content_8310692.htm.

Jiaoshou 叫兽. "Tan Kexiu li fengrenyuan hai you duo yuan?" 谭克修离疯人院还有多元 (How long until Tan Kexiu ends up in the lunatic asylum?). http://blog.sina.com.cn/s/blog_4f3a03c501007zco.html.

Kirshenblatt-Gimblett, Barbara. "Kodak Moments, Flashbulb Memories: Reflections on 9/11." *TDR (1988–)* 47, no. 1 (April 1, 2003): 11–48.

Kong, Shuyu. *Consuming Literature: Best Sellers and the Commercialization of Literary Production in Contemporary China*. Stanford, CA: Stanford University Press, 2005.

Kunze, Rui. *Struggle and Symbiosis: The Canonization of the Poet Haizi and Cultural Discourses in Contemporary China*. Bochum/Freiburg: Projekt Verlag, 2011.

Lagerkvist, Johan. *After the Internet, Before Democracy: Competing Norms in Chinese Media and Society*. Bern: Peter Lang AG, 2010.

Laji shidai 垃圾时代. "Di yi huihe: Shen Haobo VS Xu Xiangchou" 第一回合：沈浩波VS徐乡愁 (The first exchange: Shen Haobo vs. Xu Xiangchou). http://www.yanruyu.com/jhy/author/40634.shtml.

Landow, George. *Hypertext 2.0*. Baltimore: Johns Hopkins University Press, 1997.

Lanhudie Zidingxiang 蓝蝴蝶紫丁香. "Zhongguo lajipai zhuming shiren, guanshui dashi Lanhudie zidingxiang da wangyou wen" 中国垃圾派著名诗人、灌水派大师蓝蝴蝶紫丁香答网友问 (Famous poet from China's School of Rubbish and master of the School of Spam Blue Butterfly Lilac answers Internet friends' questions). http://my.ziqu.com/bbs/665167/messages/1452.html.

Latham, Kevin. "Nothing but the Truth: News Media, Power and Hegemony in South China." *China Quarterly* 163 (2000): 633–54.

Lao Touzi 老头子. "Laji pai jishi (2003 nian 3–5 yue)" 垃圾派纪事(2003年3–5月) (School of Rubbish chronicles [March to May 2003]). http://www.yanruyu.com/jhy/author/34836.shtml.

———, ed. *Laji pai minkan: Zong di er qi* 垃圾派民刊：总第二期 (School of Rubbish Journal: Second edition). Unofficial journal, Beijing, 2004.

———. "Lajipai Xuanyan" 垃圾派宣言(School of Rubbish manifesto). www.yanruyu.com/jhy/author/34926.shtml.

———. "Shi zha" 诗札 (Poetry epistles). http://hk.netsh.com/eden/bbs/6411/html/tree_4095350.html.

———. "Zhongguo laji pai shige daibiaozuo shi shou zuopin yu dianping" 中国垃圾派诗歌代表作十首与点评 (Ten representative works and commentary of China's School of Rubbish poetry). http://tw.netsh.com/eden/bbs/704883/html/tree_5753831.html.

Lao Xiang 老象. "Lao Touzi zenme le?" 老头子怎么了 (What's up with Old Man?), http://hk.netsh.com/eden/bbs/6411/html/tree_5357898.html.

Lazer, Hank. *Opposing Poetries: Issues and Institutions*. Evanston, IL: Northwestern University Press, 1996.

Li, Dian. "Naming and Antinaming: Poetic Debate in Contemporary China." In *New Perspectives on Contemporary Chinese Poetry*, ed. Christopher Lupke, 185–200. New York: Palgrave Macmillan, 2008.

Li, Hongmei. "Parody and Resistance on the Chinese Internet." In *Online Society in China: Creating, Celebrating, and Instrumentalising the Online Carnival*, ed. David Kurt Herold and Peter Marolt, 71–88. New York: Routledge, 2011.

Li, Shubo. "The Online Public Space and Popular Ethos in China." *Media, Culture and Society* 32, no. 1 (2010): 63–83.

Li Xia 李霞. "Ershiyi shiji: Wangluo niepan hanshi" 二十一世纪：网络涅槃汉诗 (Twenty-first century: Chinese Internet poetry nirvana). http://www.poemlife.com:9001/ReviewerColumn/lixia/article.asp?vArticleId=29272&ColumnSection=.

Lin, Julia C. *Modern Chinese Poetry: An Introduction*. 1st ed. Seattle: University of Washington Press, 1973.

Ling Hongfa 凌宏发. "Kang zhen shige: Minzu beiqing de yishihua biaoda" 抗震诗歌：民族悲情的仪式化表达 (Quake relief poetry: The ritualized expression of national sorrow). *Xinmin wanbao* (June 14, 2008).

Link, Eugene Perry. *The Uses of Literature: Life in the Socialist Chinese Literary System*. Princeton, NJ: Princeton University Press, 2000.

Liu Chun 刘春. "Jin 20 nian xin shi xuanben chuban de huimou yu pingshuo" 近20年新诗选本出版的回眸与评说 (A look back at and reflection on the publication of poetry anthologies in the past twenty years). *Jianghan daxue xuebao* 24, no.1 (February 2007): 16–23.

———. *Menglongshi yihou: 1986–2007 Zhongguo shitan ditu* 朦胧诗以后：1986–2007中国诗坛地图 (After Misty Poetry: A map of the poetry arena, 1986–2007). Beijing: Kunlun chubanshe, 2007.

Liu, Fengshu. *Urban Youth in China: Modernity, the Internet and the Self.* 1st ed. New York: Routledge, 2010.

Liu, Jianmei. "Gender Politics in Jin Yong's Martial Arts Novels." In *The Jin Yong Phenomenon: Chinese Martial Arts Fiction and Modern Chinese Literary History*, ed. Ann Huss and Jianmei Liu, 179–200. Amhurst: Cambria Press, 2007.

Liu Zhenfu 刘真福. "Jianguo yilai zhongxue jiaocai xin shi jiaoyu de fazhan: Xuanpian lun" 建国以来中学教材新诗教育的发展 ·选篇论 (The development of new poetry education through middle school textbooks since the establishment of the PRC: A treatise on poetry selection). *Jianghan daxue xuebao* 26, no. 4 (August 2007): 5–9.

Lu, Jie, and Ban Wang, eds. *China and New Left Visions: Political and Cultural Interventions.* Lanham, MD: Lexington Books, 2012.

Lu, Sheldon H. *Chinese Modernity and Global Biopolitics: Studies in Literature and Visual Culture.* Honolulu: University of Hawaii Press, 2007.

Lu Yang 鲁羊. "Zhongguo shitan you Yang Ke! Lun Yang Ke ji qi zhubian de 'Zhongguo xin shi nianjian'" 中国诗坛有杨克！论杨克及其主编的'中国新诗年鉴' (The Chinese poetry arena has Yang Ke! On Yang Ke and his *Chinese New Poetry Almanac*). http://blog.boxun.com/hero/2007/luyangweiji/10_1.shtml.

Luo Zhenya 罗振亚. *Ershi shiji Zhongguo xianfeng shichao* 二十世纪中国先锋诗潮 (Twentieth-century Chinese avant-garde poetry). Beijing: Renmin chubanshe, 2008.

Lupke, Christopher, ed. *New Perspectives on Contemporary Chinese Poetry.* New York: Palgrave Macmillan, 2008.

Mackinnon, Rebecca. *Consent of the Networked: The Worldwide Struggle for Internet Freedom.* New York: Basic Books, 2013.

———. "Flatter World and Thicker Walls? Blogs, Censorship and Civic Discourse in China." *Public Choice* 134, no. 1–2 (January 1, 2008): 31–46.

Manfredi, Paul. "Great Expectations: Self, Form, and the First Modern Chinese Poem." *Modern Chinese Literature and Culture* 13, no. 2 (2001): 1–29.

Mao, Zedong. "Talks at the Yan'an Forum on Art and Literature." In *China: Adapting the Past, Confronting the Future*, ed. Thomas Buoye, Kirk Denton, Bruce Dickson, and Barry Naughton, 435–39. Ann Arbor: Center for Chinese Studies, University of Michigan, 2002.

Marolt, Peter. "Grassroots Agency in a Civil Sphere? Rethinking Internet Control in China." In *Online Society in China: Creating, Celebrating, and Instrumentalising the Online Carnival*, ed. David Kurt Herold and Peter Marolt, 53–67. New York: Routledge, 2011.

Matten, Marc Andre, ed. *Places of Memory in Modern China*. Leiden: Brill, 2011.

Matusitz, Jonathan. "Deception in the Virtual World: A Semiotic Analysis of Identity." *NMEDIAC Journal of New Media and Culture* 3, no. 1 (2005). http://www.ibiblio.org/nmediac/winter2004/matusitz.html.

McDougall, Bonnie S. *Fictional Authors, Imaginary Audiences: Modern Chinese Literature in the Twentieth Century*. Hong Kong: Chinese University Press, 2003.

McDougall, Bonnie S., and Kam Louie. *The Literature of China in the Twentieth Century*. New York: Columbia University Press, 1999.

McGrath, Jason. *Postsocialist Modernity: Chinese Cinema, Literature, and Criticism in the Market Age*. Stanford, CA: Stanford University Press, 2010.

Merkel-Hess, Kate, Kenneth L. Pomeranz, and Jeffrey N. Wasserstrom, eds. *China in 2008: A Year of Great Significance*. Lanham, MD: Rowman & Littlefield, 2009.

Meyers, Oren, Motti Neiger, Eyal Zandberg, Andrew Hoskins, and John Sutton. *On Media Memory: Collective Memory in a New Media Age*. New York: Palgrave Macmillan, 2011.

Meng, Bingchun. "Regulating Egao: Futile Efforts of Recentralization?" In *China's Information and Communications Technology Revolution: Social Changes and State Responses*, ed. Xiaoling Zhang and Yongnian Zheng, 52–67. New York: Routledge, 2009.

Middleton, Peter. *Distant Reading: Performance, Readership, and Consumption in Contemporary Poetry*. Tuscaloosa: University of Alabama Press, 2005.

Miller, Carolyn R., and Dawn Shepherd. "Questions for Genre Theory from the Blogosphere." In *Genre in the Internet: Issues in the Theory of Genre*, ed. Janet Giltrow and Dieter Stein, 263–90. Philadelphia: John Benjamins Publishing Company, 2009.

Møllgaard, Eske. *An Introduction to Daoist Thought: Action, Language, and Ethics in Zhuangzi*. New York: Routledge, 2007.

Morris, Adalaide Kirby, and Thomas Swiss, eds. *New Media Poetics: Contexts, Technotexts, and Theories*. Cambridge, MA: MIT Press, 2006.

Moss, Stephen. "My Run for Oxford Professor of Poetry Was Crushed by Viral Campaign—and a Distinguished Rival." *The Guardian*, June

18, 2010, sec. Books. http://www.guardian.co.uk/books/2010/jun/18/oxford-professor-poetry-stephen-moss.

Nanfang dushibao 南方都市报 (Southern Metropolis). "'Zhongguo xin shi nianjian' shige chonghui minjian de keneng"'中国新诗年鉴'诗歌重回民间的可能 ("Chinese New Poetry Almanac": The possibility of poetry returning to the people), April 13, 2004. http://www.nanfangdaily.com.cn/southnews/tszk/nfdsb/gzzz/gzzz/200404130340.asp.

Nandu zhoukan 南都周刊 (Southern Metropolis Weekly). "Yang Ke fangtan" 杨克访谈 (An interview with Yang Ke) (2007). Reproduced on Yang Ke's blog http://blog.sina.com.cn/s/blog_48930cd801000c6s.html.

Nanfang zhoumo 南方周末 (Southern Weekend). "Langsong: Hui shi zhi zui?" 朗诵：毁诗之罪？ (Is recitation to blame for destroying poetry?). http://www.nanfangdaily.com.cn/zm/20060216/wh/dsys/200602160051.asp.

Nelson, Cary. *Repression and Recovery: Modern American Poetry and the Politics of Cultural Memory, 1910–1945*. Madison: University of Wisconsin Press, 1989.

Nie Shebo聂社波. "Dangdai shige 'shi' bing" (The "ten" diseases of contemporary poetry). http://blog.sina.com.cn/s/blog_530bd5ee0100nab8.html.

Nora, Pierre. "Between Memory and History: *Les Lieux de Mémoire*." *Representations* 26 (Spring 1989): 7–24.

Ouyang Youquan 欧阳友权. *Wangluo wenxue lungang* 网络文学论钢 (A thesis on Internet literature). Beijing: Renmin daxue chubanshe, 2003.

Owen, Stephen. *Readings in Chinese Literary Thought*. Cambridge MA: Harvard University Press, 1992.

Pang Qingming 庞清明, "Bo Yu Jian 'langsong shi shige de duantoutai' zhi waili xieshuo" 驳于坚'朗诵是诗歌的断头台'之歪理邪说 (In refutation of Yu Jian's fallacies in "Recitation is poetry's guillotine"). http://www.laren.cn/blog/2005/zhidao/archives/2006/3412.html.

Pettitt, Thomas. "Media Dynamics and the Lessons of History." In *A Companion to New Media Dynamics*, ed. John Hartley, Jean Burgess, and Axel Bruns, 53–72. Chicester: Wiley-Blackwell, 2013.

Pidan 皮旦. "Lajipai jiyao" 垃圾派纪要 (School of Rubbish synopsis). www.yanruyu.com/jhy/author/46807.shtml.

———. "Lun zuowei yinyu de laji pai" 论作为隐喻的垃圾派 (On the School of Rubbish as metaphor). http://hk.netsh.com/eden/bbs/6411/html/tree_4699615.html.

———. "Lun zuowei yundong de lajipai" 论作为运动的垃圾派 (On the School of Rubbish as a movement). http://hk.netsh.com/eden/bbs/6411/html/tree 2496931.html.

———. "2005 nian beiwanglu" 2005年备忘录 (2005 memorandum). http://hk.netsh.com/eden/bbs/6411/html/tree_6656043.html.

Pu Lizi 蒲荔子. "Xie Youshun: Shige yinggai yu shidai gandan xiangzhao" 谢有顺：诗歌应该与时代肝胆相照 (Xie Youshun: Poetry should be in tune with the times). http://news.sina.com.cn/c/2008-06-01/081615659442.shtml.

Qiu, Jack Linchuan. *Working-Class Network Society: Communication Technology and the Information Have-Less in Urban China*. Cambridge, MA: MIT Press, 2009.

Qiu Zhijie 邱志杰. *Zhongyao de shi xianchang* 重要的是现场 (The important thing is the live scene). Beijing: Zhongguo renmin daxue chubanshe, 2003.

Ren, Hai. *The Middle Class in Neoliberal China: Governing Risk, Life-Building, and Themed Spaces*. 1st ed. New York: Routledge, 2013.

———. *Neoliberalism and Culture in China and Hong Kong: The Countdown of Time*. New York: Routledge, 2010.

———. "Redistribution of the Sensible in Neoliberal China: Real Estate, Cinema, and Aesthetics." In *China and New Left Visions: Political and Cultural Interventions*, ed. Ban Wang and Jie Lu, 225–45. Lanham, MD: Lexington Books, 2012.

Renov, Michael, ed. *Theorizing Documentary*. New York: Routledge, 1993.

———. "Introduction: The Truth About Non-Fiction." In *Theorizing Documentary*, ed. Michael Renov, 1–11. New York: Routledge, 1993.

Roberts, I. D. "China's Internet Celebrity: Furong Jiejie." In *Celebrity in China*, ed. Louise Edwards, 217–36. Hong Kong: Hong Kong University Press, 2010.

Robinson, Luke. "From 'Public' to 'Private': Chinese Documentary and the Logic of Xianchang." In *The New Chinese Documentary Film Movement: For the Public Record*, ed. Chris Berry, 177–94. Hong Kong: Hong Kong University Press, 2010.

Robison, Richard. Introduction to *The Neoliberal Revolution: Forging the Market State*, ed. Richard Robison, xii–xv. New York: Palgrave and Macmillan, 2006.

———. "Neoliberalism and the Market State: What Is the Ideal Shell?" In *The Neoliberal Revolution: Forging the Market State*, ed. Richard Robison, 3–19. New York: Palgrave and Macmillan, 2006.

———, ed. *The Neoliberal Revolution: Forging the Market State*. New York: Palgrave Macmillan, 2006.

Han, Ruixia. "The Influence of Microblogging on Personal Public Participation." In *2010 IEEE 2nd Symposium on Web Society (SWS)*, 615–18. IEEE.org. 2010.

Sang Ke 桑克. "Hulianwang shidai de zhongwen shige" 互联网时代的中文诗

歌 (Chinese poetry in the age of the Internet). http://www.poemlife.com/libshow-228.htm.

Scott, David. *Conscripts of Modernity: The Tragedy of Colonial Enlightenment*. Durham, NC: Duke University Press, 2004.

Shanshangshi 山上石. "Liting Zhao Lihua: Dang xiandai shige zaoyu minzhong" 力挺赵丽华：当现代诗歌遭遇民众 (In support of Zhao Lihua: When modern poetry collided with the masses). http://bbs.tianya.cn/post-poem-114703–1.shtml.

Shen Haobo 沈浩波. "Dui Yang Ke shuo" 对杨克说 (To Yang Ke). http://blog.sina.com.cn/s/blog_48b6ff2b010009wf.htm.

———. "Huida jingbao jizhe de 11 ge wenti" 回答晶报记者的11个问题 (Replying to 11 questions from a Jingbao reporter). http://blog.sina.com.cn/u/48b6ff2b010008kv.

———. "Langsong shi shige de yi bufen" 朗诵是诗歌的一部分 (Recitation is a part of poetry). http://www.wenhuacn.com/wenxue/article.asp?classid=87&articleid=4002.

———. "Ruhe lijie xianfeng: Zai lushan xin shiji shige mingjia fenghui shang de fayan" 如何理解先锋：在麓山新世纪诗歌名家峰会上的发言 (How should we understand the avant-garde? A speech at the Lushan New Century Famous Poetry Summit). http://bbs.frguo.com/a/a.asp?B=4&ID=116874.

———. "Shei zai na 'jiushi niandai' kai shuan?" (Who's fooling "the nineties"?). In *1999 Zhongguo xin shi nianjian* (1999 Chinese New Poetry Almanac), ed. Yang Ke, 540–44. Guangzhou: Guangzhou chubanshe, 2000.

———. "Shiren nengfou zhimian shidai?" 诗人能否直面时代？ (Can poets face up to the era?). http://www.poemlife.com/Wenku/wenku.asp?vNewsId=1557.

———. "Xiao bo Yu Jian de langsong guan: Langsong shi shige de yi bufen" 小驳于坚的朗诵观：朗诵是诗歌的一部分 (A brief refutation of Yu Jian's views on recitation: Recitation is a part of poetry). http://blog.tianya.cn/blogger/post_show.asp?BlogID=510090&PostID=5742199.

———. *Xin cang da e* 心藏大恶 (A great evil hidden in the heart). Dalian: Dalian chubanshe, 2004.

———. *Yi ba hao ru* (A handful of tit). Unofficial publication, 2001.

Shirky, Clay. *Here Comes Everybody: The Power of Organizing Without Organizations*. Reprint. New York: Penguin Books, 2009.

Shoemaker, Pamela J., and Timothy Vos. *Gatekeeping Theory*. New York: Routledge, 2009.

Song, Weijie. "Space, Swordsmen, and Utopia: The Dualistic Imagination in Jin Yong's Narratives." In *The Jin Yong Phenomenon: Chinese Martial*

Arts Fiction and Modern Chinese Literary History, ed. Ann Huss and Jianmei Liu, 155–78. Amhurst: Cambria Press, 2007.

Stevenson, Nick. *Cultural Citizenship: Cosmopolitan Questions*. Maidenhead: Open University Press, 2003.

Straw, Will. "Scenes and Sensibilities." *Public* 22/23 (2002): 245–57.

Sullivan, Jonathan. "A Tale of Two Microblogs in China." *Media, Culture and Society* 34, no. 6 (2012): 773–83.

Sun, Cecile Chu-chin. *The Poetics of Repetition in English and Chinese Lyric Poetry*. Chicago: University of Chicago Press, 2011.

Sun, Helen. *Internet Policy in China: A Field Study of Internet Cafés*. Lanham, MD: Lexington Books, 2010.

Sun, Yan. *Corruption and Market in Contemporary China*. Ithaca, NY: Cornell University Press, 2004.

Tan Kexiu 谭克修, ed. *Mingtian* 明天 (Tomorrow) 1. Changsha: Hunan Wenyi Chubanshe, 2003.

———. "Zisha lushang de xiao wenren shige" 自杀路上的小文人诗歌 (Petty literati poetry on the road to suicide). http://blog.tianya.cn/blogger/post_show.asp?BlogID=341456&PostID=5679527&idWriter=0&Key=0.

Tan Wuchang 谭五昌. "Dangdai xin shi jingduanhua wenti ji xin shi jiaoyu wenti piantan" 当代新诗经典化问题及新诗教育问题片谈 (A brief discussion of the canonization of contemporary new poetry and the problem of new poetry education). http://www.xzbu.com/5/view-1235203.htm.

Tang, Xiaobing. *Chinese Modern: The Heroic and the Quotidian*. Durham, NC: Duke University Press, 2000.

Tengxun xinwen 腾讯新闻. "Jiwei shuji huo Lu Xun wenxuejiang, 'yanggao ti' shi baohong wangluo" (Party secretary wins Lu Xun prize for literature, "Baby Lamb form" poems light up the web) (October 20, 2010). http://news.qq.com/a/20101020/001964.htm.

———. "Yan Yanwen: 'Yanggao ti' shi Lu Xun wenxuejiang de siwang zhengshu" 阎延文："羊羔体"是鲁迅文学奖的死亡证书 (Yan Yanwen: "Baby Lamb form" is the death certificate for the Lu Xun prize for literature). http://view.news.qq.com/a/20101024/000015.htm.

Tian, Xiaofei. "Muffled Dialect Spoken by Green Fruit: An Alternative History of Modern Chinese Poetry." *Modern Chinese Literature and Culture* 21, no. 1 (April 1, 2009): 1–45.

———. *Tao Yuanming and Manuscript Culture: The Records of a Dusty Table*. Seattle: University of Washington Press, 2005.

Tian Xiaoqing 田晓青. "Shisan lu yanxian" 十三路沿线 (Route no. 13). In *Chideng de shizhe* 持灯的使者 (Bearers of the lamp), ed. Liu He 刘禾, 19–54. Oxford: Oxford University Press, 2000.

Tompkins, Jane. *Sensational Designs: The Cultural Work of American Fiction, 1790–1860*. New York: Oxford University Press, 1985.

Turkle, Sherry. *Life on the Screen: Identity in the Age of the Internet*. New York: Simon & Schuster, 1995.

UNESCO, "Draft Programme and Budget, 2004–2005." General Conference, Thirty-second session, Paris 2003. www.unesco.ee/dok/32C_5a.pdf.

Visser, Robin. *Cities Surround the Countryside: Urban Aesthetics in Postsocialist China*. Durham, NC: Duke University Press, 2010.

Voci, Paola. *China on Video: Smaller-Screen Realities*. New York: Routledge, 2010.

Wang, Ban. *Illuminations from the Past: Trauma, Memory, and History in Modern China*. 1st ed. Stanford, CA: Stanford University Press, 2004.

———. "What Is Political Theater? A Critique of Performance Studies." In *China and New Left Visions: Political and Cultural Interventions*, ed. Ban Wang and Jie Lu, 81–97. Lanham, MD: Lexington Books, 2012.

Wang, Ban, and Jie Lu. "Introduction: China and New Left Critique." In *China and New Left Visions: Political and Cultural Interventions*, ed. Ban Wang and Jie Lu, ix–xvi. Lanham, MD: Lexington Books, 2012.

Wang Gan 王干. "Zai feixu shang chuli de shige jinianbei: Lun '5.12' dizhen shichao" 在废墟上矗立的诗歌纪念碑—论"5、12"地震诗潮 (A poetry memorial standing tall above the ruins: On the "May 12" poetry tide). http://whj.smx.gov.cn/ReadNews.asp?NewsID=3871.

Wang Jiehong 王杰泓. "Shenti de 'chuanqi' yu 'xingshi' zhuyi de molu: Xingwei yishu yuyan lun" 身体的'传奇'与'形式'主义的末路：行为艺术语言论 ("Magical tales" of the body and the end of the road for "form'alism": On the language of performance art). http://arts.tom.com/1004/2004/5/8-53677.html.

Wang, Jing. *Brand New China: Advertising, Media, and Commercial Culture*. Cambridge, MA: Harvard University Press, 2010.

———. "Culture as Leisure and Culture as Capital." *Positions: East Asia Cultures Critique* 9, no. 1 (March 2001): 69–104.

———. *High Culture Fever: Politics, Aesthetics, and Ideology in Deng's China*. Berkeley: University of California Press, 1996.

Wang, Ning. "Cultural Studies in China: Towards Closing the Gap Between Elite Culture and Popular Culture." *European Review* 11, no. 2 (2003): 183–91.

Wang Pu 王璞. "Dui 'wangluo shige' de chubu kaocha he yanjiu" 对网络诗歌的初步考察和研究 (Preliminary investigations and research into Internet poetry). http://www.shigebao.com/html/articles/22/689.html.

Wang Tongyi 王同亿, ed. *Yuyan dadian* 语言大典 (A great Chinese dictionary). Beijing: Sanlian chubanshe, 1990.

Wasik, Bill. *And Then There's This: How Stories Live and Die in Viral Culture.* New York: Viking Adult, 2009.

Wu Wenguang 吴文光, ed. *Xianchang* 现场 (Document). Tianjin: Tianjin shehui kexueyuan chubanshe, 2000, 2001, and 2005.

Xi Du 西渡. "Shushang lichang yu yishu yuanze: Ping '1998 Zhongguo xin shi nianjian'" 书商立场与艺术原则：评1998中国新诗年鉴 (A book agent's standpoint and artistic principles: A review of the *1998 Chinese New Poetry Almanac*). http://www.hongxiu.com/zhuanti/document/view.asp?id=843.

Xiaowen 小闻. "Xinrui shiren menglie pengji 'xiao wenren shige' 新锐诗人猛烈抨击'小文人诗歌' (Sharp poets harshly criticize "petty literati poetry"). http://www.ycwb.com/gb/content/2006-07/01/content_1156642.htm.

Xiao Yu'er 小鱼儿. "Laji xiezuo qiangdang chulong, gongcheng maotou zhizhi xiabanshen" 垃圾写作强档出笼，攻城矛头直指下半身 (Rubbish writing appears with a bang, its spears pointed straight at the lower body). http://www.yanruyu.com/jhy/author/41161.shtml.

———. "2003 nian huayu wangluo shige bu wanquan shuli" 2003年华语网络诗歌不完全梳理 (An incomplete assessment of Chinese language Internet poetry in 2003). http://www.shigebao.com/shi/images/article/1066.html.

Xie Youshun 谢有顺. "Minjian yijing chengzhang wei zhuliu: Du '2004–2005 Zhongguo xin shi nianjian' you gan" 民间已经成长为主流：读2004–2005中国新诗年鉴有感 (The popular has already grown into the mainstream: Thoughts upon reading the *2004–2005 Chinese New Poetry Almanac*). http://www.nanfangdaily.com.cn/southnews/tszk/nfdsb/ydzk/200606190170.asp.

———. "Neizai de shige zhenxiang" 内在的诗歌真相 (The inner true face of poetry). In *Nanfang zhoumo* 南方周末 (Southern Weekend), April 2, 1999.

Xin, Guangwei. *Publishing in China: An Essential Guide.* 2nd ed. Farmington Hills, MI: Cengage Learning, 2009.

Xinhua 新华. "Dangdai shige weihe 'jimo'?" (Why is contemporary poetry so lonely?). http://www.hb.xinhuanet.com/zhibo/2007-11/13/content_11658533.htm.

———. "Liting Zhao Lihua, nan shiren Su Feishu luoti langsong bei juliu" 力挺赵丽华，男诗人苏非舒裸体朗诵被拘留 (Supporting Zhao Lihua, male poet Su Feishu's naked recital gets him arrested). http://news.xinhuanet.com/book/2006-10/19/content_5221600.htm.

———. "Shei hai zai xie shi, Zhongguo hai you shiren ma?" (Who still writes poetry and does China still have poets?). http://news.xinhuanet.com/mrdx/2005-12/25/content_3966626.htm.

Xinjingbao 新京报. "Xiju, yinyueren dazao 'kuajie' shige langsonghui" 戏剧、音乐人 打造'跨界'诗歌朗诵会 (Theatre people and musicians create a "boundary crossing" poetry recital). http://news.sohu.com/20060614/n243726969.shtml.

Xinlang, "10 wei shiren dengshang 'yongshibang' Sun Wenbo lie bangshou Zhao Lihua mei shang bang" 10位诗人登上'庸诗榜'孙文波列榜首赵丽华没上榜 (Ten poets climb the "mediocre poetry charts," Sun Wenbo makes no. 1, Zhao Lihua nowhere to be seen). http://news.sina.com.cn/c/2007-01-23/122211068050s.shtml.

Xu, Gary. "Where Has the Aura Gone? Reflections on Cultural Studies, Neoliberalism, and Literature as the Auratic Event." *Taiwan Academic Online* 31, no. 2 (2005): 15–39.

Xu Jiang 徐江. "Lun wei minjian" 论伪民间 (On the fake popular). http://bbs.tianya.cn/post-poem-149748-1.shtml.

Xu Jingya 徐敬亚. "Jueqi de shiqun: Ping Zhongguo shige de xiandai qingxiang" 崛起的诗群----评中国诗歌的现代倾向 (Poetry groups on the rise: Critiquing the modernist tendency in Chinese poetry). http://wxs.zhongwenlink.com/home/news_read.asp?newsid=61223.

Xu Xiangchou 徐乡愁. "Niubi shi zhuang chulai de: Da 'Shijianghu' de yi qun wei xianfeng" 牛逼是装出来的：答"诗江湖"的一群伪先锋 (Being shit hot is a pretense: A reply to the fake avant-garde of *Poetry Rivers and Lakes*). http://www.yanruyu.com/jhy/author/40634.shtml.

———. "Xu Xiangchou jianta renmin xilie" 徐乡愁践踏人民系列 (Xu Xiangchou's trample on the people series). http://www.yanruyu.com/jhy/author/63679.shtml.

———. "Xu Xiangchou laji yulu" 徐乡愁垃圾语录 (Rubbish quotations of Xu Xiangchou). http://www.yanruyu.com/jhy/author/39754.shtml.

———. "Xu Xiangchou wenxuan" 徐乡愁文选 (Collected writings of Xu Xiangchou). http://my.ziqu.com/bbs/665167/4/145.html.

———. "Zhongguo lajipai: Cong wu yue fengbao dao liu yue juexing (shijianghu lunzhan zongshu)" 中国垃圾派：从五月风暴到六月觉醒（诗江湖论战综述） (China's School of Rubbish: From May's storm to June's awakening [a summary of the polemic with *Poetry Rivers and Lakes*]). http://www.yanruyu.com/jhy/author/detail.asp?sendid=40801&page=1.

Yang, Guobin. "The Internet as Cultural Form: Technology and the Human Condition in China." *Knowledge, Technology & Policy* 22, no. 2 (March 2009): 109–15.

———. *The Power of the Internet in China: Citizen Activism Online*. New York: Columbia University Press, 2010.

———. "Social Dynamics in the Evolution of China's Internet Content Control Regime." In *Routledge Handbook of Media Law*, 285–302. New York: Routledge, 2013.

Yang Ke 杨克, ed. *1998 Zhongguo xin shi nianjian* 1998中国新诗年鉴 (1998 Chinese New Poetry Almanac). Guangzhou: Huacheng chubanshe, 1999.

———. "98 gongzuo shouji" 98工作手记 (98 work notes). In *1998 Zhongguo xin shi nianjian* 1998中国新诗年鉴 (1998 Chinese New Poetry Almanac), ed. Yang Ke, 517-520. Guangzhou: Huacheng chubanshe, 1999.

———, ed. *1999 Zhongguo xin shi nianjian* 1999中国新诗年鉴 (1999 Chinese New Poetry Almanac). Guangzhou: Guangzhou chubanshe, 2000.

———, ed. *2000 Zhongguo xin shi nianjian* 2000中国新诗年鉴 (2000 Chinese New Poetry Almanac). Guangzhou: Guangzhou chubanshe, 2001.

———. "'2000 Zhongguo xin shi nianjian' gongzuo shouji" '2000中国新诗年鉴'工作手记 (2000 Chinese New Poetry Almanac work notes). In *2000 Zhongguo xin shi nianjian* 2000 中国新诗年鉴 (2000 Chinese New Poetry Almanac), ed. Yang Ke, 633–37. Guangzhou: Guangzhou chubanshe, 2001.

———, ed. *2002–2003 Zhongguo xin shi nianjian* 2002–2003 中国新诗年鉴 (2002–2003 Chinese New Poetry Almanac). Tianjin: Tianjin shehui kexueyuan chubanshe, 2004.

———. "'2002–2003 Zhongguo xin shi nianjian' gongzuo shouji" '2002–2003中国新诗年鉴'工作手记 (2002–2003 Chinese New Poetry Almanac work notes). In *2002–2003 Zhongguo xin shi nianjian* 2002–2003 中国新诗年鉴 (2002-2003 Chinese New Poetry Almanac), ed. Yang Ke, 570-571. Tianjin: Tianjin shehui kexueyuan chubanshe, 2004.

———, ed. *2004–2005 Zhongguo xin shi nianjian* 2004–2005中国新诗年鉴 (2004–2005 Chinese New Poetry Almanac). Guangdong: Haifeng chubanshe, 2006.

———. "2004–2005 'Zhongguo xin shi nianjian' gongzuo shouji" 2004–2005'中国新诗年鉴'工作手记 (2004–2005 "Chinese New Poetry Almanac" work notes). In *2004–2005 Zhongguo xin shi nianjian* (2004–2005 Chinese New Poetry Almanac), ed. Yang Ke, 320–21. Guangdong: Haifeng chubanshe, 2006.

———, ed. *2006 Zhongguo xin shi nianjian* 2006中国新诗年鉴 (2006 Chinese New Poetry Almanac). Guangdong: Huacheng chubanshe, 2007.

———, ed. *2007 Zhongguo xin shi nianjian* 2007中国新诗年鉴 (2006 Chinese New Poetry Almanac). Guangdong: Huacheng chubanshe, 2008.

———, ed. *2008 Zhongguo xin shi nianjian* 2008中国新诗年鉴 (2008 Chinese New Poetry Almanac). Guangdong: Huacheng chubanshe, 2009.

———, ed. *2009–2010 Zhongguo xin shi nianjian* 2009–2010中国新诗年鉴 (2009–2010 Chinese New Poetry Almanac). Chongqing: Chongqing chubanshe, 2011.

———. "Lushan shihui" 麓山诗会 (Lushan poetry meeting). http://my.clubhi.com/bbs/661473/messages/45404.html.

———. "Nanfang ribao fangtan: Nianjian, minjian, Guangdong" 南方日报访谈：年鉴, 民间, 广东 (Interview with *Southern Daily*: Almanacs, the Popular, Guangdong). http://blog.sina.com.cn/u/48930cd8010004a1.

———, ed. *Zhongguo xin shi nianjian shinian jingxuan* 中国新诗年鉴十年精选 (Ten year selection from the Chinese New Poetry Almanacs). Beijing: Zhongguo qingnian chubanshe, 2010.

———. "Zhongguo shige xianchang—yi 'Zhongguo xin shi nianjian' wei lizheng fenxi" 中国诗歌现场—以'中国新诗年鉴'为例证分析 (Live scenes of Chinese poetry: A case study analysis of the *Chinese New Poetry Almanac*). http://www.sydao.net/shownews.asp?newsid=3066.

———. "'Zhongguo xin shi nianjian' de jiazhi duo nian hou hui gengjia mingxi" '中国新诗年鉴'的价值多年后会更加明晰 (The value of the *Chinese New Poetry Almanac* will be clearer in years to come). http://www.ycwb.com/xkb/2007-11/08/content_1675666.htm.

Yang Xiaomin 杨晓民. "Wangluo huanjing xia de shige xiezuo" (Poetry writing in an online environment). *Shikan* 7 (1999).

Yeh, Michelle, ed. *Anthology of Modern Chinese Poetry*. New Haven, CT: Yale University Press, 1994.

———. "Chinese Literature from 1937 to the Present." In *The Cambridge History of Chinese Literature*, ed. Kang-i Sun Chang and Stephen Owen, 565–696. Cambridge: Cambridge University Press, 2010.

———. "Contemporary Chinese Poetry Scenes." *Chicago Review* 39, no. 3/4 (January 1, 1993): 279–83.

———. "The 'Cult of Poetry' in Contemporary China." *Journal of Asian Studies* 55, no. 1 (February 1, 1996): 51–80.

———. "Frontier Taiwan: An Introduction." In *Frontier Taiwan*, ed. Michelle Yeh and N. G. D. Malmqvist, 1–54. New York: Columbia University Press, 2001.

———. "Introduction: From the Margin." In *Anthology of Modern Chinese Poetry*, ed. Michelle Yeh, xxiii–lv. New Haven, CT: Yale University Press, 1994.

———. *Modern Chinese Poetry: Theory and Practice Since 1917*. New Haven, CT: Yale University Press, 1991.

———. "'There Are No Camels in the Koran': What Is Modern About Modern Chinese Poetry?" In *New Perspectives on Contemporary Chinese Poetry*, ed. Christopher Lupke, 9–28. New York: Palgrave Macmillan, 2007.

Yeh, Michelle, and N. G. D. Malmqvist, eds. *Frontier Taiwan*. New York: Columbia University Press, 2001.

Yi Sha 伊沙. "Da 'Nanfang dushibao' si wen" 答'南方都市报'四问 (Replying to four questions from *Southern Metropolis*). http://www.poemlife.com/PoetColumn/yisha/article.asp?vArticleId=16687&ColumnSection=1320.

———. "Wo zuo gu wo shuo" 我做故我说 (I do therefore I speak). http://blog.sina.com.cn/s/blog_489db097010006b9.html.

———. "Zuo da de 'Shi jianghu'" 做大的'诗江湖' ("Poetry rivers and lakes" made big). http://blog.sina.com.cn/s/blog_485dc33401000be3.html.

Yu, Haiqing. "Blogging Everyday Life in Chinese Internet Culture." *Asian Studies Review* 31, no. 4 (December 2007): 423–33.

———. *Media and Cultural Transformation in China*. New York: Routledge, 2009.

Yu Jian 于坚. "Chuanyue hanyu de shige zhi guang" 穿越汉语的诗歌之光 (The light of poetry, cutting through the Chinese language). In *1998 nian Zhongguo xin shi nianjian* (1998 Chinese New Poetry Almanac), ed. Yang Ke, 1–17. Guangzhou: Huacheng chubanshe, 1999.

———. "Langsong" 朗诵 (Recitation). http://www.zgyspp.com/Article/ShowArticle.asp?ArticleID=653.

———. "Shiren he wei?" (What are poets for?). In *Zongpi shouji* (Notes of the palm bark), Yu Jian, 235–38. Shanghai: Dongfang chuban zhongxin, 1997.

———. *Zongpi shouji* 棕皮手记 (Notes of the palm bark). Shanghai: Dongfang chuban zhongxin, 1997.

Yu, Pauline. "Poems in Their Place: Collections and Canons in Early Chinese Literature." *Harvard Journal of Asiatic Studies* 50, no. 1 (June 1, 1990): 163–96.

Yue Gencheng 乐根成. "Zai shou jie lushan xin shiji shige mingjia fenghui xinwen fabuhui zhici" 在首届麓山新世纪诗歌名家峰会新闻发布会致词 (An address at the press conference for the First Lushan New Century Famous Poets Summit). http://www.villachina.com/2006-06-12/730288.htm.

Zhang, Chunhou, and Edwin C. Vaughan. *Mao Zedong as Poet and Revolutionary Leader: Social and Historical Perspectives*. Lanham, MD: Lexington Books, 2002.

Zhang, Jeanne Hong. *The Invention of a Discourse: Women's Poetry from Contemporary China*. Leiden: CNWS Publications, 2004.

Zhang Jiayan 张嘉谚. "Di shige yundong: Wangluo huayu geming de qianchao" 低诗歌运动：网络话语革命的前潮 (The Low Poetry Movement: The frontline in the Internet discourse revolution). http://www.poemlife.com:9001/ReviewerColumn/zhangjiayan/article.asp?vArticleId=31052&ColumnSection=.

Zhang, Lijia. "Mad Dog: The Legend of Chinese Poet Guo Lusheng." *Manoa* 14, no. 1 (July 1, 2002): 105–13.

Zhang, Qinghua. "The Return of the Pioneer: On Shi Zhi and His Poetry." Trans. Jonathan Stalling. *Chinese Literature Today* 1, no. 2 (2011): 6–12.

Zhang Taozhou 张桃洲. "Shige de fei langsong shidai" 诗歌的非朗诵时代 (Poetry's era of no recital). http://news.xinhuanet.com/book/2006-02/17/content_4192995.htm.

Zhang Xin 张新. *Ershi shiji Zhongguo xin shi shi* 二十世纪中国新诗史 (A history of twentieth-century Chinese New Poetry). Shanghai: Fudan daxue chubanshe, 2009.

Zhang Xinyu 张新煜. "Zhongguo dangdai xingwei yishu de meixue zhi si" 中国当代行为艺术的美学之思 (Thoughts on the aesthetics of Chinese contemporary performance art). http://arts.tom.com/1004/2004/5/13-42393.html.

Zhang, Xudong. *Postsocialism and Cultural Politics: China in the Last Decade of the Twentieth Century*. Durham, NC: Duke University Press, 2008.

Zhang, Yingjin. "From Counter-canon to Hypercanon in a Postcanonical Age: Eileen Chang as Text and Myth." *Frontiers of Literary Studies in China* 5, no. 4 (2011): 610–32.

Zhang, Zhen. "Bearing Witness: Chinese Urban Cinema in the Era of 'Transformation.'" In *The Urban Generation: Chinese Cinema and Society at the Turn of the Twenty-First Century*, ed. Zhen Zhang, 1–48. Durham, NC: Duke University Press, 2007.

———. "Transfiguring the Postsocialist City: Experimental Image-Making in Contemporary China." In *Cinema at the City's Edge: Film and Urban Networks in East Asia*, ed. Yomi Braester and James Tweedie, 95–118. Hong Kong: Hong Kong University Press, 2010.

———. *The Urban Generation: Chinese Cinema and Society at the Turn of the Twenty-First Century*. Durham, NC: Duke University Press, 2007.

Zhao Lihua 赵丽华. "Lu Xun jiang he Lu Xun goupi guanxi dou meiyou" 鲁迅奖和鲁迅狗屁关系都没有 (The Lu Xun prize has dog fart all to do with Lu Xun). http://blog.sina.com.cn/s/blog_4aca2fbd0100lvw3.html.

———. "Wo yao shuo de hua" 我要说的话 (What I want to say). http://blog.sina.com.cn/s/blog_4aca2fbd010005r5.html.

———. "Zhao Lihua huida Yangcheng wanbao caifang" 赵丽华回答羊城晚报采访 (Zhao Lihua replies to an interview with the *Yangcheng Evening News*). In *Shige yuekan: Xia ban yue* 诗歌月刊:下半月 (Poetry monthly: Second half of the month) 13 no. 1/2 (2007): 168–72.

Zhao, Yuezhi. *Communication in China: Political Economy, Power, and Conflict*. Lanham, MD: Rowman & Littlefield, 2008.

Zheng, Yongnian. *Technological Empowerment: The Internet, State, and Society in China*. Stanford, CA: Stanford University Press, 2007.

Zhou, Yongming. *Historicizing Online Politics: Telegraphy, the Internet, and Political Participation in China*. 1st ed. Stanford, CA: Stanford University Press, 2005.

———. "Living on the Cyber Border: Minjian Political Writers in Chinese Cyberspace." *Current Anthropology* 46, no. 5 (2005): 779–803.

Zhou Zan 周瓒. "Da dizhen yu wenxue biaoda" 大地震与文学表达 (The big earthquake and literary expression). http:// mythicizer.ycool.com/post.2880492.html.

———. *Touguo shige xiezuo de qianwangjing* 透过诗歌写作的潜望镜 (Through the periscope of poetic writing). Beijing: Shehui kexue wenxian chubanshe, 2007.

Zhu, Jiangnan. "The Shadow of the Skyscrapers: Real Estate Corruption in China." *Journal of Contemporary China* 21, no. 74 (2012): 243–60.

Zhu, Ying. *Two Billion Eyes: The Story of China Central Television*. New York: The New Press, 2012.

INDEX